Mothers as Keepers and Tellers of *Origin Stories*

Edited by Kerri S. Kearney and B. Lee Murray

DEMETER

Mothers as Keepers and Tellers of Origin Stories
Edited by Kerri S. Kearney and B. Lee Murray

Copyright © 2019 Demeter Press

Individual copyright to their work is retained by the authors. All rights reserved. No part of this book may be reproduced or transmitted in any form by any means without permission in writing from the publisher.

Demeter Press
140 Holland Street West
P. O. Box 13022
Bradford, ON L3Z 2Y5
Tel: (905) 775-9089
Email: info@demeterpress.org
Website: www.demeterpress.org

Demeter Press logo based on the sculpture "Demeter" by Maria-Luise Bodirsky www.keramik-atelier.bodirsky.de

Printed and Bound in Canada

Front cover artwork: Michelle Pirovich
Typesetting: Michelle Pirovich

Library and Archives Canada Cataloguing in Publication
Title: Mothers as keepers and tellers of origin stories / Kerri S. Kearney, B. Lee Murray, editors.
Names: Kearney, Kerri S., 1966- editor. | Murray, B. Lee, 1951- editor.
Description: Includes bibliographical references.
Identifiers: Canadiana 20190148780 | ISBN 9781772582123 (hardcover)
Subjects: LCSH: Mother and child. | LCSH: Motherhood. | LCSH: Storytelling. | LCSH: Families.
Classification: LCC HQ759.M68 2019 | DDC 306.874/3—dc23

For You

The particular human chain we're part of is central to our individual identity. Even if we loathe our families, in order to know ourselves, we seem to need to know about them, just as prologue. Not to know is to live with some of the disorientation and anxiety of the amnesiac.

—Elizabeth Stone

Acknowledgments

It is a privilege to thank those who have made this book possible. We begin with Andrea O'Reilly, editor-in-chief of Demeter Press, who has consistently guided and supported us. We also thank the other members of the team at Demeter Press who provided guidance and support throughout the process.

We thank the peer reviewers who took the time to read our book and provide such valuable feedback. The encouragement they provided was very much appreciated.

We thank Hollie Turner for her assistance in editing chapters and Janelle Hanson for her assistance with the introduction to this book.

We are very grateful to our contributors who worked diligently through the process of writing and revising and then revising again. We appreciate their cooperation in using autoethnography as methodology and admire their courage in writing very personal and sometimes very difficult and challenging stories. Of course, we understood the task of editing this book could be very challenging and demanding work at times (and it was), but we were not expecting how the stories would move us in such an evocative and exciting way. Through sharing and working together, we created relationships with people we have never met and feel we now know. It has been our honour.

Finally, we thank our own networks, both personal and professional, whose support makes it possible to use our voices and our experiences in service to others.

Contents

Introduction
Kerri S. Kearney and B. Lee Murray
11

Chapter One
In the Beginning: Stories (Un)Told of Adoption and Origin
Kate Greenway
19

Chapter Two
Connecting the Dots in Family Stories:
Embedded Feminist Perspectives
Evonne Garnett
45

Chapter Three
Who Wants to Know?:
An Autoethnography of How and Why a Mother May
Craft Audience-Dependent Stories of Origin
Elizabeth Cralley
69

Chapter Four
Single Mothers Storying the Absent Father and
Values-Based Cartooning
Penelope Mendonça
99

Chapter Five
A Familial History of Alcoholism and Depression:
An Imagined Interaction with My Daughters
Sarah LeBlanc
137

Interlude
The Secrets of Your Conception
Sagashus T. Levingston with Kerri S. Kearney and B. Lee Murray
159

Chapter Six
Magic Carpets and Baloney Boats:
An Origin Story Told By Two Moms
B. Lee Murray
169

Chapter Seven
Three Mothers of a Metis:
(Re)Creating Complex Origin Narratives
Michael Howard
211

Chapter Eight
Once Upon a Time: Storytelling Origin Stories
Kerri S. Kearney
229

Postlude
Kerri S. Kearney and B. Lee Murray
259

Notes on Contributors
261

Introduction

Kerri S. Kearney and B. Lee Murray

This book is about origin stories and the role of mothering as a part of creating, telling, retelling, positioning, and holding onto those stories. Because the book is about origin stories, it is also naturally about secrets—those told and those held. And it is about love and the situations and circumstances mothers navigate in attempting to honour their personal values, protect those they mother, and try to bring some loving order to the messiness of human lives.

Mothering, in this book, refers to acts of mothering, not to biology, legalities, or social standing (Walks and McPherson). Rather, the mothers in this book—whether they be the authors or actors in each story—came to mothering through avenues not aligned with patriarchal views of what creates the role of mother, in which only the man, woman, and their biological child are the stars of the show.

We came to edit this book through first travelling through our individual mothering journeys and then through being co-travellers as, over the years, we have written together about this experience called mothering. We first met at the 2010 conference for *Association of Research on Mothering* (now *Motherhood Initiative for Research and Community Involvement*) in Toronto, Canada, when Lee joined the audience for Kerri's presentation. In speaking afterwards with Andrea O'Reilly, editor of the *Journal of the Motherhood Initiative*, we asked that our individual manuscripts in an upcoming journal publication be placed back to back. As a birthmother, Lee's piece explored the secrets she kept around the birth of her son Dave when she was a frightened teen (Murray, "Secrets"); as a mother who adopted two of her three children, Kerri's piece detailed the birth of her second child and her meeting with her child's birthmother (Kearney and Bailey). Together, they presented a unique positioning of both birthmother and mother-by-adoption perspectives. We were each intrigued by the other's journey, and knowing each other and being in ongoing conversation presented information opportunities to ask questions that perhaps we would not have dared to ask the birthmother or mother of our own children. Those questions each of us asked of the other produced answers that, at various times, made each of us scratch her head in confusion or sometimes say, "Yes, me too!" A collaboration, and a friendship, was born. Our premise for this book was born from our conversations, our experiences, Lee's dissertation work on secrets of mothering (Murray, "Secrets"), and Kerri's ongoing work with former foster youth in college.

Together, we vehemently reject the idea that there is an essential, real mother to be discovered; indeed, we assume that an individual's desire to know his or her original story is separate from the desire to be in relationship with the actors from that story. There is very limited academic or social exploration about nontraditional mothers' decisions about origin stories, yet this is a type of mothering labour that occurs beneath and beside more recognized types of mothering tasks and behaviors. This book is one way to encourage dialogue about mothering roles and origin stories and to challenge the beliefs, values, and ways of thinking about being mothers and sharing (or not sharing) these stories with the next generation.

The authors of the chapters in the book are mothers by adoption, by unintended pregnancy, and by "unnatural procreation." For those of us who are not in culturally different relationships, we may enjoy the privilege of not being asked some of the questions about our children's origins—a privilege that others may not have. In recognizing this privilege, we must acknowledge that our stories reach beyond the personal to the cultural and socio-political. Despite what may be our desire to make decisions based solely on the wellbeing of our children, we, and they, sit within cultures of great influence and, sometimes, of great judgment. Thus, as writers and readers, we move back and forth between the personal and the cultural, as the boundaries rapidly merge and blur. We are a part of the cultures in which we reside. From both a personal and cultural perspective, there is complexity in every secret and the possibility, or not, of maintaining each piece of the secret.

Shame, blame, guilt, and/or fear may disrupt disclosure. And although the healing that comes from telling secrets is an oft-promoted outcome, no one can truly reassure mothers that revealing complex origin stories will, indeed, be positive. Mothers often cannot predict the outcomes, even for themselves.

The perceived risks of sharing origin stories were further highlighted for us during the proposal and writing processes for this collection, and we acknowledge part of that might have been related to our encouragement of autoethnographic approaches. Some authors just couldn't bring themselves to actually put their stories on paper. Others who had their pieces accepted withdrew during the process; two noted that they were withdrawing their chapters because other actors in their stories were very uncomfortable. One author's older child provided permission before the chapter was written. Kerri talked with her teen daughter before contributing her chapter, and, similarly, Lee spoke with her son and his family about the manuscript she wrote. One author, who chose to include her story in the collection, said that she was asked by others if she was sure she wanted to publish her story "out there where anyone can read it." With more than one author, we provided gentle but consistent encouragement to reach more deeply, to explain, to explore, and to share more than perhaps they were originally comfortable with. We saw the struggles the authors had with how much to reveal unfold vividly on the pages of rewrites and in email conversations. Frustration was a part of the journey for some. One author simply said, "This has been the most difficult thing that I have ever tried to write."

Although we greatly value all people who willingly choose to share part of themselves in research, the vulnerability associated with authoring the types of chapters in this book is, we believe, significantly different. Whereas many qualitative (non-autoethnographic) works present anonymized data and findings, the data in these chapters are us—our stories, wounds, would be's, should have been's, and so sorry's. Kerri imagines that we, the authors and editors, are figuratively but collectively holding hands (and our breath) as this book goes to publication, and our inner worlds are out there for anyone to see. For even in our individual efforts, there is strength in numbers and in shared experiences.

We truly honour the value and importance of every person's origin story for it plays a role in his or her understanding of who they are. And we are in awe of the authors who wrote about creating, keeping, telling, and retelling origin stories, as well as the impact of origin stories, in this brave and sometimes revealing book about a rarely discussed aspect of mothering.

The first chapter of this volume, "In the Beginning: Stories (Un)Told of Adoption and Origin," details Kate Greenway's personal adoption story. Kate questions her origin, her sense of self, and, ultimately, her place in society as a whole. She expresses uncertainty about who she is and how she will handle questions about where she got her physical appearance. Kate weaves a narrative that takes us through a gauntlet of emotions: fear, uncertainty, shame, acceptance, love, understanding, and trust. Her attempts to name how she fits into a socially acceptable or common narrative of birth resonate with the soul and emphasize how some secrets may injure the sense of self. Kate addresses the secrets that have defined her origins and eventually she provides hope through her own sense of having found peace with her adoption story.

In the next chapter, "Connecting the Dots in Family Stories: Embedded Feminist Perspectives," Evonne Garnett explains how family stories become childrearing practices within a Mennonite tradition. Her origin story focuses on the importance of growing up with female role models who interpreted and lived their experiences while also teaching her how to create her own sense of self. Her perspective as a child growing through adolescence as well as an adult reflecting on the influences shaping her personal agency are connected through the stories, or dots, of her family. Evonne shares how a minor choice can influence a lifetime and future generations by the sharing of stories in a family. Embracing the knowledge of a legacy, Evonne finds that feminism has not one definition but many and that emulation is not always the most sincere form of appreciation.

A visceral account of giving birth to her two children is narrated by Elizabeth Cralley in "Who Wants to Know?: An Autoethnography of How and Why a Mother May Craft Audience-Dependent Stories of Origin." Through gut-wrenching descriptions and naked emotional communications, Liz shares her in-the-moment thoughts, feelings, and struggles of giving birth twice in a foreign country where she does not speak the language. Addressing the question of how childbirth stories are crafted, Liz creates three possible narratives for each of her two children: a narrative for herself, a narrative for others, and a narrative for her child. Recognizing the societal pressure to craft a sanitized birth story, she evokes an understanding of childbirth that is often missing in the literature. Acknowledging the possibility of coping with the trauma associated with birth through humour and talking Liz crafts a story of strength, curiosity, and engagement.

Sharing her research on mothering, Penelope Mendonça in her chapter "Single Mothers Storying the Absent Father and Values-Based Cartooning" uses values-based cartooning as a visual representation of single mother origin stories. Pen is frank and discerning in describing how many mothers hesitate to share their stories. Her chapter discusses assumptions commonly made about a father or sperm donor; the societal drive for a nuclear family; and the marginalization of single mothers. Through presenting these challenging and thought-provoking stories, Pen makes visible an often silenced group.

Sarah LeBlanc's chapter, "A Familial History of Alcoholism and Depression: An Imagined Interaction with My Daughters," grips readers by instantly putting them into Sarah's position. How does a mother explain the choice to have biological children while knowing they may inherit alcoholism or depression or both? Sarah imagines how the future conversation with her daughters will go, what questions her daughters may ask, and what she will teach them about different coping techniques than the ones she learned. Sarah candidly addresses the tendency to sweep problems under the rug or run away from confrontation. In her piece, Sarah weaves together her family history, her own personal research, and the imagined conversation with her teenage daughters to create a story that brings to light many of the fears associated with the origin stories of children.

This book contains a special treat in the form of an interlude, which provides an opportunity for readers to pause and reflect on what they've read so far. This interlude includes a narrative by Sagashus T. Levingston, "The Secrets of Your Conception," with Kerri S. Kearney and B. Lee Murray. Sagashus's work is frank and unapologetic as she writes about how, as a strong woman, she survived and even thrived through tough times. However, she also acknowledges the challenges of positioning her choices as a woman, many of which were outside generally accepted social politics, as teachable moments when it comes to helping her children understand the impacts on their origins.

B. Lee Murray's chapter, "Magic Carpets and Baloney Boats: An

Origin Story Told by Two Moms," presents a script of an actual conversation involving her (as birthmother), her son, and his mother. Lee self-narrates throughout the script with inserted italics about her own feelings and thoughts as she transcribes the experience. The resulting narrative reveals the many moving and complex pieces that created the pathway to adoption and that continued well into the child's adulthood years, and highlights the mixed emotions and unasked questions for each participant in the adoption triangle. The lack of information Lee received about her son was reflected in the worry she felt for many years until she met her son for the first time and finally knew he survived and was happy. Lee's narrative includes answers to her son's curiosity about his birth father and explores the need that seemed to emerge, for both birthmother and child, to consider where their paths may have unknowingly crossed prior to meeting many years after her son's birth.

In "Three Mothers of a *Metis*: (Re)Creating Complex Origin Narratives," Michael Howard narrates an origin story from a father's perspective when he writes about three mothers who affected his son's life: his son's biological mother, the state of Washington as mother, and his wife. The harrowing process of adopting and navigating the many systems and mass of information provided by the state (much incorrect), and facing the frustrations inherent in the process of determining who to trust in an open adoption are all present in his narrative and create a complex coming-of-age story about choices—choices made by the mother, father, birthmother, and son.

In the final narrative, Kerri S. Kearney invites the reader to share in origin stories through children's storybooks in "Once Upon a Time: Storytelling Origin Stories." Kerri discusses how she used the power of the written word to create access to an origin story for each of her three children, two of whom were adopted. Although Kerri acknowledges that the storybook concept may increase the risk of idealizing the birth family, this concern is balanced by the reader's experience of wonder and magic in each page of her daughter's origin story. The artist, Kira, deftly uses the drawing of a window to share the feelings of being a part and yet separate from the world. The story itself, a tale of decisions made without regrets, transports the reader into the hopes and dreams of both birthmother and mother. The collection closes after Kerri's work with a postlude intended to provide another space for readers to reflect on their own reactions and thoughts.

As we come to the end of the long stretch of time between the initial formulation of this volume and its publication, we, as editors and friends, can't help but look back on the journey with our co-authors. From strangers to collaborators about this complicated, challenging, and beautiful journey called mothering, as a group, we hope that this collection touches the readers' hearts and creates new dialogues and understandings about diverse acts of mothering.

Many blessings to each of you!

Works Cited

Kearney, Kerri Shultz, and Lucy E. Bailey. "An Adoptive Mother's Reflections on Mothering and Grief: Another Voice from Inside the Adoption Triad." *Journal of the Motherhood Initiative,* 2010, vol. 1, no. 2, 2010, pp. 150-164.

Murray, B. Lee. "Secrets of an Illegitimate Mom." *Journal of the Motherhood Initiative,* vol. 1, no. 2, 2011, pp. 137-147.

Murray, B. Lee. "Secrets of Mothering." Dissertation. University of Saskatchewan, 2010.

Murray, B. Lee., and Kerri S. Kearney. "Twice Shamed and Twice Blamed: Assumptions, Myths and Stereotypes about 'Giving up a Child' and 'Taking in a Child.'" *The Mother-Blame Game,* edited by Vanessa Reimer and Sarah Sahagian, Demeter Press, 2015, pp. 237-255.

Walks, Michelle, and Naomi McPherson. "Preface." *An Anthropology of Mothering,* edited by Michelle Walks and Naomi McPherson, Demeter Press, 2011, pp. ix-xii.

Chapter One

In the Beginning: Stories (Un)Told of Adoption and Origin

Kate Greenway

> [This] contains a story and several other things. The other things might be connected within the story, or they might not; they might be connected to stories that haven't appeared yet. It's not easy to tell.
>
> —Pullman, preface to *Lyra's Oxford*

I want to tell a story about adoption, identity, and origin, as revealed in narratives told and untold to me by my birthmother and mother by adoption.[1] It's my story and their story, and as in all stories, it is both an individual and a collaborative construction (Kellas).

I was adopted at birth. In 1962, my parents, a doctor and nurse with four children, living in a mid-size Ontario town, brought me, a baby girl, home just before Christmas. This act shaped my life in ways that I never really considered—until I began a search for my origins—since "adoptive family stories are related to individuals' senses of self" (Kranstuber and Kellas 195). Because I am a woman who has lived under closed adoption legislation and because my birthmother and adoptive mother also lived under the same conditions and because I have been both a searcher and a nonsearcher of origins, I believe I am well positioned to tell my story of origin. I know mine is a historically and culturally specific discourse of adoptive identity, yet it is one that has not changed as much as the forces of modernity would have us believe. It is a story of the lingering effects of the adoptive policies of yesterday that privileged one familial model—the nuclear family—and marginalized generations of women and their children who could not reap the benefits of openness and new attitudes to adoption, as this was not their lived realities.

I do, however, note that my story is not just about lingering effects of bygone policies. Some adoptions today are still arranged with some degree of closure; this phenomenon is not just of the past. This may be at the request of either the relinquishing or adopting parents, who might not wish to engage upon their journey of family forming with full disclosure of their circumstances, ongoing contact with the other parties, or the negotiation of boundaries and complications of co-parenting. Agencies working with children in foster care might advise a closed adoption if there are problematic histories or individuals involved who could cause harm. Children of international adoption may also lack full access to knowledge and records of their first families, particularly if they are in the care of the state prior to adoption, perhaps because of war, displacement, famine, or natural disasters. Indigenous children in residential schools, refugees, survivors of genocide, and the disappeared of Central and South America or the Balkans, to name just a few, may have similar difficulties in coming to terms with the unresolved absences in their lives—the loss of family connections, history, documentation, and answers. Perhaps, then, my story may also resonate with those children and adults involved in such contemporary traumatic circumstances or in closed adoptions by someone else's choice.

Historically "adoption has been susceptible to varying conceptualism of childhood, from a state of passive receipt of care, to emerging views of children as people with rights that extend beyond fundamental needs for nurture and psychological parenting" (Douglas and Philpot 66). Prior to the Second World War, children labelled illegitimate were still being thought of in terms of the social breakdown they were thought to represent. In 1939, *The American Journal of Sociology* opined that "the bastard, like the prostitute, thief, and beggar, belongs to that motley crew of disreputable social types which society has generally resented, always endured. He is a living symbol of social irregularity, an undeniable evidence of contra moral forces; in short, a problem" (Davis 215). Yet by the end of the war, with a desire to return to a stable society focused on rebuilding family and prosperity, with pronatalist agendas, and with a number of children needing parents due to the ravages of war, adoption made many women and children subject to certain accompanying policies. One such adoption policy was ensuring confidentiality so that families could raise their adoptive children as if they were genetically their own.

In Canada, Manitoba and Ontario began closing adoption records in the 1920s; records were to be sealed and kept in the care of the courts and the registrar general. Once the adoption was finalized in the court, a new birth certificate with a new name was issued, eradicating (at least in public paper) the original ties with the birth family—"a true labor of imaginative 'transubstantiation'" (Gonzalez 257). Such is not surprising, since as Margaret Homans notes, "adoption is a fiction-generating machine" (5). Based on recommendations from adoption practitioners and such groups as the Child Welfare League, these were seen as protective safeguards to allow for the safety and wellbeing of the adopted child and to prevent any interference from the original parents once the adoption had taken place.

Whether it was the intent of either set of my parents or not, confidentiality allowed for the alleviation of social and moral reprobation for women like my birthmother, who was ensured her secret would not follow her; she could move on from what society deemed her mistake, especially in the upper-middle-class and conservative social strata she moved within. Confidentiality allowed my adoptive parents, and others like them, security in feeling that the adopted child was now irrevocably theirs, with singular loyalty to them, and no chance of birthparents or birth relatives changing their minds in later years and coming to collect their offspring. This was a fear my adoptive mother said she held closely until the final revocation of the consent waiting period had expired, and she could celebrate with what my brother remembers as a rare glass of wine. Through such protective safeguards, my parents and others like them could maintain the real or imagined story that theirs was a superior family to that of the original parents, and no one could contravene that notion. Confidentiality also defended me from "bastardy," from knowledge of unsavoury conception circumstances, and from the perceived moral degeneracy of (unmarried) birthparents. Confidentiality also protected me from marginalization from others by providing me a new clean place in the social order. It allowed a simpler origin story. It protected me from a birthparent who may try to intervene later in my life and any potential conflicts stemming from this relationship. It was, as denoted in the period, in the "best interests of the child."

In order for a couple like my parents to adopt me, they had to apply through either public means (i.e., the Children's Aid Society) or private means. During the period surrounding my relinquishment, the requirements and eligibility criteria in practice for public adoptions were restrictive, cumbersome, and often arbitrarily applied:

> [In the 1950s] adoption agencies set up forbidding guidelines and standards in order to choose the most 'worthy' parents out of the many who applied to adopt. Only those who were considered young enough, in perfect health and free from any chronic illness, financially above average, married for the first time and to a man or woman of the same race and religious faith, who didn't have and were able to prove they couldn't have children, were considered eligible to adopt a child. (Raymond and Dywasak 4)

My adoptive parents, who already had four children and were over forty, were considered ineligible by Children's Aid, even suspicious for wishing to add to their family.

My sister remembers my parents' reactions to that decision: "I know there was a sense of disgust on their part. Mother thought, 'For heaven's sakes, we have a perfectly good income, and why wouldn't you want to adopt somebody into a family with siblings; it would show we have a track record of being able to do this.' She was very indignant about it. And dad was really indignant about it. About somebody judging him." Thus, they looked to adopt privately.

Private adoption had advantages for both mothers. For my adoptive mother, its focus on the placement of newborns, its expedited timelines (as relatively few newborns were available for public adoption as compared to the number of families wishing to adopt), and its less strict acceptance criteria made adoption possible for her. My oldest brother told me the following: "[Mom and dad] went through a friend essentially. I've forgotten who the doctor was. Basically, the doctor presented the idea of adoption to the [birth] mother and she said yes, and that was the only process."

With private adoption, my birthmother could obtain medical care, shelter and food, as well as a placement with little or no delay (as little as a few days versus potentially several months or more); she could even have input as to where and with whom I was placed, with no questions asked (Solinger 177). In opting for a placement managed independently by doctors and lawyers, as mine was, my birthmother could avoid public services, institutions, and the accompanying compromises of freedom, invasions of privacy, pressures to reveal the father's name, and authoritarian approaches to rehabilitation.

As I am a product of this era of closed adoption and secrecy, the recent opening of adoption records in Ontario in 2009 has done little to alleviate the lingering questions I have about biological family and origin, particularly because in cases of private adoption like mine, very little paperwork was required, and, thus, little documentary evidence is attainable because it does not exist.

My brother reminds me: "That's one of the reasons you don't have a lot of records about medical history and that kind of stuff because it wasn't a process adoption. It was pretty much 'Do you want to do it?' 'Yes, okay, we're on the way.'" Openness in adoption to greater degrees is now more the norm, but it is a norm I will never experience, and there are many like me for whom access to information may not grant us any greater understanding of who we are and where we came from: we are reliant on the custodians of the story, which for many like me, are not now, nor may have ever been, accessible or willing to talk.

Betty Jean Lifton has claimed that "the obsession to find out who you are is universal" and that for the person adopted it is an attempt "to recreate yourself, to give birth to yourself under another set of circumstances" (*Lost and Found* 4). Not all persons who were adopted wish to find out more information about their origins, and, initially, I fit into this category and was disinterested in further detail. Yet later in life, I became one of those who desired more information, without really knowing why. To connect? To satisfy longing? To find something missing? To understand my own story? Paris DeSoto explains many adoptees' urges to search in similar terms: "Although an adoptee's search for origins may start out as a search for identity it ultimately becomes a search for narrative" (194). With such a lack of information, I am reliant on pieced together stories, and seeing mothers as "communication-brokers" (Freeark 3). These artefacts have been left to me and my imagination to generate a narrative of any coherence or substance: my own creation myth, one that I can live with.

Origins

> Men can do nothing without the make-believe of a beginning.
> —Elliot and Hardy 1

As an adoptee, in what ways is my story of origin told? I can say that I was born, but all the details of my entrance into the world are shrouded in uncertainty. A child raised in a biological family likely has access to multiple oral and material accounts of their origins, birth, and connection to family—corroborated by evidence in the form of birth certificates, hospital records, photographs or videos, all of which bind the child to their family in tangible and intangible ways. I am not able to tell of my origin except through the mediation of another: my birthmother, Children's Aid, government officials, or my mother by adoption. These are the gatekeepers of my own chronicles—those who may not divulge fully or have access to these stories, or who may choose not to tell at all. I had no visual, oral, or documentary evidence of my origins at all other than my amended birth certificate and the story of being brought home until I received my adoption order in my thirties and my original hospital record in my forties.

Archetypal narratives, such as Moses, Oedipus, and fairy tales, "give imaginative expression to our preoccupation about origins and identity" (Douglas and Philpot 8), as they are tales of children with unknown or questionable pedigrees. Surely I cannot help but "evaluate [my] own story based on how it compares to an 'ideal' story" (Vangelisti et al 338), and I wonder about the unintelligibility of my origins. Perhaps my own access as an adoptee to narrative authority depends on my being able to tell the story, however fragmented, of my beginnings. But are my origins, as an adoptee, simply fictions?

The idea of no origin and no truth, takes up Foucault's theory of genealogy: "It is not the search for origins, and is not the construction of a linear development.... The beginnings of things are not in some identity, some whole, some 'truth', but in numerous accidents, events, oppositions ... we are always 'made up' not of a solidity and wholeness but of the fragmentary" (82). Even though, as Foucault suggests, the seeking of origin is impossible and doomed to failure, I nonetheless persist and attempt to negotiate a complicated layer of stigma and labelling stemming from myself, theorists, and the public.

The disconnection from my birthmother erases knowledge of part of my being. I do not have a creation myth. I do not know the specifics of my conception, gestation, or birth. Was it a difficult or an easy labour? Did my birthmother hold me or even see me before I was given away, and who controlled this decision? When did she know what she would name me? I know only after recently receiving my original unaltered birth certificate what my birth weight was, a figure that is the essence of any birth announcement. Issues of "identity and difference ... emerge when dislocations deny the possibility of a seamless narrative of origin" (Yngvesson and Mahoney 78). I have no details; I possess only uncertainty and conjecture. My origin story does not really begin with my birth; mine is a different natality.

I also have the problem of having to integrate my social and biological worlds in ways that others do not. The cultural importance of knowing my heritage and my ancestry, which is then joined to a timeline and family history, is somehow invested with the notion of wholeness—a complete self-identity. Note the explosion of ancestry.com-like advertisements, in which so-called false histories are corrected to what is presented as the immense life-altering satisfaction of their clients. The problem, though, for me is that I start with fragmentation as a baseline: those who begin the task of examining their adoptive identities begin with the unavoidable knowledge that large pieces of their backgrounds concerning who they are and where they came from are missing. As Jackie Kay explains, being an adoptee "you have a sense of difference quite strongly" (qtd. in Gish 172). With my fair skin and red blonde hair, I have often been asked if I am English, or Scottish; without opening up a much deeper conversation, I find it difficult to formulate a satisfactory reply. This balance between acknowledgment of difference, but not pathologizing it, is akin to finding the balance between the sel(f)ves of the adoptee. Even as a subject I am not sure what story I am telling in relation to the world.

Telling: Stories of My Adoptive Mother

> I think the adopted person's identity is even more fluid than a person who is not because everything that is behind them is moving ... the past is unknown to them... [and] constantly open to dreams, imagination, fantasy and interpretation. It's something that can be re-invented: the possibilities for the adopted person to constantly reinvent themselves are endless.
>
> —Kay qtd. in Gish 174

My parents told my siblings of my pending adoption in an exceptionally rare family meeting. Discussing adult choices with children was never their norm.

My sister recalled: "I knew they were looking to adopt, but I wasn't sure how far along in the process we were because then all of a sudden, things moved very quickly. But I was, what, ten, so much of that was adult conversation."

She continued: "I know we were told ... as a group before you were on the scene because it had to explain why this person—you—was going to be there. It wasn't a highly emotional kind of conversation; it was quite matter of fact."

She recalled my mom saying that "this is something we're thinking about doing, stay tuned, we'll let you know."

My sister also remembers that "mom and dad were excited, so we weren't involved in worrying about it, and mom liked having babies. So it was a good thing. It was a positive thing. It was an upbeat thing."

I wonder if my sister's unrelenting positivity is for my benefit: "The stories we remember and tell about our lives reflect who we are, how we see ourselves, and perhaps, how we wish to be seen" (Cole and Knowles 119). I accept that my adoption was a welcome and unhidden event in our family. I know it wasn't a problem, and I never felt as such. Yet since this occurred in the 1960s, I'm not sure whether I believe that all of the reactions from my relatives, parents' colleagues, and neighbours were as open, positive, or nonjudgmental as my siblings present them to be.

I have always known I was adopted. My adoptive parents were careful to never keep it secret. They never wanted the "you were adopted" traumatic reveal. As soon as I could talk, I would tell people I was adopted, much to my parents' relieved approval. Their strategy was somewhat foiled when after pronouncing this publicly on countless occasions, I asked what "adopted" meant. A little later in my cognitive development, I understood that it meant I was chosen, selected—a special status conferred with all its rights and privileges. I was not abandoned. I was not unwanted. That was the story I told. Freud might have examined my diction a little more skeptically.

Adoptive mother Jennifer Gilmore muses

> What is the narrative arc of my son's birth and how much of that narrative bears repeating? The story of a biological child's birth is the story of when his mother's water broke, or how his mother was rushed to the hospital, the duration and pain or ease of labour.... Our story is longer and it is shorter.... Is that story— the story of my son making his way to us—not the story I should tell? (qtd. in Gross)

I was told my equivalent of this narrative with "the phone call"—my entrance story and an adoptive substitute for tales of pregnancy, gestation, labour, and delivery in biological births. On a weekend in mid-December, 1962, my parents hosted a formal Christmas party. Carloads of perfumed holiday guests filled the rooms, women in oh-so-politically incorrect muskrat stoles and mink wraps, men sporting tweed hats and smoking Export A cigarettes. My father told of the glamorous gown my mother wore that left "little to the imagination," as he remembered it. Amid Frank Sinatra and Tony Bennett blaring on the imitation wood hi-fi and the clinking of ice cubes in highball glasses was a phone call taken in the study: a doctor from Victoria Hospital in London, where my father also worked, phoned to say they had a baby girl a few hours old who was in need of a family. And then a deliberately provocative birth announcement was placed in the paper the following day: "Dr. and Mrs. R.E. Greenway announce the arrival of their baby daughter, Kathryn Isabel, on December 12," news that must have surprised the more than slightly hungover guests gingerly drinking their black coffees the following day. My origin story balances on a single call, with no warning, and a chance of fate; my entire gestation and birth into this family lasted less than twenty-four hours.

The decision to tell this adoption story, early and often, was not in keeping with the norms of the day. David Kirk is generally credited with critiquing the assumption that confidential adoptions were beneficial, and introduced his theory of "shared fate" in 1964. He proposed that adoptive parents, himself being one of them, must acknowledge the differences between parenting a biological child and parenting one by adoption. He suggested such communication would allow for open and healthy discussion about the differences in being an adoptive family: "Advocates of disclosure want[ed] to see the issue discussed openly so that there [was] no shame or secretiveness about the adoption ... it is something of which to be proud and in which the child should rejoice; these parents feel the child will learn a little at a time by the frequent discussion of adoption with others in their social network rather than a revelatory moment" (Isaac 154). Sally Sales observes that this might have left the door open to further contact or initiate a relationship with birthparents, which was, ironically, at the same time that the ability to access birthparents was severely restricted in Canadian law (77).

Telling children about their adoptive origin in the 1960s mostly consisted of a verbal disclosure made by the adoptive parents based on whatever scant information they had been provided and might be willing to share. The most common method of telling was the chosen child story, in which the parents imparted a more or less reassuring fairy tale of the child's specialness and the parents' desire to possess that particular child over all others. Part of the distinction of the story was the difference in the type of motherhood—biological versus adoptive: "One is a mother because she had to be, one because she wants to be" (Berebitsky 87); choice is, thus, offered as comfort.

My sister recalled the following: "Mom explaining to me that she would tell you that you were adopted but that it wasn't a discussion. And then on another occasion her saying to me that later you might decide to find out who your real [biological] parents were and that was okay. She did say she was going to tell you that you were adopted and the difference was that she'd picked you out special and that's why you came home to us."

My mother tried to keep the subject of adoption open in order "to normalize adoption ... [and] help manage [my] uncertainty, not just to provide information" (Colaner and Kranstuber 253), and, later, she encouraged me to search for my birthmother. It was I who resisted. Perhaps I worried subconsciously about the potential loss of specialness.

The process of telling the adoption story by adoptive parents, according to Meredith Harrigan, "serves four main functions: to offer positive reinforcement, create familiarity with adoption-related talk and knowledge, convey a complete history for their children, and prevent their children from fantasizing about various aspects of their adoption" (36). But there are fundamental problems with this assessment of the adoption story, which is, just that, a story. In private adoption of the 1950s or 1960s, it was likely a chance opportunity that brought the parents and child together, as in my case. My parents had little to no choice in becoming parents to a particular child, beyond accepting or rejecting the offer to adopt me. Like most adoptions, if they involved choice at all, it was choice under some form of restrictive conditions. The fiction that a complete history is possible, even from more robust records than mine, does not allow for the complexity of multiple narrative lines, the absences and losses. Thus I, like many adoptees, invented various scenarios and substitutes as well as conceivable backgrounds and trajectories—every possibility surrounding what might have been and who I am.

In the 1950s and 1960s, it was proposed (but not universally accepted) that it might be best for the child's healthy emotional development to understand their origins. But telling them involved sending some often conflicting messages and was fundamentally a process of "the sustaining of two quite distinct positions regarding the adopted child's birth family: the child should make a complete break with their original family and yet, s/he should be 'told' of the adoptive status" (Sales 77). David Kirk observed that many adoptive parents rejected his idea that the adoptive family was different from the biological family, yet by telling the child they were adopted, the persons were nonetheless acknowledging a difference (qtd. in Isaac 187). Marianne Novy also recalls being told of her adoption and how she was supposed to understand that there was nothing wrong with it, yet by the silences imposed on further discussion of her adoption, she absorbed a different conception: "I was given up so I could be better taken care of; I was chosen, but I shouldn't tell others. Our family was different from others in how it was formed, and I was different from other people, and if I wasn't allowed to talk about them, these couldn't really be good kinds of difference" (3). Sally Sales concurs: "Secrecy and disclosure work together within a field where original kinship has to be simultaneously accepted and refuted" (192).

In my case, the story before the entrance–the origin story–contained two parts full of gaps, omissions and mystery. My adoptive mother told me all she knew: I was born in the county of York, Ontario, and my birthmother was a secretary, both facts I later discovered were not quite correct. The obstetrician who delivered me knew of my birthmother and worked with my father. He knew that my parents had been rejected by Children's Aid and were looking for a daughter—a story of coincidence and chance. And in the second part of the story, I was left with two items: a grey and yellow wool blanket with a Harrods's label on it and a lacy white knit layette. The importance of these items cannot be underestimated: bequeathed to me by a birthmother I never knew, they were gifts beyond measure. They hint at connection, love, and, perhaps, family background: objects speak when people are absent. My adoptive mother kept my blanket and layette in pristine condition, saved carefully in a cedar chest constructed by her own grandfather. And tucked into the lid of the chest was a small folded note to a woman she knew would never receive it: "These were on Kate when we brought her home from the hospital. They were supplied by her natural [biological] mother. God bless her wherever she is and our thanks for allowing us to share her baby." She made this symbolic gesture because she had no other recourse; she had no information about my birthmother. Yet she still reached out to the universe. And only she and I will ever know she wrote this letter. How I wish my birthmother could read her words. From time to time now, I sit on the floor, pull my blanket and layette out of my own linen closet, and remember the mother I knew and the mother I did not.

As Marianne Novy explains, in her unpacking of adoption rhetoric, there are two basic adoption plot myths, and they operate at the ends of two different poles. One plot centres on the adoptee finding their original real mother and recreating a sense of identity. The other promotes seeing the adoptive mother as real; the curiosity of the adoptee is satisfied, and they have no further desire to search for their original parenthood. Reunion or return—there does not seem to be room for anything but this binary for the adoptee. For the mothers, there is also the problem of overcoming of labels and perceptions. The birthmother may be seen as less than three dimensional, even imaginary, often providing only a character foil or becoming the object of a search rather than being a subject in her own right. Her story may be suppressed or stigmatized. Stories about adoptive mothers can display them as secretive about their child's adoption or as disapproving or disappointed about a child's wish to search for their birthmother or birthfamily, or as a stalwart parent to whom a child returns; alternatively, the adoptive mother is lauded as exemplary, as an altruistic rescuer. Her own fears, failures, desires, and conflicted feelings with regards to mothering are rarely discussed.

Both women who were my mother come with potential distinguishing prefixes. The nomenclature of mothering in adoptive circumstances is problematic, as it attempts to codify an identity and a place in a hierarchy while marginalizing complex relationships. The intent behind the word "mother" and the manner in which it is received also matters. Some may consider a term neutral or even positive, whereas others may find the same word demeaning or offensive; connotations change over time as well. The language of the 1950s and 1960s was clearly disparaging. The "unwed mother" pejoratively pointes out the absence of religious or state normalization, and "natural mother" invites the binaries of "natural" versus "unnatural" mother, as does the term "real mother." "Birthmother" equates and limits the act of mothering with biological gestation and delivery, and as with "biological mother," it also suggests that "other mothering" is somehow secondary if not consanguineous. A child of a "biological mother," with its scientific connotations, sounds like a mere product of living tissue and may invite comparisons to the infertile other adoptive mother. "Adoptive mother" feels like an unwieldy apologia—a second-best status highlighting an artificially constructed relationship. More recent examples include "first mother," which numerically implies a primacy that the second mother cannot possess, as does "original mother." "Other" mother is just that—other. Is it possible to find language that complicates and celebrates family building rather than reducing the strata of relationships and statuses involved in it?

Adoption is partially about a tension between differing notions of mother and the construction of "good" and "bad" mothers, which is perhaps made easier when the original cannot or will not provide for the child's upbringing. However, it is made more precarious if through social institutions, laws, and processes of systemic mistreatment, she is convinced or coerced into relinquishment or if the adopting mother is similarly indoctrinated into the necessity of having children to complete a family. As an adopted daughter, which model of motherhood am I supposed to assimilate? All of these are (m)other. And how am I to think and speak of these women?

I prefer instead the language my adoptive mother instinctively selected: she was 'sharing' a baby somehow, with a woman she would never know: yet both as mothers.

Keeping: Stories of My Birthmother

> If you are adopted, a hush falls around you, the conditions of your move into the world and into language. Decisions are made about which stories to tell and which to keep silent, what to reveal and what to keep sealed. This hush is a pact, an unarticulated presence.
>
> —Jones 119

One of the key differences in family formation in adoption is that paper and law, not blood, enforce ties. I am part of a specific kinship group by decree, and I am bound by a contract that with one stroke of a pen, confers motherhood upon one woman and removes it from another and with it, potentially all other familial records and links. Now, it is only through the words of others that I can build some kind of sense of a birthmother I never knew. It is the rare papers, not the mother, and the marks upon them, that link me to her and lead back through the past. Words themselves become the substance and more real than the figure of the woman and the ghost family I seek. The tracing of the autobiographical through fragments and snippets of official writ— information doled out in parcels by others who have the capacity to withhold, deny, or assist in the release of information—is a process with which I am familiar, especially under sealed records that serve "as a symbolic battleground for conflicting perceptions of the nature of kinship, identity and attachment" (Wegar qtd. in Muller and Perry 7). Like many of my era, the type of closed adoption I experienced almost served as a type of surrogate witness protection program: identifying documents were closed and impenetrable, if they were even kept at all. Many were lost, and new histories, new birth certificates, and new families were issued, reinforcing the acceptance of a patrilineal order legitimizing children through the passing on of the father's name.

My father never really spoke about adoption to me. Not that it was avoided, but it was not a topic of conversation. After mom died, I wanted more information, and I had to work up the courage to broach the subject and, specifically, to ask his permission to open the private lawyer files. He retrieved the same little bits of information I had heard over the years—my birthmother was a secretary, she had lived in Toronto, and the obstetrician who delivered me knew of her. That is all he knew, perhaps all he wanted to know. He did agree to sign for the release of information. In the age of openness and apparent reconciliation, I was not allowed to search my own identity without permissions: parental, paternal, and legal. In frail health already by this time, had my father passed away earlier, I do not know if I could have accessed them. Does one's own history hinge on the permission given or withheld by another?

There are still many gaps and silences in my history and past that have not yet, and may never be, filled.

> Historically ... adoption has operated under the principle that nurture conquers nature and that a child can thrive when transplanted to a new environment. How does that familiar notion fit with the outburst of searching, the spreading of petitions for access to unrevised birth certificates, and the calls for open adoption of the past twenty-five years? Today's arguments [urge] proper nurture requires nature. (Modell 186)

To access my nature, however, I never have direct access to the stories of my birthmother and my conception or birth. I gradually learned through my independent research—unlocking files from lawyers and government agencies, such as the Adoption Disclosure Registry, and making eventual albeit tangential and brief contact with my birth family—that my mother gave birth as a woman in her thirties. She had a successful career that offered opportunities for advancement in a world not yet aware of women's rights: she was not the young, frightened naïve girl of the literature and propaganda. Although she was unwed and unable to bring me up as a single mother in the milieu of the day, she made her own decision to cut off contact with my birthfather; to some extent, she exercised what agency she could.

The most surreal part of acquiring the few original documents regarding my adoption, which occurred when I was in my thirties, was learning my original name—Martha Anne. It is the first time I have seen or known this information about my alter ego, my other self. This is who I might have been. With the signing of my order of surrender, this name was replaced, erased, and buried. In one of only two encounters I had with cousins of my birth family, who provided some of the precious narrative nuggets about anything even tangentially connected to my past that I am greedy for, I learned that Anne is also my birthmother's middle name. While not daring to keep me, my birthmother nonetheless enacted a small claim and connection. I never will know why Martha. "The gaps produced in adoption stories are moments of revelation when the 'might-have-been-otherwise'... are exposed" (Yngvnesson and Mahoney 88), and my names become a symbol of an alternate self and lost identity; not knowing the story of my naming is another part of the story of "I was born" I am left without.

We intuitively associate our identity with our name: "One of first ways parents actualize their parental role following the birth of a child is the choice of the child's first name.... This act of ascription is a means of self-definition for the parents.... The name is a 'thread of continuity' that leads back to the point of origin" (Hoffmann-Riem 237). However to me, the whole idea of birthmothers naming a child to be given away seems bizarre. Names are so intimate, a form of attachment and claiming, and yet birthmothers in the 1960s were urged not to bond, perhaps not to even see the child. Is naming, therefore, an act of subversion or protest, a small gesture of defiance? Or is there a kind of Biblical reverberation signifying rebirth? If it is a legal requirement to name the baby for identification purposes and to signal their personhood, then the elimination of that name must function in reverse. How then are these ideas of the giving, removal, and re-giving of names reconciled?

It was equally poignant to see my birthmother's full name and signature for the first time and to note the way her capital letters point up crisply, the slant of her cursive, the long loops of her descenders. In her signature, she is affirming, under what I assume were the disapproving eyes of male authority, that she was the *unmarried* mother—an appendix added in handwriting to the official writ as if a fact not to be forgotten or forgiven—who signed away all rights to this child. The signature of one mother is required for dismissing the claim to motherhood, whereas another signature is required to grant motherhood: everything seems to hinge on the act of putting pen to paper on a legal document, one name traded for another, one mother traded for another. I was told by my birthmother's sister-in-law, whom I met only twice and almost a decade ago now—another tenuous tie to family that has unravelled—that a single letter was written to me in her later years by my birthmother and was reported to be in her apartment when she died. I assume if her "only daughter," my half-sister, cleared out these contents, then it was destroyed. This biological half-sister expressed her desire to the sister-in-law to never know me, and I cannot help but think she is yet another barrier to my origins. I mourn this loss of a connection to her and of hearing my birthmother's words. I envision what it may be like to have the privilege to know my birthmother's thoughts and to hear her story, and mine, from her own lips.

My birthmother never told anyone who my birthfather was, and, thus, I will never know his identity. The sister-in-law affirms this, and the blank space on my birth certificate reaffirms this, as does the story recounted to me by the adoption counsellor who spoke to her in person. She rejected him; I do not know if he would have rejected me. The name of my birthfather is missing from all official documents and from any oral account of my adoption, which forever prevents me from knowing about half of my parentage, half my origin. I may have only represented a mistake that was apparently solved for him, and with no genetic testing in the 1960s, he would have been labelled only the putative father. He could have denied his involvement, yet, equally, I might also have been a child lost to him—one he knew of but had no way of finding if he had wanted to. I will never know. My birthmother's decision stops any knowledge of half of my genetic being.

This denial of the birthfather, or refusal to name him, was not uncommon, and it speaks of the wounds inflicted by illegitimate pregnancy during this time period. If the telling of the pregnancy, or the process of relinquishment, involved rejection or denial from her partner, a birthmother may not want to relive this hurt and distress. If her child resembles the birthfather, this may reopen old wounds, and the child's face or voice may be more than she can bear. Lee Campbell et al.'s study of reunion corroborates this tendency: they find that an incredible eighty per cent of biological mothers did not wish to discuss the biological father (8). These women may have worked very carefully to put this past behind them or to reconstruct a new self, only to have their equilibrium thrown by an encounter with someone who could conceivably turn their reinvented life into a lie.

For the birthmother in the 1960s, such secrecies surrounding adoption purported to provide a kind of closure. They offered security and anonymity for herself and her family. It was believed the mother could reclaim her place in society, perhaps rejoin her education, work, or social circle without gossip or censure. She could rest assured that no one in her future would ever need to know of her past. It represented a kind of inviolable contract. Confidential adoptions supposedly allowed the birthmother to relinquish and then move past her grief and shame. She could forget that she had given up her child and not have to worry that she would see her child in close proximity raised by others.

However, there are tensions. The birthmother was told that relinquishment was a solution to her problem and that she would be redeemed and rehabilitated; moreover, because she was an unfit parent, she was doing the right thing in giving up her child. And as for her own psyche, she would put this episode of her life behind her and move on. Yet a birthmother might have been forced into secrecy against her wishes; knowing that her transgression was a secret might only have reinforced her sense of shame and guilt. Because the act was a secret once, many birthmothers felt that it would always have to be one, as she feared the rejection of family, spouse, children, friends, coworkers, or any others who might not forgive her past sins. Secrecy prevented a birthmother from knowing the fate of her child: who adopted the child, how they fared, if they were adopted at all, or even if they subsequently perished. Researchers Harold Grotevant and Ruth McRoy note that such lack of information can inhibit a birthmother's grief resolution and may contribute to relationship difficulties in her future as well as prolonged feelings of loss, mourning, and attachment issues. Secrecy could equally be a coping mechanism for a mother who told no one about her baby's adoption because as long as she kept her secret, "she alone would have absolute control over it" (Schooler and Norris 8).

If a birthmother told her story at all, she could not be sure of its reception, and telling would not reverse years of secrets and lies. She might tell it "to seek meaning, understanding, and peace within adoption memories; to compensate for activities deemed abnormal by the larger society; [or] to justify [her] motherhood as valid" (Keisel 20) and her loss as real. I reflect on the duplicity that women had to resort to if they had conceived a child out of wedlock and how or whether a birthmother might decide to tell her story. I wonder how many times my birthmother might have wanted to tell her husband or her daughter. I was in my thirties before I learned from a counsellor at the Adoption Disclosure Registry (an ineffectual governmental agency that placed those birthparents and adoptees who sought each other on contact lists that took upwards of a decade to activate) that my birthmother finally told her secret for the first time more than forty years after my birth to her family—a husband, and a female child born not long after I was. Perhaps she felt her hand was forced with the mediated contact I established through the Adoption Disclosure Registry and told out of fear of being discovered. Perhaps she wished to change her own narrative of motherhood. Or perhaps she wished to disclose the secret she held for so many years in the face of imminent death. I will never know. In any case, this would have been a terrifying emotional journey that must have cost a great deal. I do not know how her family reacted. With her silence, I am left to fear what many birthmothers fear is true of mine: she suffered rejection, disapproval and blame. I think the reaction of these key people in her life must have contributed to her continuing hesitation to make contact with me. Her betrayal may have been seen doubly, and her shame reinforced. I was told by my birthmother's sister-in-law that my half-sister, upon learning of my existence, declared that she wanted nothing to do with me. All I can attest to for certain was that my birthmother never broached the subject of contact with me again to her family, and I never would meet her. Her telling may have undermined trust in a woman who essentially lied to the two most intimate people in her life for as long as she had known them. Her telling may have jeopardized her status as wife or mother, or as a moral person. Her telling may have bred resentment and unresolved conflicts. But her telling was untold to me.

I learned about my birthmother's death via a meeting with birth relatives, the sister-in-law who married my birthmother's brother, and two cousins, her children. I was given some anecdotes, personality traits, explanations, and even a few photos. I must revise the stories I thought to be real, the half-truths, and the imaginings. I learn something of my birth narrative. In June of 1962, when my birthmother was thirty-four years old, the wife of my birthmother's brother and my birthmother shared a room during vacation at the family cottage; in late August, they were assigned separate rooms. The sister-in-law attributed this to a falling out of friendship; in hindsight years later, she realized it was so my birthmother did not have to undress in front of her, as her secret pregnancy had begun to show.

As she drew near to delivery, my birthmother went away on an extended trip with granny, the matriarch who regularly travelled on cruises around the world. They spread the story that they were going to London. The assumption was London, England, which they indeed visited, but they also travelled to London, Ontario, the city of my birth. By not specifying which London and going to both, they would not slip up if asked where they had been. Thus, a lie became true. Another snippet of an origin story revealed to me in the conversation with my birth family relatives was that my layette blanket was grey and yellow because my birthmother did not know what gender I would be: no pinks or blues in the symbolism of the times. I used to wonder what clues this blanket held and how to decode its meaning—an object at least once held by the mother who gave birth to me. That she cared enough to leave me with a remnant of herself selected by her own hand and no doubt on the same London journey has always given me comfort. Now, I have one more small piece of understanding. One more piece of origin story.

I remember the mediated written conversation through the required adoption counsellor of the then Adoption Disclosure Registry system of my initial and only contact with my birthmother, where I learned she cried when learning of my existence and my desire to connect with her. She was glad to hear I grew up with siblings. I had two dogs—beagles. "Oh my" was her response.

And the single sentence from that interview I cling to: "There is never a day goes by when I don't think of that child." This is, ultimately, the origin story my birthmother gave to me.

The Use of Adoption Stories

> The story of adoption is a ghost story, full of fantasy, mystery, and missing persons, who, for the most part, are 'as if' dead.
> —Lifton, "Ghosts" 71

Hannah Arendt suggests that to tell one's story is an act of freedom; it is "a discursive practice in which material realities and imaginary possibilities coexist" (qtd. in Buss 2). In the act of telling my story, I assemble what I consider to be a comprehensible and true narrative—the transmission of selfhood and identity. But Sidonie Smith posits that "there is no essential original, coherent autobiographical self before the moment of [such] self-narrating…. Any hint of the disparate, the disassociated, is overlooked or enfolded into a narrative of synthesis" (108). I may assume a coherence that did not exist or a linearity that explains the destination without considering the detours. Are some stories, familiar to my mouth, passed on through birth and adoptive mothers more fabrication than substance? Has retelling smoothed the edges and burrs? And if I have to let go of some of my stories will I be "susceptible to experiences of dislocation, disenfranchisement, disarray, dissonance in [my] daily lived experiences as [I] face the loss of stories that [I] have used?" (Leggo in Schwartz 19). Which are more useful, the adoption stories I tell, or the ones that were told to me?

"We need to compose and tell our stories as creative ways of growing in humanness," (in Swartz 2) writes Carl Leggo. Yet my story is not whole or unbroken; it does not point backwards seamlessly or situate me within a context that can be fully grasped. It is full of silences and imaginings, as I try to make sense of my adoptive identity, origins, and the lives of the women who nurtured me in person or from afar. Counter-narratives to that of the dominant discourse can open spaces to position such stories differently in social discourse, not as shameful or as mere victim testimony. Adoption stories may not reclaim a past or find answers to unknowable questions; instead, they may allow for eventual acceptance of omissions and fictions without a drive for closure and an understanding of the arbitrariness of all families and the contingencies of identity. They may allow for empowering narratives that have often been silenced to be heard: the stories of imperfect motherhood. And within these narratives can be found accounts of beginnings—however partial, incomplete or unknowable—that nonetheless may help all those seeking an origin story that they can live with.

Endnote

1. I have referred to her as my mother by adoption or adoptive mother only in this chapter and for purposes of clarity. She was, and will always be, my mother. Likewise the term "adoptive parents" is used in this chapter only for clarity purposes.

Works Cited

Baldassi, Cindy L. "Quest to Access Closed Adoption Files in Canada: Understanding Social Context and Legal Resistance to Change." *Canadian Journal of Family Law,* vol. 21, no. 2, 2005, pp. 211-266.

Berebitsky, Julie. *Like Our Very Own: Adoption and the Changing Culture of Motherhood, 1851-1950.* University Press of Kansas, 2000.

Colaner, Colleen Warner, and Haley Kranstuber. "'Forever Kind of Wondering': Communicatively Managing Uncertainty in Adoptive Families." *Journal of Family Communication,* vol. 10, 2010, pp. 236-255. doi: 10.1080/15267431003682435.

Cole, Ardra L., and J. Gary Knowles. *Lives in Context: The Art of Life History Research.* AltaMira Press, 2001.

Buss, Helen M. *Repossessing the World: Reading Memoirs by Contemporary Women.* Life Writing Series. Wilfrid Laurier University Press, 2002.

Davis, Kingsley. "Illegitimacy and the Social Structure." *American Journal of Sociology,* vol. 45, no. 2, Sept. 1939, pp. 215-233. ezproxy.library.yorku.ca/login?url=http://search.proquest.com/docview/58466544?accountid=15182.

Campbell, Lee H., et al. "Reunions between Adoptees and Birth Parents: The Adoptees' Experience." *Social Work,* vol. 36, no. 4, 1991, pp. 329-335. ezproxy.library.yorku.ca/login?url=http://search.proquest.com/docview/215269717?accountid=15182.

de Soto, Paris. "Genealogy Revised in Secrets and Lies." *Imagining Adoption: Essays on Literature and Culture,* edited by Marianne Novy, University of Michigan Press, 2001, pp. 193-206.

Douglas, Anthony, and Terry Philpot. *Adoption: Changing Families, Changing Times*. Routledge, 2003.

Eliot, George, and Barbara Nathan Hardy. *Daniel Deronda*. Penguin Books, 1986.

Freeark, Kristine, et. al. "Fathers, Mothers and Marriages: What Shapes Adoption Conversations in Families with Young Adopted Children." *Adoption Quarterly*, vol. 11, no. 1, 2008, pp. 2-23. doi: 10.1080/10926750802291393.

Foucault, Michel. "Nietzsche, Genealogy, History." *The Foucault Reader*, edited by Paul Rabinow, Pantheon, 1984, pp. 76-100.

Gish, Nancy K. "Adoption, Identity, Voice. Jackie Kay's Inventions of Self." *Imagining Adoption: Essays on Literature and Culture*, edited by Marianne Novy, University of Michigan Press, 2001, pp. 171-191.

Gonzalez, Macarena Garcia, and Elisabeth Wesseling. "The Stories We Adopt By: Tracing 'The Red Thread' in Contemporary Adoption Narratives." *The Lion and the Unicorn*, vol. 37, no 3, September 2013, pp. 257-276. doi:10.1353/uni.2013.0021.

Gross, Terry. "Fictional 'Mothers' Reveal Facts of A Painful Adoption Process." *Fresh Air. National Public Radio*, May 22, 2013. www.npr.org/2013/05/22/184264231/fictional-mothers-reveal-facts-of-a-painful-adoption-process. Accessed 7 Nov. 2019.

Grotevant, Harold D., and Ruth G. McRoy. *Openness in Adoption: Exploring Family Connections*. Sage Pub., 1998.

Harrigan, Meredith Marko. "Exploring the Narrative Process: An Analysis of the Adoption Stories Mothers Tell Their Internationally Adopted Children." *Journal of Family Communication*, vol. 10, pp. 24-39, 2010. doi: 10.1080/15267430903385875.

Hoffmann-Riem, Christa. *The Adopted Child: Family Life with Double Parenthood*. Routlege, 2017.

Homans, Margaret. "Adoption Narratives, Trauma, and Origins." *Narrative*, vol. 14, no. 1, Jan. 2006, pp. 4-26.

Isaac, Rael Jean. *Adopting a Child Today*. 1st ed. Harper & Row, 1965.

Jones, Stacy Holman. "(M)othering Loss: Telling Adoption Stories, Telling Performativity." *Text and Performance Quarterly*, vol. 25, no. 2, Apr. 2005, pp. 113-135.

Kellas, Jody Koenig. "Narrating Family: Introduction to the Special Issue on Narratives and Storytelling in the Family." *Journal of Family Communication*, vol. 10, 2010, pp. 1-6.

Kiesel, Suzan G. *Natural and Not: Articulating Mother(hood) Within the Adoption Triangle*. Dissertation, Southern Illinois University, 2008.

Kirk, David. *Shared Fate: A Theory and Method of Adoptive Relationships*. 2nd ed. Ben-Simon Publications, 1984.

Kranstuber, Haley, and Jody Koenig Kellas. "'Instead of Growing Under Her Heart, I Grew in It': The Relationship Between Adoption Entrance Narratives and Adoptees' Self-Concept." *Communication Quarterly*, vol. 59, no. 2, April-June 2011, pp. 179-199.

Lifton, Betty Jean. "Ghosts in the Adoptive Family." *Psychoanalytic Inquiry*, vol. 30, 2010, 71-79. doi: 10.1080/07351690903200176.

Lifton, Betty Jean. *Lost and Found: The Adoption Experience*. Dial Press, 1979.

Pullman, Phillip. *Lyra's Oxford*. Alfred A. Knopf Books for Young Readers, 2003.

Modell, Judith Schachter. *A Sealed and Secret Kinship: The Culture of Policies and Practices in American Adoption*. Vol 3. Berghahn Books, 2002.

Muller, Ulrich, and Barbara Perry. "Adopted Persons' Search for and Contact with their Birth Parents I: Who Searches and Why?" *Adoption Quarterly*, vol. 4, no. 3, 2001, pp. 5-37. ezproxy.library.yorku.ca/login?url=http://search.proquest.com.ezproxy.library.yorku.ca/docview/61464393?accountid=15182.

Novy, Marianne. "Reading Adoption: Family and Difference in Fiction and Drama." *Women's Studies,* vol. 36, 2007, pp. 213-218. ezproxy.library.yorku.ca/login?url=http://search.proquest.com.ezproxy.library.yorku.ca/docview/36763993?accountid=15182.

Raymond, Louise, and Colette Taube Dywasuk. *Adoption and After*. Harper & Row, 1974.

Sales, Sally. *Adoption, Family and the Paradox of Origins: A Foucauldian History*. Palgrave Macmillan Studies in Family and Intimate Life. Palgrave Macmillan, 2012.

Schooler, Jayne E., and Betsie Norris. *Journeys after Adoption: Understanding Lifelong Issues*. Bergin & Garvey, 2002.

Schwarz, Lorin. "About Wishes and Invitations: Four Meditations on Life Writing with Carl Leggo." *Vitae Scholasticae*, 2006. www.freepatentsonline.com/article/Vitae-Scholasticae/173922137.html. Accessed 7 Nov. 2019.

Smith, Sidonie. "Performativity, Autobiographical Practice, Resistance." *Women, Autobiography, Theory: A Reader,* edited by Sidonie Smith and Julia Watson, University of Wisconsin Press, 1998, pp. 108-115.

Solinger, Rickie. *Wake Up Little Susie: Single Pregnancy and Race before Roe v. Wade.* New York: Routledge, 2000.

Vanelisti, Anita L., et al. "Family Portraits: Stories as Standards for Family Relationships." *Journal of Social and Personal Relationships*, vol. 16, no. 3, 1999, pp. 335-368.

Yngvesson, Barbara, and Maureen A. Mahoney. "'As One Should, Ought and Wants to Be': Belonging and Authenticity in Identity Narratives. *Theory, Culture & Society,* vol. 17, no. 6, 2000, pp. 77-110.

Chapter Two

Connecting the Dots in Family Stories: Embedded Feminist Perspectives

Evonne Garnett

My sister and I are chatting long distance about an opportunity to write an exploratory manuscript discussing the birthing stories of my maternal grandparents' generation and how these stories influenced our understanding of feminism. We come from a long line of "true-blue" Mennonites on both sides of our family. All of the family tree branches going back for many generations include only Mennonite people. Mennonites marry Mennonites: mine is the first generation to break that tradition.

I am proud of my heritage, as the Mennonite culture has a rich diversity of languages, food, and music. This culture is well known for balancing patriotism with pacifism, and both values are held with equal measures of passion. No one can outwork a Mennonite; the work ethic permeates everything, and a pragmatic utilitarianism is instilled in children from the time they are very young. However, no culture is without its shortcomings, and running like a speed boat through the waters of Mennonite culture is a patriarchal ideology. Its noble purpose is to maintain family structures, but a consequence is the growing distance between the values and dreams placed on boys and men, as opposed to those given to girls and women. Boys are raised to be men and to become leaders of their home and community, and they are encouraged to pursue education and become public servants. Women are useful as child bearers, gardeners, cleaners, and cooks. My sister and I have been immersed in this conservative culture. But with breaks in tradition also come breaks in worldviews, which have been fed, in part at least, by our family's birthing stories, handed down for two generations.

"Oh, I don't think I'd use the word feminist to describe our Great-Aunt Mary," my sister says.

"You wouldn't? Why not? Because she certainly took control of her own life," I say surprised.

"She would not have articulated that though," my sister continues. "Not like that. She must have been in her seventies, I guess, when we were kids, eh? How many little old women knew how to put up and take down storm windows? She did those things because she had to, not because she was making some feminist statement. She didn't even know what the word feminism meant!"

"But I think that's the point," I reply. "She took control of her own life, of her own choices. In order to live the life she chose she had to learn how to do all those things that *men* were supposed to do for her. Isn't that what feminism is? Isn't it all about having choices?"

I propose that my mother's family birthing stories have served like a dot-to-dot activity in which the dots are anchoring points: they appear random until they are connected to create a meaningful image. By examining my mother's use of language in these stories, their contexts, and the ideologies transmitted by them, I can trace an evolution of feminist ideology that has permeated my patriarchal landscape. This emergent image has influenced the shape of my identity, the foundation upon which I have made choices and constructed a life. This chapter has four "dots" of its own that discuss the language of particular birthing stories and draw out their meanings. The first section introduces the idea of discourse analysis generally and also introduces the reader to my mother's family. The second section, broken into four parts, analyzes the stories from my mother's paternal family. The third section, in six parts, examines my mother's maternal family stories. The stories from these two sides of my mother's family are contrasted, and the result of the ensuing contradictions is the subject of the fourth and final section of this chapter. Stories transmit meaning. They communicate values. They evolve with each telling. I have been influenced by stories, and the result is a shift in my personal identity. On a larger scale, however, stories are capable of shifting cultural values and of changing the culture itself by influencing individual ideologies, identities, and choices.

Looking for the Dots

Sara Mills, in her book *Discourse*, writes that "critical discourse analysts [are] those linguists who analyse text from a political perspective" (118). My mother, had she been given the opportunity, would have been an extraordinary critical discourse analyst, of the ethnographic variety. No event of her life passed by without eventually undergoing an examination of its meaning. Mills continues, saying that

> [analysts] argue that language is a central vehicle in the process whereby people are constituted as individuals and as social subjects, and because language and ideology are closely imbricated, the close systemic analysis of the language of texts can expose some of the workings of texts and, by extension, the way that people are oppressed within current social structures.

I heard my mother tell family origin stories, but where she got them from is a mystery, although I suspect she did a lot of eavesdropping when her mother, aunties, and grandmothers talked among themselves in their kitchens and gardens. Mom never failed to pair a story with a lesson to be learned from it, and those lessons heavily featured the inequitable power structures of the Mennonite culture in which she grew up. In Mennonite culture, men have power over women and girls by virtue of their sex. The stories my mother learned as a child influenced her ideology, which highlighted the uneven power structures and informed her childrearing choices. She strove to eliminate these differences in her childrearing. These choices, combined with her storytelling, shaped my ideology. Through the stories Mom told, I learned to interpret the world. They formed my own feminist worldview by which I would navigate my way, one choice at a time, through the tangle of cultural intersections that tattoo my life—dots branded into the skin of my ideology.

Mom's Paternal Stories: An Explicit Voice Claiming Freedom of Choice

My Great-Aunt Mary, my mother's paternal aunt, was an icon for me when I was young. Stories of her rebellious prowess captured my imagination, particularly as she was raised Mennonite. In those days, to be a Mennonite female who rebelled against the gender roles was to be a person of superhero proportions. When I was dragged to her house by my mother for tea, all I saw was a scrawny leathery woman, no taller than my own mother, barely strong enough to hold up a cigarette in her frail hands. However, in my mind she was an Amazonian—a woman who fought against the waves of a cultural ideology that told her who she ought to be. She worked hard for the opportunity to live a life of her own choosing. My Great-Aunt Mary spurned dresses and skirts, choosing instead to wear her father's coveralls to break wild horses her brothers were afraid to approach; she drove the stone boat to town to fetch the doctor when her brothers were too panicked to make a clear-headed decision about what to do in a crisis. She turned down a proposal from the love of her life, telling him she refused to bear children but, if he'd wait thirty years until she was past "the childbearing age," she'd marry him then. He waited, and she embraced her independence well into her mid-life, and married my Uncle Jake after her menopause. She supported herself through the early twentieth century, bought her own house and lived in it alone, and eventually dragged my mother (her niece) out of an abusive situation; she showed my mother her how to live independently and make choices of her own.

Through my mother's storytelling I learned to love Great-Aunt Mary. I loved the idea of her. I declared out loud that I would also control my own life; I'd provide for myself, and no one could tell me what kind of woman I ought to be. My mother's storytelling encouraged me to live less bound by patriarchal restraints than she had been. So I was taught a version of feminism from my mother who learned it, in part, from Great-Aunt Mary. Where did Great-Aunt Mary's ideas about making her own choices come from? The story came and went through my childhood, but the essentials of it remain the same: Mary made a choice when others may not have even noticed one existed.

Great-Aunt Mary's Birthing Story

This story came to my mother from either Great-Aunt Mary herself, or from one of Mom's aunts, or possibly from her grandmother, Great-Aunt Mary's mother. So it is at least a third-generation story, and, as such, full of imaginings before it even made it to me. This story, told to me by my mother, fixed itself in my head as a signpost. Mom never included the details, as I have narrated them; she left that part up to me. I tell it here as I have imagined it, identifiable through italicized text.

Mary was told to go outside to play and to not come back in until she was called. The house was full of strange people, and Mary's mother had been in bed all morning. Even her father wasn't acting like himself. Mary had no choice—a child among all these adults. She went outside, but she did not play. Lingering around the house, maybe kicking stones, or rubbing the dogs' bellies, Mary could hear when her mother started screaming.

I imagine that she rushed back into the house but was turned around at the door: "This is no place for children. Now be obedient and stay outside!" I can hear the door slam behind her on its wooden frame. Mary went around the house and on tiptoe looked inside her parents' bedroom through the window, still listening to her mother crying and screaming. From her vantage point, she could see her mother's feet pointed towards the window where Mary's voyeurism had her rooted to the spot. At the sides of the bed, adults were rushing about, one of them perhaps putting a rolled towel in Mary's mother's mouth through which came sounds that lodged themselves in Mary's ears as a tortured gagging. There was blood spilling out from between her mother's legs, and Mary's view provided a clear picture of the whole traumatic process as her brother launched himself into the world at her mother's expense. At the end of the day, Mary vowed she would never ever go through that; she would live a life without children if that's what childbearing meant for women. Mary was six years old.

Stories Out of Context

As I have worked through this story and other family stories, I have wrestled with my thoughts to assemble them into some kind of order and to connect those dots in order to understand the context of the larger storylines. It's been a struggle to articulate why these have meaning for me or how they have influenced my worldview. I have always understood at some visceral level that family stories have personal significance, and the task of writing about these stories has forced me to analyze their influence on me. Like those childhood dot-to-dot activities, stories, like dots scattered on a page, appear random but connected have meaning. I often refer to Michael White and David Epston's book, *Narrative Means to Therapeutic Ends* to look for connections between the dots. Even with the assistance of other writers, including Diane Setterfield and Sara Mills, this chapter has been difficult for me to write. However, characters from within the pages of a story always do have difficulty clearly seeing the subplots and story arcs. Writing the stories down and reorganizing their themes on paper, long conversations with my sister and husband, brooding walks, and one-sided discussions with my Alzheimer's-afflicted mother—these have helped to clarify the message that the dots had to tell. I had to be patient with my own process.

There are many stories about my Great-Aunt Mary, but the story just told is the most relevant to my development as a feminist. As a young girl, I was not explicitly thinking about my intellectual position on feminism, but I was watching the women around me and learning about what it means to be female in a patriarchal world, even if I could not possibly have put that into words of any kind. Concepts form in abstract ways even while they are informed by concrete experience. White and Epston write that "stories are full of gaps which persons must fill in order for the story to be performed. These gaps recruit the lived experience and the imagination of persons" (13). My young imagination was more than up to the task of filling in any gaps my mother's versions left out. White and Epston continue: "Thus, in two senses, [storytelling] introduces us to an intertextual world. In the first sense, it proposes that persons' lives are situated in texts within texts. In the second sense, every telling or retelling of a story, through its performance, is a new telling that encapsulates, and expands upon the previous telling" (13).

My sister would very likely tell the story of Great-Aunt Mary's experience watching her brother being born differently than I do; her imagination and experience are quite distinct from mine. As a young girl I imagined the birthing scene, trying to understand what that birthing scenario must have been like. In my grade six health classes, during the sex education segment, having babies was presented as a clean and sterile experience with smiling women in green hospital gowns and tiny pink babies gurgling and wrapped in white linens, handed over by doctors and nurses in pressed uniforms under bright lights. The distance between this and Great-Aunt Mary's experience was beyond my grasp, and so just like any child with an imagination, I went for the worst case images: people yelling and rushing around in thinly disguised panic, blood gushing everywhere from between my great-grandmother's legs, producing yet another male into the world to control and manage the universe from his privileged position as son. I do not know whether Great-Aunt Mary took this feminist position as a child or whether it evolved in her thinking as she grew; I do know that by the time the story reached my ears it was firmly linked to Great-Aunt Mary's resentment towards male dominance in Mennonite culture and her decision to not bear children herself.

I heard these stories out of context: their meaning in the 1910s when they occurred could not possibly be understood by a child hearing them in the 1940s when my mother took hold of them, nor could I as a child in the 1970s possibly grasp their original significance. White and Epston explain that "every new reading of a text is a new interpretation of it, and thus a different writing of it.... What a person knows of life they know through 'lived experience'.... In order to make sense of our lives and to express ourselves, experience must be 'storied' and it is this storying that determines the meaning ascribed to experience" (9-10). I grew up in a mid-sized city, close to hospitals and birth-control clinics, but Mom grew up in the 1930s in a tiny town near the farm where Great-Aunt Mary's experience occurred. My mother had been in that bedroom, looked through that window, knew the baby birthed there as her uncle, and loved Mary's mother, my great-grandmother, with passion. Mom likely had a much clearer understanding of this origin story, the story of her uncle's birth, having experienced more of its context firsthand, and would have needed much less imagination than I did to fill in the details of setting and character. As a result, her interpretation of it may have landed much closer than mine to the interpretations of those who lived it. The distance between a child's interpretation of experiencing something this traumatic and a child's interpretation hearing about it two generations later covers quite an expanse of subjective ground.

For Mom this short anecdote served as a foundation for her feminist stance that "women are good for much more than childbearing!" She firmly taught me that I had choices as a girl. I grew up under the umbrella of that mantra and it was drilled into me from my early years—just because I had female reproductive organs didn't mean I had to use them. I remember this "dot" being around in my childhood, but it wasn't for years that it came into focus for me. This anecdote brings into real life the point White and Epston make when they write that "since we cannot know objective reality, all knowing requires an act of interpretation" (2). As a child the meaning of Great-Aunt Mary's experience outside that window was interpreted for me by my mother. In time I would overlay my own interpretations over my mother's story and create a new version of the story, layering meaning over meaning to suit the context in which I was living. In the end, the concept of choice has been the real-world application of this story.

Stories as Foundations for Living Out Worldviews

As a young woman, when I was engaged to be married, Mom stopped me in the kitchen, where she was making Sunday soup, to tell me that I was under no obligation to provide grandchildren for her: "You do what you want, Evonne. If you want to have children, good, but don't do it for me. Your brothers have provided all the grandchildren I could want. If you never have children, you have my blessing too." Something inside me notably clicked when she said this: a gate opened in my mind that I hadn't realized had been closed. Despite my loud feminist declarations, I had still taken for granted that I would have children. Doesn't every woman get married and have babies and make a family? Isn't that the point of getting married, I asked myself. Mom never thought so, but she rarely articulated it directly to me, nor, I suspect, even to herself. Instead, she told stories. I doubt she intentionally fashioned the stories to instruct me in feminism—Mom would not have even counted herself a feminist. She was far too practical for that. However, her thinking bled through her stories whether she meant for it to or not, and I clearly understood the underlying messages when she relayed these narratives.

I don't think Mom explicitly linked Great-Aunt Mary's story with her own version of feminism. By telling me that I could choose a different path, she connected me with Great-Aunt Mary's route through life, and, by doing so Mom revealed choices I hadn't noticed existed. As a result, when the doctor informed my husband and me that there was no point in his prescribing birth control because only by a miracle would we ever have children, I reacted in a way that I had not expected: I thrust my fist into the air and shouted, "Yes!" I was immensely relieved of a burden I had assumed was mine to bear without exploring my own feelings about the matter.

Here is where the interpretation of the origin story became ideologically lived out. If Mom had told different family stories, ones that emphasized the necessity of childbearing, perhaps I would have felt grief or guilt over this news. If Mom had told the birthing stories differently, with shame or with scorn, perhaps I would not have felt any freedom to choose my response in that moment. In a sense, I had no choice about not bearing children or about not birthing my own origin stories, but because this choice was illuminated by my mother through her storytelling, I was free to choose, even in those moments when it appeared that choices were taken from me.

Stories as Shifts in Cultural Practice

My mother's instruction to me about how personhood for women is not connected to motherhood created options for me within the context of my own life. In reflecting on that moment of learning that I was unlikely to bear biological children, I realized that my mother's interpretations of Great-Aunt Mary's experiences gave me childbearing or not-bearing choices that I recognized as decisions apart from my identity as a woman. I was differently equipped for this moment than perhaps other women because of the ongoing guidance of Great-Aunt Mary's stories. The stories shifted something in my mind. White and Epston assert the following:

> In order to perceive change in one's life—to experience life as progressing—and in order to perceive oneself changing one's life, a person requires mechanisms that assist her to plot the events of her life within the context of coherent sequences across

time—through the past, present and future—the detection of change is vital to the performance of meaning. (35)

I perceived an interpretive change: I became aware of a new thinking that resulted in actual changes in my actions. I was granted personal agency—"the meaning that [people] attribute to events that determine their behaviour" (White and Epston 2). My understanding of my choices and my interpretation of what it means to be feminist spring directly from this seminal story of Great-Aunt Mary. How I respond to the choices presented to me and—even more so, how I interpret what my choices are—is in part a result of the meaning I gleaned from my mother's storytelling, starting with Great-Aunt Mary's experience of her brother's birth.

When I was a child I wasn't thinking about having and raising a family. I never wanted to play with babies and never dreamed of having my own children. I didn't talk about being a mom because Mom never talked about me being a mom. She talked about me being a reader or a writer or a lawyer; the "mom" part was my assumption because all the adult women I knew were moms. However, once I understood that a whole new set of choices was available to me, the possibility of a cultural shift also opened up. As I sorted through a newfound set of options, I noticed a path that was formerly too obscure to be noticed, let alone chosen. This new path held a possibility for shifting cultural practices and norms in small ways and in daily decisions. I was suddenly aware that I did not have to take the obvious and well-worn path of my Mennonite ancestors. Great-Aunt Mary laid out a whole new set of dots for the next generations. The practical application came immediately at the time of hearing that I would not likely bear my own children, as a choice: I framed this as "I would have chosen to not bear children anyways, had I thought of that as a choice." However, I could not have articulated this at the time. The awareness of the new set of dots took more time to emerge.

Cultural practices become the norms that inform our choices. The reverse is also as true: our choices influence norms, which shift cultural practices. In my particular case, my initial understanding of my mothering choices came from my observations and interpretations of the experiences of other women in my mother's family. It was assumed given the cultural practices in my family that I, as a female, would embrace motherhood. That was the normal practice, and, looking around at other families, I did not observe even one adult female, other than my Great-Aunt Mary, who was not a mother or who was not planning on becoming a mother. So the cultural practices became norms, which then informed the boundaries of my perceived choices. My Great-Aunt Mary, though, was the single anomaly: she spurned motherhood and chose a life free from childbearing. Granted, her choices were based on what could conceivably be a mildly traumatic childhood experience: watching her own mother's birthing struggles. Still, she carved out a new choice and challenged the norm, which encouraged me when I learned I was not going to be bearing my own children to explore what choices I had for narrating this experience. My choice added another example to the norm, which, in turn, challenged the cultural practice. It took four generations for the cultural practices around childbearing norms to fully shift. My great-grandmother bore her children on the farm; her daughter, my great-aunt, challenged that cultural practice by making a new choice; my mother told me this story opening the possibility for another choice outside the norm; and I, the fourth generation, embraced that choice, also challenging the norm and, finally, changing the cultural practices around childbearing options. I have, on my mother's side, another cousin who has chosen to not have children. Together we are, to my knowledge, the first generation in my mother's family tree to choose to not bear children without any stigma attached to that choice. This is feminism—to have a choice free from stigma. The stories told about childbearing practices in my mother's family have allowed for those shifts to occur. Stories change cultural practices and norms, which inform choices; and choices, suggested by stories, in turn influence cultural practices and norms. Stories count.

Mom's Maternal Stories: An Implicit Voice in the Absence of Choice

White and Epston tell us that "persons can be invited to investigate their family and community archives ... in an attempt to locate previously established knowledges" and that "persons are able to appreciate their unique history of struggle" (32). I love this language, as it invites me to explore my family history to find what my family knows about women's childbearing choices in our cultural community and to learn about our struggle to carve out choices for ourselves and what it means to be female, or, perhaps even more significantly, a female person in a human family. I need to tuck myself into those pages and become a character in my family lore. I have no children of my own, but I'd like to be seen as the Great-Aunt Mary figure when my nieces and nephews tell their children our family stories.

Stories Bear Seeds That Enable Feminist Worldviews to Sprout

On my mother's maternal side, the origin stories are more subtle. There are no feminist pioneers on this side of the family. These ancestors were more traditionally entrenched, perhaps, and didn't speak of such things as childbirth. Babies were born in back rooms, and the shades were drawn so no peepers could get a glimpse of what really happened in there. Any birthing stories told on this side of the family were hushed up. Birthing stories exist on this side of the family, of course, but there's space between them, and connecting the dots takes patience. I wouldn't call any of these stories feminist, except that all apply to females exclusively but not in any liberating sense. The feminist stance has come through because of the interpretations these stories gained through the generations. No one told them with the intent of liberating anyone, but people's attitudes about them came through in the telling, and those attitudes, particularly my mother's, taught me how to interpret the morals of the stories. The connecting of these dots—the interpretations of the meanings of these stories—has been a process and not a singular revelation.

Dianne Setterfield's character Vida Winter in *The Thirteenth Tale* says that "a birth is not really a beginning. Our lives at the start are not really our own, but only the continuation of someone else's story.... When I was born I was no more than a sub-plot" (Kindle locator 870). My mother's origin stories on her maternal side are tangles of subtext that influence my developing ideology in ways that are difficult even now to articulate. Vida Winter explains to her audience the following:

> The beginning is never where you think it is. Our lives are so important to us that we tend to think the story of them begins with our birth. First there was nothing, then *I* was born.... Yet that is not so. Human lives are not pieces of string that can be separated out from a knot of others and laid out straight. Families are webs. Impossible to touch one part of it without setting the

rest vibrating. Impossible to understand one part without having a sense of the whole. (Kindle locator 864)

So the story of how the birthing stories on this side of the family have influenced my mother's ideology, her practices in childrearing, and, therefore, my own brand of feminism is more implicit and, as a result, more complex. Children aren't consciously analyzing their cultural contexts for ideological meaning. Certainly I wasn't. I will tell the following story as I remember it coming together in pieces for me. Since family stories influence ideologies, which are acted out in the real world, I will begin with my becoming aware of those ideologies. The origin stories that largely influenced these views and actions come at the end of my narration because, for me, that was the sequence of my awareness—the way in which I connected the dots between lived experiences, interpretations, and the stories that founded them.

Worldviews Are Unspoken But Enacted as Childrearing Practices

Every Saturday morning of my childhood was spent doing chores. No one was exempt. My mother wanted her boys (my brothers) to learn how to keep house to spare her future daughters-in-law from having to bear that burden alone, and she wanted her daughters to be equipped for independence. "What's good for the goose is good for the gander!" She did her best to keep gender roles from entering into the picture.

Except that gender most certainly did, realistically, enter into her administration of the chores. If we were out of honey, I would volunteer to go down to bring up the five-gallon pail of honey bought straight from the beekeeper at the farmers' market: "No, Evonne. You let your brother Bruce do the heavy lifting." If my sister or I was experiencing menstrual discomfort Mom would call for one of the boys: "Waine! Bring the vacuum cleaner up those stairs so Evonne can do the rugs up there." If Dad was trimming trees and called upon one of his daughters to help haul the branches to the alley, Mom would intervene: "George, get one of the boys to help you with the heavy work." I remember being divided in my opinion about this: anything boys can do I can do better, certainly, I thought, but there was also a quality of smugness knowing I was getting out of something that I was certainly capable of doing. What I was less aware of was the subconscious perception that there were gender roles in work and play and that lines were being drawn around what I could attain or aspire to and what I should leave well enough alone. I was subject to a variety of conflicting discourses, struggling with a kind of cognitive dissonance because "texts are not determined by one discourse alone … there may be several different discourses at work in the construction of a particular text, and these discourses are often in conflict with one another" (Mills 89). Certainly, the applied gender roles were discordant with the message that I had choices and should use them. White and Epston suggest that "we prune, from our experience, those events that do not fit with the dominant evolving stories that we … have about us" (11-12). During my preadolescence, I struggled with what that dominant story was. Was I merely a girl and limited to girls' work and play or did I have choices that would allow me to dominate any field? None of these thoughts were explicit, of course. I was a child. The following memory in particular sheds light on my mother's dual thinking regarding parenting girls: she bought an Easy-Bake Oven for her girl, but it was to be a toy. Mom wasn't emphasizing that I actually learn how to bake—I was to learn how to read. But then, what was the Easy-Bake Oven for?

I outgrow the Betty Crocker Easy-Bake Oven Santa had brought for Christmas, and I want to try my hand at real cooking. I run down the stairs, taking them two or three at a time and land with a thump in the hall outside the kitchen. Mom is standing by the stove, having already started supper. "Mom, can I help?"

She sighs, chronically tired, and turns to look at me, hands on her hips. "No, Evonne."

"But Mom, I can help! I want to learn how to cook!" I plead.

"Evonne, any damn fool can learn how to cook. If you can read a cookbook you can cook." She is adamant. "What you need is an education. Now go back upstairs and do your homework or read your books."

The toys I remember receiving included a my-size teddy bear in a wicker rocking chair; a Barbie with a red sports car and a red chest full of Barbie clothes, which Mom had made; and then, later, a doll as big as I was with her own walk-in closet and a whole wardrobe of clothes, also hand sewn by Mom. There were gender-neutral toys as well: puzzles and Lego sets, bicycles and toy instruments. And always, always books: the Hardy Boys, which I snuck out of my brothers' rooms, and for us girls, Trixie Beldon and Nancy Drew, girl detectives to balance all the boy stories. In my selection of gifts, there were never the so-called boy toys that my three older brothers received—ball gloves or airplane models—and I didn't miss them. I understood there are realms where boys rule and realms that belong to girls. It wasn't something I consciously questioned. I was immersed in Mom's choices about how to parent without being aware even then that she was making choices. I'm not sure even she was aware she was making choices.

Becoming Aware

The effects of Mom's subtly conflicted messages about gender roles weren't evident to me at the time, but looking back, I can see how I struggled with them as a girl. In this memory, I am acting out those contradictions, although I could not have put the conflict into words at the time.

My grade seven class bursts through the gymnasium emergency exit onto the playground. I am a fast runner and am easily in the middle of the pack. We arrive breathy and excited just to be out of the building and under the sun. Our male teacher tells us we'll be playing soccer and my stomach sinks. I know my mother will not want me playing soccer—it's a rough game. There's pushing and shoving. People fall hard or get a ball kicked to the gut.

The teacher chooses two team captains who will pick their teams and my hand goes in the air. I tell him, "I'm not allowed to play soccer. My mother won't like it."

"What is the problem with soccer, Evonne?" Hands on his hips, he believes girls should play sports.

"It's too rough. I'm not supposed to play. I could get hurt." I avoid looking at him. This sounds weak, even to me.

He makes a face, and I know he's not happy, but he allows me to sit it out and watch. As the game progresses, I see that Audrey and Linda in particular are as competitive as the guys are. They are excited to be playing, and I wonder at that.

It didn't occur to me to question my mother's influence in this—my first remembered reluctance to participate in boys' play. If I had questioned my position, had thought that I could do this with any skill or talent, perhaps I would have resented not being allowed to play. Perhaps I would have played, a rebellious move, and not told Mom about it. Instead, I opted out of it altogether, and it never came up at home because it wasn't something to discuss. I don't remember ever even thinking about bringing this topic up with my mother; I didn't struggle with it. Girls didn't play sports. I wondered at these girls who were playing sports, as though they were creatures whose world was so foreign to me that it simply wasn't approachable.

As children, my sister and I were protected from any rough work or play. We weren't allowed to skate in case we took a hard fall; cycling and swimming were permitted, but when our swim coach suggested we take up weights, Mom objected. This fearfulness was passed down to us through generations of gender-based ideology. Even my grandfather did not permit Mom, his daughter, to do any men's work because she was a "sickly" child. White and Epston explain that "the meaning we ascribe to any event is determined and restrained by the receiving context for that event, that is, by the network of premises and presuppositions that constitute our maps of the world" (2). In my twelve year old being, there were all kinds of "premises and presuppositions" planted there by the stories I'd heard from my mother, but, of course, I hadn't the awareness at that age to connect the dots of any of these ideas of boys' versus girls' play to family narratives. My mother, in telling her stories, was engaging in a kind of personal discourse analysis herself, for her own reasons, and her processed worldview was reflected in her telling, but all this was implicit. I was getting the message but wasn't connecting the dots. Yet.

The Middle Generation Serves as a Conduit for Interpreting Stories

Before I was born, these birthing stories were boiling away on a backburner in my mother's mind. She was processing them, extracting meaning, and boiling them down to an essential reduction. Some of the stories were hers, and some belonged to the generation before her, but together they simmered until they became meaningful, even if they weren't articulated as such by her. Once Mom had children of her own, she regurgitated these birthing stories from her ancestors and fed them to us; she did the bulk of the processing even though we were left to interpret what remained of them after she handed them over. I don't even remember the context of the following story or which circumstances prompted Mom's retelling of this story. It stands by itself in my memory, and although my sister and I both heard it many times, Mom didn't intentionally set it in any context particularly. We understood this story to be meaningful for her, and we understood that she meant it to be instructive for us. The precise interpretations were not discussed. There was no discussion of the story's explicit meaning; she never asked, "do you understand what this story means for you, Evonne?" It was simply a story, told forcefully, with emotion and intensity. Its interpretation was ours to make.

Mom sits me down and tells me how she wasn't allowed to go to school, being born female; how her father took her little face in his hands and told her she was born "just a girl" and not good for much more than bearing children; that women are cursed by God and that even the Bible says if it weren't for women, there'd be no sin in the world; that girls are here to test men and have babies. She told me that her father pulled her from school to work in the kitchen because only boys need to get an education: "What do you need to go to school for?" he questioned her. "You can read already and do enough math to cook and write home to your father after you're married. What more do you need?"

Being born a girl was a huge theme in my mother's childhood, and the origin stories she heard from her family elders are rife with the message that it is disadvantageous to be born female. Mom disagreed, strongly, and emphasized the message again and again that girls are just as valuable as boys: "*It's not true, Evonne. Boys and girls are equal, and both are good. Girls aren't born just to have babies. Go to school. Get an education.*" Remembering these episodes, though, doesn't explain how she juggled both the idea that women were good for more than women's work yet intentionally sheltered her girls from men's work. Mom raised me with a feminist duality that made sense to her because feminism wasn't a word she used, particularly not for herself. Mom was more or less oblivious to feminist rants: she was cooking meals for her family, cleaning the house, doing laundry, and raising children. Mom supported women's rights to break out of gender roles and, simultaneously, spurned any ridiculous notions that women's work had less value than men's. To Mom, women's bodies clearly had a baby-making purpose: ovaries and wombs are for procreation. Mom knew that when she had daughters they would become women, likely marry, and most probably become mothers. She understood that childbirth is a rigorous process that requires physical strength and health. Making sure that her daughters' female apparatuses were functioning well meant her girls would have easier childbirths if they chose parenthood, and Mom felt she was taking care of pragmatic concerns by sheltering us from men's work.

Mills writes that "discourse also constructs certain events and sequences of events into narratives which are recognised by a particular culture as real or important events" (48). As I listened to the knotted web of family stories my mother selected to tell, I absorbed her own responses to her family stories. Her interpretations of these family narratives were teaching me to understand what was important, what was significant, and what was of value. White and Epston state that "if we accept that persons organize and give meaning to their experience through the storying of experience, and that in the performance of these stories they express selected aspects of their lived experience, then it follows that these stories are constitutive—shaping lives and relationships" (White and Epston 12). Mom emphasized our equality with men, but for her, equality didn't at all imply sameness. These apparently contradictory positions were fluid in Mom's mind: girls don't have to have children to be valuable, but they most likely would have children, and that's of equal value as long as it's a choice.

Mom acted as a conduit between the generation that bore the stories and my generation, which received them in due time. Her interpretations and reinterpretations filtered those narratives for me and shed light on which meanings I was to take away from them. Without seeing all the dots at that point, I understood that equality meant freedom of choice. The fact that these narratives, my ancestors' stories and my own experiences, contradicted each other's meanings wasn't something I could articulate at that time. I hadn't a sense of the whole yet, so the experiences of my childhood were piled up, stacked like books on a shelf, waiting to be assigned their place in my thinking.

Contradictions Serve to Connect Discordant Dots

To understand how Mom balanced the contradictions in her narratives, it must be recognized stories happen in a historical context. The story of Great-Aunt Mary's fierce determination to choose for herself was influenced by the thinking of her day, just as the story of Mom's mother's family was influenced by the dominant ideology of that time. (White and Epston 18). Here, White and Epston are referring to the differences that retelling makes in the interpretation of the story from one generation to another. This applies to Mom's telling, which certainly reflected her interpretations and was contrasted with the interpretations she'd heard from her mother. However, White and Epston's point can also be applied across cultures—my mother's maternal and paternal extended families held very different interpretations of Mennonite culture and values. There were real contradictions. This is important to understand because the same criteria cannot be used for understanding Mom's maternal birthing stories as for her paternal birthing stories. Although both are contextualized in Mennonite culture, in actual practices and ideological stances, the two were worlds apart. To legitimately interpret these stories, the lens of the sociopolitical context in which they both occurred and were interpreted must be used. Even here, the socio-political contexts shift: the cultural practices and norms of the day in which the stories occurred had already shifted by the time they were retold to my mother, whose interpretation and practices caused shifts again by the time they were told to me. Stories are complex: they are set in sociopolitical contexts, told in cultures that have shifted those contexts, and interpreted by others whose contexts are different again. The Mennonite family into which my Great-Aunt Mary was born was not the same Mennonite family into which my mother's mother was born. Therefore, the stories themselves and the discourses they contain have to be interpreted in their own right. Having understood this, the two sides of my mother's family provide something like a literary foil, one for the other: the two contrast each other, and in so doing, highlight the lessons that the other has to offer.

Mom wanted to raise her daughters to have options. For Mom, the key component of feminism, if she were to articulate it, would likely be the power of choice. For that to be valid, I needed both the option to bear children and the option to not bear children in equal portions. Therefore, it was merely good sense to make certain that those options were equally viable and realistic. Mom wielded stories from both sides of her family like suggestive textbooks and used her childrearing practices like implicit lessons to ensure that her daughters would understand that they had choices, like Great-Aunt Mary, but unlike Mom's mother and grandmothers. However, should we choose to follow in the footsteps of Mom's mother and grandmother that would be fine—provided it was a free choice.

Mother's Maternal Mother: My Grandmother Helena's Story

These experiences and lessons came to me in the order presented as I remember them. These lessons were not linear but were dots disconnected, and without analysis, they would appear as random episodes in my childhood. However, examining them in the light of my grandmother's birthing stories creates deeper levels of meaning that I was unable to sift through as a child. Only as a young woman, nearly an adult, did I begin to understand the interpretive context that my mother provided for me with these stories. I tell the story that follows as a composite of all the times Mom told this story to me, and, naturally, I have used my own filters and lenses to present it here.

Despite the stern cultural expectations that her mother produce a first-born son, Helena, my maternal grandmother, was born a girl. Helena's father, evidently not one to let mere facts stand in his way, raised her as he would a son.

"Helena! Are you ready? The sun's rising, and there's work to do," her father called. Helena pulled on her boots and trudged out of the house after her father to the barn. Helena's mother raised each child to have a specialty: one learned to do the mending and did all the needlework for the whole family; one managed the cooking, and it was she who'd fed Helena that morning because it was Helena who learned how to plow the fields beside her father.

It was Helena who lifted the plow when it became wedged beneath fieldstones; it was Helena who hauled those stones out of the way through the soft, freshly turned soil to the side of the field, making large piles of rocks; it was Helena who managed the weight and the power of the plow through the furrows in the fields; and it was Helena, being the work beast, who spent her strength so that the family could sell the crop at the end of the season and eat of it themselves. All this because her origin story went wrong: she should've been a boy.

When my grandfather John proposed to my grandmother Helena, she did not love him, but she needed to get away from her father's brutality, so she agreed. They were married, and she bore three children. The first child was born without any skin on her abdomen, and she died within a day. Their second child, a son, was born without any skin on parts of his face and without a roof in his mouth. He lived to fulfill the role of eldest son. The third child, my mother, was born without any abnormalities; however, my grandmother did not shed her placenta when my mother was born: it was left where it was and to its own devices. When my mother was nine, Helena died of cancer from the abandoned placenta.

The doctor who performed the autopsy declared, in his Second-War-War-era wisdom, that my grandmother *"had muscles where no woman should have them. She should be unable to bear children at all!"* This doctor was shocked to learn this woman had three children. He insisted it was impossible because she had developed "unnatural muscles" for a woman, a result of her being a farm labourer and a daughter instead of a son. Presumably, these muscles were the reason that the miserable placenta wouldn't come forth. The doctor's version of this story so influenced my mother that she absorbed the idea without question. My own grandfather, Helena's husband, and my mother's father, blamed my mother for it all because she was born a girl.

My mother was very young when she heard these stories of my grandmother giving birth to my mother and her two siblings. White and Epston write that the "interpretation [of stories has] real effects" and that "the evolution of lives and relationships occurs through the performance of such stories or narratives" (11-12). Mom's understanding of feminism as a practice of having choices meant that she embraced equally both the idea that women are physically created to bear children and the idea that woman are good for much more than bearing children. Consequently, her parenting included decisions in which girls were kept from men's work in case they chose childbearing as well as practices that prepared her girls for a life beyond childbearing, much as boys are. I was protected from men's work, and, at the same time, I was led to believe that I could partake and compete in a man's world. The birthing stories Mom heard as a child, and those experiences that she had at the hands of her father as a result of her own birth story, had real effects, which resulted in her own dichotomous child-raising practices in which she shielded me from anything that would threaten my choice to bear children, or not. I grew up in a household in which my sister and I only did work meant for girls; we were forbidden to experience the robust physical world of men but were simultaneously taught that we were good for much more than women's work and that we could, if we chose, partake in a man's world. Feminism, for my mother, was always all about having a choice.

In retrospect, I am amazed at her ability to juxtapose both traditional and nontraditional positions easily and to never question the contradictions they raised. The effects of these birthing narratives meant she was in some ways fierce about what she wanted for her daughters, and since these values and ideologies were expressed through stories, they weren't explicitly examined for continuity. There was no analyses: the lessons within the narratives spoke for themselves. For Mom, both sides of this equation made equal sense and there was no contradiction. As an indication of this, allow me a final story that reveals this dichotomy. It is this story—my own story—that sparked the understanding in me that there are two streams of thought feeding into the peculiar feminist ideology under which I was raised.

Connecting the Dots

I am twenty years old, attending university, and my mother is bursting with pride at a daughter who not only graduated from high school but is pursuing post-secondary education. On this occasion, I bring home a new boyfriend who observes that the lawn needs mowing. I point him to the garage where the mower resides, but he challenges me to do it myself. I'm a little shocked. "I've never mown a lawn in my life! I don't even know how to start the mower!" I say. It wasn't one of my duties as a girl in the home.

He's appalled and states: "That's ridiculous! Girls can mow lawns as well as guys!"

I'm delighted at the idea of a man who isn't bothered by a woman who can do men's work. I think how proud Mom will be that I've picked a man who can let go of gender roles. I get the mower, and he shows me how to begin. He is standing on the driveway, hands on his hips, pointing out spots in the lawn where my job is uneven. Looking up, I see my mother in the kitchen window. The look on her face is brooding and dark. I know in an instant where her mind has gone. I see an opportunity to challenge women's roles, to exert my freedom to choose, and to fulfill my potential as a woman. My mother sees her mother, a first-born girl, pulling a plow through a field while the men watch; her mother lifting field rocks and carrying them over fresh plowed soil; her mother burying a daughter; and her mother dying from having muscles where women shouldn't have them if they want to give birth. My mother sees patriarchy and dominance where I see feminism and freedom of choice. I smile and wave at her, but she retreats into the shadows.

I began to understand that feminism is not merely "anything he can do I can do better"—an adolescent mantra in which my mother let me indulge. I began to see that feminism, for my mother, was about both breaking away from the power structures that confined women to certain submissive roles while still maintaining that women's childbearing rights and functions were honourable and of value. Mom would not have given up the one in order to attain the other. For Mom, they were a package deal. To lose the freedom and honour to bear children would be, for her, as catastrophic as losing her personhood merely because she was female. As a young woman, I misunderstood: I interpreted all the stories to mean I had to challenge my own perceived weakness. I had to attain everything men could attain in order to prove my worth. However, this interpretation is simply another way of saying that childbearing functions are dishonourable, while men's duties or roles are of more value, and, therefore, I should pursue male things. This does a disservice to my mother's interpretation, which embraces equality: both men and women play honourable roles. The key to feminism is the choice to pursue either or both.

Furthermore, the shadow of my boyfriend in the driveway, arms folded, watching and directing while I mowed the lawn, flashed my mother back to the stories of her mother pulling the plow while her father watched and directed. That her mother should have had to fulfill the roles of a first-born son at the expense of her childbearing potential infuriated my mother. Her interpretation of my new boyfriend's stance was a direct result of her family's birthing stories, whereas my interpretation of the same stance was a direct result of my mother's dichotomous childrearing practice, itself partially a result of her family's birthing stories. In this way, family stories manifest themselves as childrearing practices, which, in turn, result in differing interpretations between the generations. Here again, cultural practices and norms both inform and are informed by personal choices, and individuals' interpretations of those choices.

My family's origin stories are a part of my history, they are a part of my present life, and they are a part in the construction of my family's future. White and Epston explain this as such: "Since all stories have a beginning (or a history), a middle (or a present), and an ending (or a future), then the interpretation of current events is as much future-shaped as it is past-determined" (10). Each story told to my mother, and eventually to me, influenced her cultural understanding and worldview, which informed how she determined to raise her daughters. The real effects of the family origin stories translate into changed ideology, which becomes childbearing and childrearing practices that inform the culture of the next generation. The choices I make are, in reality, the real effects of the shifting discourse passed down for generations, and so it will be for the generations to follow.

White and Epston begin their text with this statement: "Some have argued that power doesn't really exist, but that it is something constructed in language and that those who experience its effects have participated in 'bringing it forth'" (1). The discursive power of origin stories in my family has birthed real children. The actions I take, based on my understanding of the choices I have, have as their DNA the birthing stories told to me by my mother, about her mother, and her aunts, and their mothers. The real effects of this, as well as the enacted truth that stems from these stories, are evidence of their power.

My sister and I are reflecting often these days, as Mom is struggling with the effects of Alzheimer's. My sister tells the stories of how we were raised one way, and I tell them another, but Mom's dichotomous fight for our right and freedom to choose is always a central theme. Vida Winter says, in Setterfield's novel, that "all children mythologize their birth. It is a universal trait. You want to know someone? Heart, mind and soul? Ask [her] to tell you about when [she] was born. What you get won't be the truth; it will be a story. And nothing is more telling than a story" (Kindle locator 396).

Nothing is more telling than a story.

Works Cited

Mills, Sara. *Discourse the New Critical Idiom*. Routledge, 2008.

Setterfield, Dianne. *The Thirteenth Tale*. Kindle editions. Vintage Canada, 2006.

White, Michael with David Epston. "Story, Knowledge, and Power." Michael White, David Epston. *Narrative Means to Therapeutic Ends*, edited by Michael White and David Epston, W.W. Norton & Company, 1990, pp. 1-37.

Chapter Three

Who Wants to Know?: An Autoethnography of How and Why a Mother May Craft Audience-Dependent Stories of Origin

Elizabeth Cralley

People with children are often quick to say that having a baby will change your life. They conveniently fail to mention that the experience of giving birth to a baby may do the same. Certainly, nobody coaches anyone on how to present the story of a harrowing childbirth that occurred in a foreign country where the mother did not speak the local language well. I know because I had two chaotic, confusing birth experiences in rapid succession, both during my husband's three-year diplomatic tour in Latin America, and no one passed along any tips on how to share these events with others or how to make any sort of sense of these experiences for myself. I remember vivid details from the birth of my first child, my son Carson; however, many of these details would never make it into a story I would tell. To put it into context, the story of my son's arrival would only capture what happened at the time of delivery and not the twenty-two horrible hours leading up to it or the terrible wait afterwards. The wait afterwards was punctuated by two events: learning my baby was alive and later learning that the tests indicated he was not expected to have suffered brain damage despite a period of oxygen deprivation. The actual birth went like this:

"It's time to push," my doctor said in accented English. I could hear him just fine, but I could only see the top part of his eyes, along with his round tortoise-shell glasses and curly grey hair. I trusted him absolutely. He cared for me throughout my pregnancy and did his best to help prepare me for labor and delivery in a foreign country. Aside from my husband, however, he was the only person in the room who spoke English. The shift had just changed, and I did not recognize anyone else.

There was no anesthetic to attenuate the pain. The epidural had failed. Still, I was ready to push. After twenty-two hours that only seemed to get worse by the minute, I wanted to be done.

Suddenly, two nurses crowded in on both sides of me and started pushing on my stomach with their hands. I was confused. Why were they trying to push my baby out of me? I was pushing just fine on my own. With every contraction, they crushed down even harder. I felt like they were arm wrestling each other across my body with their elbows digging into my pelvic bones. Worse, the alarm on the fetal monitor started sounding off.

After what seemed like forever, my doctor said cheerfully, "Your baby has hair..."

I inhaled sharply. I was exhausted but excited. He could see my baby!

"What colour is it?" I asked.

Instead of answering me, he looked up and past me. He was focused on something else. The machine behind me squawked even louder.

"Oh no," he said. "Don't do that!"

I was surprised. Was he scolding me? "I'm not supposed to know his hair color?" I asked.

Then my doctor's focus came back around to me. He looked me straight in the eyes and very calmly said, "I am going to have to help you have your baby."

Now he used his firm tone—the same one he used when he banned me from travelling to the Amazon earlier in my pregnancy so that I would not contract any of the myriad jungle diseases that could threaten my health or that of my baby. I tried to comprehend his words, but I did not really understand.

"I need to do an emergency C-section," he continued.

I nodded. Words like "emergency" made me inclined to agree to whatever the doctor suggested.

The fetal monitor started blaring a new tone. My doctor's eyes flicked to the monitor screen, and he jumped to his feet.

"No!" He shook his head. "There's not enough time!"
He sprinted from the room.

Before I could start to wonder where he went, he burst back in. He paused for a moment, gave me a kind but somewhat sad smile, and in that soft, gentle voice that made me fall in love with him as my doctor and trust him with my baby's life, he said, "I'm sorry."

I had no time to ask what he was sorry about before he sliced me apart and started yanking my baby out with forceps. I grabbed my husband with a death grip and sucked in great gulps of air. I heard myself shrieking and snorting. A tremendous suction noise escaped from inside me, as my doctor wrenched the baby towards the gaping exit wound he had created. It sounded like someone pried a giant squid's tentacles off a glass wall only it was inside my body. The nurses kept trying to put my hands back on the handles of the bed, and I kept grabbing for my husband.

When my baby finally came free, I felt no relief. Chaos reigned in my mind. Pain ripped through me.

I had been split in half.

My ears were ringing at a deafening volume, and although I knew people were speaking, I struggled to hear what they said. Sweat rolled down my face. My vision blurred. Seconds later, my doctor placed my baby on my stomach. His skin was gray and wrinkly, and his tiny hands covered his face. He was perfectly still.

The doctor swiftly cut the umbilical cord and held it out towards my husband. I saw a mangled, snakelike, slippery-looking tube. I looked away.

"It's tied in a true knot," I heard my doctor say. He was standing right next to me, but he sounded very far away. He was more animated than I had ever seen him. Somehow, this knot made everything clearer to him, although nothing was clear to me.

His words hung in the air as a team of people in scrubs burst through the door. They collected the cord, scooped my motionless baby off my belly, and grabbed my husband by the arm. Just as quickly as they arrived, the flurry of scrubs disappeared, dragging my husband and baby off with them. Everything was wrong, and I was terrified.

I had a question, but I could not form the words.

Was my son even alive?

After fumbling my way through many awkward and probably less than diplomatic conversations in the early weeks and months after each birth, I settled on a basic version of what to tell others. However, it took me countless hours of private and deliberate reflection to craft meaningful and coherent stories for myself, ones that I believe also promoted my personal growth. All along, I drafted and edited in my mind exactly what I would tell my children once they were old enough to ask. Thus, I created several stories that varied according to whom I was talking.

I use autoethnography to explore what it means to be a mother of two children whose chaotic and dangerous arrivals while my husband and I lived overseas led me to craft multiple, authentic stories of origin. Following Carolyn Ellis's explanation of autoethnography as part self and part culture, I draw from diary entries, medical records, photographs, and my own memory to explain how and why these different versions emerged. I focus less on story content than I do on how cultural scripts, prior expectations, concern for the protection of the various parties involved, and the emotional labour of trying to make meaning from these experiences helped shape the processes. I share this information so that others may better understand how and why some mothers present different stories of origin for different audiences, disclosing or withholding specific details based on who wants to know.

Different Types of Stories

I have three stories of origin for each child, and I consider all six to be authentic accounts of events. They are just different versions, restoried deliberately for each audience. The creation parts of the stories are fixed; my husband and I created each child first in our hearts. It's the arrival parts that are audience dependent. I categorize these stories of origin into three groups: stories for the self, those for others, and ones carefully and lovingly crafted for each child.

Each type of story serves a different purpose. The stories that help me understand, process, and make meaning of the confusing and terrifying events that occurred are "stories for the self." The versions that I consider socially acceptable to share with inquisitive adults are "stories for the other." Those stories I have created for my son and daughter are "stories for the child." Each story differs in levels of protection and detail. The lowest levels of protection and highest detail are afforded to stories for the self, moderate levels of protection and significantly less detail are included in stories for the other, and the highest levels of protection and only selective details are used in stories intended for the child. However, I recognize that these stories may change over time, especially as my children age. What I describe in this chapter reflects my perceptions at this point in time, which is eight years after the first birth. Because I believe that stories for the other rely on powerful cultural scripts and help situate the other two types in contrast, I consider them first.

Stories for the Other

When I became pregnant, we were living overseas and an entire continent separated me from my mother. Talking on the phone about childbirth would have seemed awkward to me even if I had not lived so far away so, as for somewhat pragmatic reasons, most of the knowledge I acquired about childbirth came from books I ordered from the Internet. I favoured Vicki Iovine's confessional-style book, *The Girlfriend's Guide to Pregnancy*, over other helpful but more sterile ones, such as Heidi Murkoff and Sharon Mazel's informative and frequently updated *What to Expect When You're Expecting*. I poured over both when I was pregnant, trying to find answers to my questions within them, and considering how many copies have been sold, I could not have been the only one drawn to reading them. Judith Lothian and Alyson Grauer suggest that women in the United States today often learn about the more intimate details of childbirth from books, television, and the Internet. This was true for me, even though I was away from the U.S. at the time.

These books provided me with invaluable information that I could process at my own pace, and although some of the material made me uncomfortable, I was comfortable with what I felt I had learned. These books probably also set some of my expectations about how labour and delivery would unfold. Additionally, I had taught college students about prenatal development in dozens of courses, so I already knew a fair amount about the developing baby. True, the actual bodily processes of labour and delivery were a bit sketchier for me, but I believed that I had a solid enough understanding of the physiological aspects that I could power through what would be an intense but finite period of time. I was healthy, educated, and excited, and I had the best doctor in the entire host country delivering my care. I did not feel compelled to seek out detailed stories from other women, although in retrospect I should have.

At forty years old, I was an older mom to be with plenty of friends and acquaintances who had given birth. I knew the broad brushstrokes of their stories, but strong social norms kept me from asking direct or personal questions. Even if I had asked, I believe that the same norms might have kept mothers in my social circles from divulging too much detail in response. These artificial barriers kept our conversations about childbirth socially proper, which seemed especially important in my role as a U.S. diplomat who was planning to give birth overseas. Implicit pressure to be like a female James Bond, who could navigate dangerous events across land, sea, and air only to arrive at a cocktail party on time and looking fabulous, discouraged me from asking other female diplomats who had given birth in foreign countries to tell me how they had experienced the process. For all intents and purposes, they appeared to discreetly give birth and then pop back into the social circuit in glamorous gowns ten seconds later, positively glowing with happiness and pride. From an outsider's perspective, they made it look so easy that it appeared that there was nothing challenging to it. Thus, I did not find out much about how other women who gave birth away from home really felt, whether they were elated or terrified or some combination of both, and I own the fact that I never really sat anyone down and asked.

Of course, that doesn't mean that I never encountered any stories of childbirth. I have heard dozens of those from both close friends and strangers. But they all fit within what I call "stories for the other"; these stories are nicely packaged versions of events that tell the entire tale of a child's birth from start to finish in the space of a short elevator ride. Why? I imagine it is because these are the socially acceptable versions to share and because sometimes the people who ask are only being polite. In my case, any woman from the host nation who asked about my experience giving birth away from home was guaranteed to get a short and diplomatic story from me—one that admitted some nervousness on my part but also complimented the wonderful, caring people of the host country who helped bring my children into the world. I acknowledged the ties that would bind our family with their country and culture forever, and I professed sincere gratitude for being so blessed.

The stories I told ranged from untrue ("everything went just fine") to true, but they lacked detail, and specific parts I deliberately omitted. For example, I was reluctant to discuss the behaviour (some of which was abhorrent) of a few of the people who were involved in the birthing events, and I purposely avoided disclosing the terrible risks my husband and I were forced to take in trying to handle numerous, serious medical crises. Despite my negative experiences giving birth, I felt protective of the people and culture of the host country, and if I suspected the person asking simply wanted to hear how "behind" or "unsophisticated" the medical care was in the country, I closed the discussion rapidly. I did not want to lie, but I felt I would be betraying the host country people and culture to tell much more to people who seemed to have alternate motives for inquiring, which is why, in part, I will not name the country here. I would have been happy to report how wonderful everything was, if that had legitimately been the case, but it was not, so I could not. Still, when somebody asks a woman to tell a birth story, she (the narrator) often feels compelled to share something about how her child was born. However, she may also try to make sure that the story content does not offend anyone's sensibilities. In my experience, these stories can be both dramatic and true to events, but they keep the audience from feeling too uncomfortable while listening, and they do not make the inquiring party regret having asked. This is part of an implicit social contract. Stories for the other are distilled specifically for the audience, with the impurities either removed or refined. This distillation allows for some interesting details to be shared but provides a layer of protection for the privacy and dignity of individuals involved.

The stories I get when I do ask other women about childbirth now that I am back in the U.S. are the same type of intriguing but socially sanitized stories that I hear myself telling back to them. They follow a prescribed pattern, and in my experience growing up in the U.S., the "every new mom is already a supermom" script mandates that these stories resolve the same way: regardless of how it all really went down, out came a live, healthy baby, and for this, the new mother gives thanks. The supermom would also be expected to be happy and adjusting well, always pleased to sacrifice even more of herself for her child. Societal pressure to be grateful for the child despite the circumstances of birth may push some mothers (and fathers), certainly me, to downplay or outright omit negative events that occurred during the process. We, they and I, spin terrifying circumstances into clever short stories, deflecting the discussion away from feelings of fear, vulnerability, or even shame at having failed already as a mother, and redirecting it back to expressions of gratitude. Perhaps ironically, I always suspected that a key element in recovering from the trauma I experienced would be in how I reconciled the deep feelings of shame, so hiding these feelings might even have been detrimental. Regardless, these brief narratives told to others often use elements of drama and humour, both inviting the audience to read between the lines just a bit and simultaneously discouraging anyone from asking a lot of follow-up questions. Stories for the other sound something like the composite examples below, all of which I created by combining memorable elements from actual stories that were told to me. Although the use of composites (and pseudonyms) means that these are not verbatim stories for the other, the elements they contain are authentic and they stay true to the pattern of the original versions I heard.

Annabelle's Story

My husband, dratted bastard, was in lower Manhattan when my water broke, so he missed the whole thing. The Ethiopian cabdriver who was taking me to the hospital had to pull over on the way, and he delivered Junior. It was a bit tricky, given that the cab ended up blocking two lanes of traffic, and it was afternoon rush hour in New York City, but Junior turned out great, and our new friend, Hakim, even came to the baptism.

Hannah's Story

Back then, we lived on a ranch out west. When I went into labour, my husband and I loaded into the truck to make the one-hundred-mile trek to the nearest hospital. We only made it halfway though because it wasn't safe to keep on driving through a record-breaking blizzard. Our blessed child came into the world in a warm, cozy gas station that was still open. Luckily, my husband had birthed plenty of calves on the farm, and our son was born in the aisle with all the paper towels. Our "Baby Boy Bounty" is doing fabulous, and thank you so much for asking!

Christina's Story

We decided we wanted to try having a water birth for our child, but things didn't go exactly the way that we planned (nervous laughter). Long story short, it ended up that our baby girl was born in a whirlpool in the dark. We weren't counting on the labour taking so long or the whirlpool breaking down or the power going out in the birth center, but what can you do? Besides, little Serenity is the light of our lives, and she already knows how to swim.

Often told in chronological order, my experience is that the narrator first describes the setting and actors, along with the basic problem, which, of course, was that the baby was on the way. Then the narrator casually makes a few statements that suggest an additional problem or two might have arisen. If the experience was particularly eventful, an even bigger problem is tacked on. If the narrator is also a good storyteller, the problem may be presented in dramatic fashion to ensure that the tension mounts towards the climax (but only very briefly because, after all, it was an infant's life on the line). The narrator then leaps forwards in time, skipping over an ambiguous number of hours or days and unpleasant details, to describe the lightning-fast problem-solving actions that were taken, often by men, that led to victory in the end. The conclusion is then accompanied by effusive expressions of gratitude for the gift of a child. These stories map neatly onto what Jennifer Lilgendahl describes as Western culture's focus on triumph over adversity—no matter what anyone throws at the mother during childbirth, in these stories for the other, she emerges victorious and holding a beautiful baby in the end.[1]

In my experience, the narrator omits (or admits but immediately dismisses) any feelings other than minor worry as irrelevant, essentially conveying that these emotions are unworthy of inclusion or notice at all. It is a story, after all, rather than some sort of therapy session. If the audience does look shocked, surprised, or disturbed in any way after hearing the story, the narrator may try to repair the damage by offering reassurances that a) it all turned out well and that b) mother nature has a way of helping women forget about all the bad parts. As Robert Sternberg notes, some stories net cultural approval, but others do not, and Susan Ayers et al. suggest that as a common event, childbirth is subject to cultural norms and expectations, with the birth leading to some sort of positive outcome. Again, regardless of how it all really went down, in most cases out came a live, healthy baby, and for this, the new mother gives thanks. Once the narrator is done presenting the story and/or reassuring the audience, she may say something to signal that the topic is closed.

Enough about Me. Let's Talk about You!

Few people I know discuss details of the truly rough stuff from childbirth, especially if the audience members are expecting a baby. Who wants to scare a pregnant woman or her partner? Still, Jane Savage suggests that women who have given birth are essentially tasked with sharing their stories with other women, and pregnant women are expected to listen; in this way, sharing information about childbirth may help explain some of its unknown aspects and also reduce fear. However, I imagine that some women who had negative birth experiences may feel that they are doing these parents to be a kindness by keeping silent rather than divulging frightening events (this describes me). Other women may stay silent because they do not actually know some or all the details of their birth experiences due to anesthesia or sedating medication (this also partially applies to me). Perhaps others fear that the audience will see them as unappreciative of the precious gift of life if they reveal any deeper level of detail regarding the emotional circumstances of the delivery (here again, this describes me). Maybe, like me, some women feel ashamed or even flawed that their experience deviated markedly from the script, and even worse, they may feel personally responsible for anything and everything that went wrong along the way. Like me, some women may feel as though they failed at one of the most fundamental tasks of being a woman. These all seem like reasonable motives for providing minimal detail in stories for the other, which also affords protection for the dignity and privacy of the key players, not to mention the comfort of the audience who listens.

There also may be motives that stem from normative influence. Indeed, Dan McAdams and Kate McLean caution that "narrators should not go on so long and obsessively as to slide into rumination, for good stories have satisfactory endings" (234). This implies that the stories themselves and the details the narrator includes are subject to some sort of judgment or evaluation. Thus, stories for the other may be challenging for women who did not experience a lot of positive events.

These mothers are expected to weave authentic stories that end well, which requires them to consider all of the events that transpired and then to step outside of themselves and consider how others may react to the stories they tell. As a two-step process, the woman first must confront and pass judgment on the events herself, which falls at least partly under the domain of stories for the self, and then she must start crafting what she thinks is an appropriate story to tell others. Other considerations also problematize the narration of a trauma-associated origin story. For me, my children's privacy was of concern, as was a prickling and an uncomfortable sense that what I shared could, at a later date, be restoried and told to my children by others—an act that would reduce my power to frame my children's experiences and perhaps impact their conceptions of self. So perhaps withholding some details could be viewed as an intentional act of protection of my children.

Perhaps there were also some perceived elements of protection of self, as I decided what to share with others or not. In first evaluating my own experiences before deciding what to tell others, I graded myself against the theoretical U.S. supermom standard. I admit this is an absurd but perhaps culturally common thing to do. I would say that I flunked my first childbirth experience. I was overconfident in my resilience and was unaware of how clashing cultural norms (especially those involving my high-status role as a U.S. diplomat but low-status role as just another labouring woman in the world) may contribute to resentment and mistreatment by some female hospital workers. I was also unprepared for any sort of medical crisis involving my son. I did not know how to speak the language well, which made everything worse, and in a high-risk emergency delivery, it almost cost my son's life. In fact, it would have if it had not been for the heroic efforts of my (male) doctor. Moreover, little of what happened involved much diplomatic behaviour on my part. That is the gist of what happened the first time around, and these events are documented (in Spanish) on various medical charts, written in my diary, and permanently seared into my mind. After considering these events myself, I decided that these were not the sorts of details I wanted to share in stories for the other.

I also needed to confront the actual events from my daughter's birth before I could decide what to tell others about her birth. I would give myself an A+ on a much more diplomatic performance (if you can call childbirth a performance) during my daughter's delivery thirteen months later (same doctor, same hospital, and many of the same female personnel from one year before); I had learned how to communicate better in Spanish and was much more assertive with everyone (especially the female nurses) during labour and delivery. Due to unknown reasons, however, I gave birth prematurely, and without the heroic efforts of my (male) doctor (again), that time I might have died. Even worse, our daughter's life was in perilous danger, and we had no real idea for the first week or so if she would really survive. Thank goodness, she did. Therefore, we did. We then moved from one medical crisis to another over the following six months until we returned to the U.S. at the end of our tour. Thus, even though I had a (somewhat) more satisfying labour and delivery on the second go around, I probably still deserve a failing grade in the end. Again, these details are ones I deliberately decided to withhold from others, partly because the details seemed to centre more around me than my baby.

Still, a small part of me wonders, "although it isn't all about me, isn't at least some of it about me? I am a new mom who is willing to do the best for my child but does that mean I am expected to fade into the background?" Even as I write this, I am reminded that the normative script tells me that it is not about me, and perhaps even worse, I am now violating another social norm by writing this down for others to read. The script I know says to be thankful for the positive outcome. And thankful, I am. I have two happy, wonderful, beautiful children, and I am blessed and forever grateful to have them. The script does not make room for the birthing mother's emotions, though, so the problem is that although I am grateful for and love my children, their more complete stories of origin include the troubling fact that I had a horrible time getting them here. These birth experiences badly damaged me. That is the literal truth. But the details of my feelings of fear, vulnerability, helplessness, anger, and outright betrayal by several women who were supposed to be helping are all a part of a story that most other people will never come to know. Although I have acknowledged some of these details here, I wrestle much more deeply with the demons in those details during my private contemplation in the stories for the self. In the stories for the other, I am not supposed to ruminate too long or convey a story without a satisfactory conclusion. So after first confronting the events myself, I must take the second step in the process where I consider how the stories I tell may be judged and present suitable stories for the other. Therefore, other people, especially pregnant women, get the short and sanitized version—the one that is more socially acceptable to share.

Yes, I gave birth to both of my children in a war-torn country where I did not speak the language, and due to my diplomatic status, I was under tremendous pressure to keep my composure, but by golly I did it! And I have two healthy, precious children to show for it. Never mind the details. You, supermom to be, should just think positive thoughts while you are growing a person, and if by chance, your baby is delivered by a cabdriver who is taking you from the whirlpool birthing centre to a hospital one hundred miles away after the power goes out in a blinding snowstorm, make sure you choose the gas station aisle with the paper towels in it when you stop to give birth. It makes a little less mess and a lot better story.

So... when are you due?

Stories for the Self

Although I cannot speak for how other women craft their stories for the self, I can say that the process for me included quite a bit of heartache, countless hours of contemplation in the dark of night, and various combinations of therapy and medication. I typed more than two hundred pages of text, trying to understand exactly what had transpired. I struggled to make meaning of it all within the greater context of my life, my understanding of my adult self and my own origins, and how I had responded to the clashing cultural forces that played a powerful role in how everything unfolded. I consider these emotional, evocative, and (eventually) coherent stories to be truthful accounts of both my son's and daughter's origins. They are laden with detail and spare no person's behaviour from scrutiny, especially my own. These accounts are for me. They help heal me from the wounds. The following excerpt reflects some of my feelings about my daughter Sydney's birth.

If my birth plan for Carson was just to have him arrive safely, then my birth plan for Sydney was to avoid a repeat of the horrors that happened with Carson. I was going to get a chance at a delivery do over, and I was determined not to mess it up.

As it was, my water broke at 9:00 p.m. on a Monday evening in December. I was in labour five weeks early. Brian, my husband, was at a black-tie dinner for the diplomatic corps when I called to let him know that the game was on. I had seen my doctor earlier that day. The ultrasound had shown the umbilical cord wrapped around my baby's neck, and I'll admit that I worried more than a bit about her health (especially because we came so close to losing Carson due to a knot in the umbilical cord depriving him of oxygen). I refused to allow myself to worry about me this time around. I could and would handle her delivery just fine. As long as she stayed healthy and managed to execute a few somersaults to unscramble the umbilical cord, she and I would do well. I was so happy and confident that her birth would be easy that I didn't even consider it possible that anything would go wrong. Hadn't the worst already happened with Carson? As far as I was concerned, as long as she slipped free from the cord, then my daughter and I would be fine.

When my doctor asked how I was feeling that morning I had told him that I felt great, although I somehow felt less pregnant at that point than I had when I was only six months along. He gave me an odd look and said that my comment made him a bit nervous. He urged me to call if anything out of the ordinary happened, so I don't think he was surprised to have me call him that night.

When we got to the hospital, I found that the on-call doctor spoke only halting English, but my Spanish had improved, so we communicated well enough. He checked to make sure my water had broken, although I questioned why this was necessary given that I had practically sloshed my way through the waiting room. As he removed his gloved hand from my insides, a gallon of amniotic fluid splashed onto the floor (quite near my suitcase I might add), and he nodded. Brian was so shocked that he grabbed some paper towels and started to wipe up the floor. This surprised the doctor who said not to bother. I didn't care much one way or the other. I figured they would probably hose it down a drain or something. I was only thinking about how I was well on my way to meeting my daughter.

I went to a large shared room where I joined a collection of other women in various states of labour. I was hooked up to an IV for antibiotics and, of course, a fetal heart monitor. The alarms kept going off, and I kept calling the nurse to check it. I had been through this with Carson. I wasn't going to be shy about pestering people to check this time around. Brian was so tired that he kept climbing on the narrow bed with me to try to sleep. I was angry about the idea that while I was undergoing stronger contractions, he was trying to nap on my bed.

When I asked for an epidural, they chucked him out and I was relieved.

He went to the cafeteria and then came back when they were done, but he only stayed long enough to say that he was going out to the hall to find a place to sleep. He said he would come back in an hour. I suggested thirty minutes. He agreed and left.

My contractions progressed rapidly over the next twenty minutes and the low level of the epidural that the anesthesiologist had started me with wasn't enough. I had just decided to ask for more pain killers when I felt a burning sensation between my legs and a strong urge to push. I rang for the nurse.

"Esta llegando la bebe," I said. *The baby is coming.* I was pleased that I could remember how to speak some Spanish while my baby crowned. Of course, it might not have been the most eloquent way to phrase it, but I think it got the point across, because she immediately got the on-call doc who checked again to confirm that what I said was true. He took a quick peek between my legs and said, "DON'T POOSH!"

Technically, I didn't push for the time that it took them to move me down the hall to the delivery room. However, my body was busy pushing on its own with every passing contraction. As they slid me to a different bed for delivery, I saw my doctor off to the side. Several nurses were helping him don his scrubs.

"How are you doing, Liz?" he asked.

After knowing him for two years, I didn't have the heart to tell him that I go by either Beth or Elizabeth. It seemed so endearing that he called me Liz that I always let him.

"Just super," I said, with perhaps a tiny amount of sarcasm.

I smiled, though, because I was confident this time around. It didn't mean I was comfortable, just that I was sure I could push this baby out without a problem.

At that point, I realized that Brian had appeared by my side in his scrubs, too. I found out later that my OBGYN had stumbled upon my husband asleep in a hallway while my doctor was racing to get to the delivery room. The on-call doctor had phoned my OBGYN at home and said delivery was imminent and that he should hurry or he might miss it. In my opinion, both my doctor and my husband were damn lucky they showed up in time.

Naturally, I did not get any more painkillers. When my doctor told me to push, I pushed a mere three times before my daughter punched her way out (fist first) from the inside. It was 3:49 a.m. We did it. She had arrived safely, and I was still in one piece. There was no snorting, wailing, slicing, or yanking. The cord was not wrapped around her neck. There was no knot in it. I had a moment to revel in her delivery as a complete success.

Then my doctor placed my daughter on my stomach. The experience was nothing like it had been with Carson. I was shocked but in an entirely different way.

Sydney was the tiniest baby I had ever seen.

I cupped my left hand around her head and torso for a nanosecond before somebody whisked her away and tossed me a paper towel. I found that I didn't want to wipe off my hand because I might be wiping away the evidence that my teeny-tiny daughter had lived and that I had touched her, if only for a short time.

Immediately after she disappeared, I sensed that something had gone wrong once again. Brian could too. I wasn't split in half, but my doctor was up to his elbows inside me, rearranging my internal organs and talking quietly to himself in Spanish. After about ten minutes, he told us that there was a problem and that he would have to put me under general anesthesia.

The next thing I recall was someone saying "respira profundo," which I took to mean something akin to "take a deep breath." As they wheeled me to the recovery area of the maternity ward, I pushed the uncomfortable oxygen mask off my face to ask Brian about Sydney. He squeezed my hand and said the doctors were "taking care of her" in the NICU. He had stayed with me.

I was stunned. I thought Sydney would be brought to me at any minute so that I could nurse her. Instead, my baby had been admitted to the NICU because she needed intensive care. I had failed all over again.

This is just part of the story for the self, and it reflects much lower levels of shame than the early versions did. I believed I had failed a second time, not just myself but my child. These deep feelings of shame were so powerful that weeks passed before I could start to even face my own feelings. When I did start to confront my feelings about both birth experiences, it was in the dark of night, sitting alone with a computer on my lap. I deliberately tried to write my way through what I was feeling about both children's arrivals in developing these stories for the self.

Perhaps I should clarify, though, that although these stories are for the self, I did share them (eventually) with my husband. Because he is the father of my children and my best friend, I asked him if he wanted to read what I wrote. He did, and we talked about it numerous times after. We questioned each other on our thoughts and feelings, and we discussed things that I remembered that he did not recall or that he never knew (because he was not present all the time). We also looked at photographs together that provoked mixed emotions of anxiety, sadness, happiness, and relief. Our conversations and his support helped me work through and resolve some lingering negative emotions. However, I experienced such anguish at times that I wondered if I ever would recover. The process of crafting these coherent stories for the self help me claw my way up from the depths of despair a few inches at a time, repairing and reshaping my fragile sense of self and searching for and embracing a greater purpose in my life.

Eventually, we started focusing on the parts we found humorous and did not mind sharing with others. We discussed and tried to settle collectively on what was appropriate to share with others, which was also part of my process (and his) of crafting stories for the other, and the use of humour was especially important. Humour helped me, perhaps because it allowed psychological distance from the events and allowed me to reframe stressful events into ones I could laugh about. For example, we zeroed in on how my husband almost missed our daughter's birth because he fell asleep on a random bench in a hospital hallway after I refused to share my gurney with him so that he could "take a quick nap" while I laboured. "Who tries to share a labouring woman's gurney?" I would ask, which always made us both smile, and then we would agree that he was lucky he showed up in time to see his daughter arrive. This helped us both cope with the events and provided some psychological distance for us from the frightening events that had taken place.

I can review these *stories for the self* much more dispassionately now that I have physical distance from the location of events (more than two thousand miles), years of joyful memories created with my growing children, and a more robust understanding of how everything fits within my reconstructed self-concept. It took a long time, though. While we still lived overseas and our children were both infants, I tried to be more academic about it. I researched as much as I could about trauma associated with childbirth to learn what had been published on the topic. I found discouragingly few articles in the databases I searched back in 2009. I did find some articles in the medical field, and a few informative ones written (Ayers; Ayers and Pickering; Beck). However, I did not come across much that either validated that I was not alone in my experiences or that coached me on how to cope with the aftermath. Perhaps, I failed to find relevant work not because it was not out there but because I was searching databases remotely from overseas.

After we returned to the U.S. in 2010, I found much more research, including studies on childbirth trauma and even on posttraumatic stress disorder (PTSD) following childbirth. Indeed, a 2014 meta-analysis by Rebecca Grekin and Michael O'Hara found the incidence of postpartum PTSD to be 3.1 percent. It never occurred to me before I gave birth that it might be a traumatic rather than triumphant experience, which reflects my naivety at the time as well as how strongly I bought into the supermom script. However, I knew within hours after my son's emergency delivery that the person I had always known myself to be was destroyed. I summed it up as succinctly for my husband as I could. I leaned off the edge of my narrow hospital bed and touched his forearm with a trembling hand.

I am broken.

Consistent with what Gill Thomson and Soo Downe found in their qualitative research on birth experiences, women who had experienced traumatic births "referred to themselves as 'broken,' 'empty' and with 'parts missing'" (107). Even though I knew about PTSD and had even lectured on the symptoms in many psychology classes, I lacked the insight to understand it as it might apply to the freshly "broken" version of me, perhaps because of the pressure to perform as the idealized birthing mother I struggled to make meaning of the childbirth events, and on top of that, I struggled to understand why doing so was such a struggle.

I powered through the early months of my son's life just trying to be the best mother and diplomat that I could be, and when I became pregnant again only a few months later, I was elated. We wanted more children, and we wanted to have them close together. In retrospect, maybe part of my delirious joy was because I was also still off kilter from my normal self. I was confident that nothing could be worse than what I had gone through with Carson. I was just wrong. Although my daughter's delivery was quicker and more satisfactory, the first few weeks of her life trumped all previous challenges. I thought everything would be better after my daughter was born, but instead it was worse. I had constant flashbacks that exhausted and overwhelmed me, nightmares that made me afraid to fall asleep even though I was desperately tired. I had a chronically high level of arousal such that a change in either baby's breathing pattern grabbed my attention even from three rooms away. There were angry outbursts and emotional numbing to the pain and suffering of others (such as the people of Japan who experienced a devastating earthquake that killed more than fifteen thousand people and displaced several hundred thousand more). I had a strong aversion to any television storylines that dealt with childbirth (such as Lynette's character in my then-favourite show *Desperate Housewives* giving birth while being held hostage and completely dependent on her capturer to ensure her baby's survival). I also had a tendency to avoid looking at or taking photos of my daughter that showed any medical equipment attached to her which seemed symbolic of vulnerability, and I experienced a marked decrease in my own sensations of pain.

My own experience with traumatic childbirth is less important to me, though, than how the situation I was in and prevailing norms of silence prevented me from helping myself sooner or from getting beneficial assistance from others. I believe that this happened in part because I was a diplomat in a foreign country and in part because it was so difficult to craft coherent stories that made any kind of sense to me. Research by Ayers et al. indicates that after traumatic birth events, narratives become more coherent and shorter over time, and this was certainly true for me. I trimmed my original two hundred pages down to 175, and then I formatted it in the more familiar manuscript style of a book. In doing so, I was better able to connect my emotions and experiences to a whole collection of other life experiences that helped me reconstruct a coherent and continuing life narrative that could accommodate these events rather than allowing the specifics of these two key life events to subsume my life narrative. Despite my initial memories of my children's births being formed in highly emotive circumstances, I believe that repeated contemplation and reflection helped consolidate them and restructure them to become more consistent with the format and storage of other important autobiographical memories from my life.

Reflecting now on how the meaning-making process transpired for me, I can see that I followed what McAdams and McLean identify as a redemptive sequence. I needed to and did take events that were emotionally negative and transform them into events that led to positive outcomes related to the self. Lilgendahl has identified three steps to this sequence: acknowledge, analyze, and then transform the self, and these steps fit into my stories for the self. Although I was unaware at the time that I might have been engaged in such a process, it makes sense in retrospect when reflecting on the past. I considered myself to have failed during my first child's birth, and part of my determination to have a more satisfying experience and be in more control the second time linked back to the storyline of triumph over adversity.

In a qualitative study including interviews of fourteen women who experienced trauma with the birth of their first-born child, Thomson and Downe's research supports the possibility of "redemptive" birth experiences with later-born children. The redemptive birth could help move a woman "from a state of disgrace to a state of grace" (107). They identify four themes, which include resolving the past in order to prepare for the future as well as being connected, redeemed, and finally transformed. I recognize, however, that believing that I was transformed by either (or both) birth experiences, and the subsequent struggle to make meaning from them, may reflect only the clarity of hindsight or changing perspectives over time. I want to acknowledge that thinking that I have been transformed and that I am somehow now better for having experienced what I did may reflect yet another layer of my naivety because I seem to have gotten it wrong so many times before. But what I really hope is that I actually am a different (and better) person.

Last, I was surprised to learn in my research that women with PTSD who were participants in Ayers et al.'s study reported negative interactions with staff who were involved in traumatic childbirths. I think that if I had known about that information sooner, it might have helped me be better able to process what I perceived to be terrible betrayals by several other women. The following excerpt describes one such encounter that I wish I could forget.

My doctor admitted me to the hospital around 6:00 p.m. the day before my first baby was born. An exam showed that the baby was no longer growing and my amniotic fluid was low. The doctor spoke fluent English and cared for both foreign diplomats and wealthy local women, so I think he had some sway at the hospital. He set me up in the only private labour-

delivery-recovery room available at the hospital so that my cervix could "ripen" overnight (with the help of a medicated insert). He would induce labour the next morning with Pitocin. He said that the OBGYN on call would remove the insert at 3:00 a.m., and then he attached a fetal heart monitor around my gigantic belly with thick Velcro straps and left for the night.

I sent Brian home at about 9:00 p.m. so that he could get some real sleep, but by 10:00 p.m., I wished he had stayed. I became convinced that I would have the baby that night, as I experienced contractions that were strong and frequent (which I thought defined "going into labor"). The alarm on the fetal monitor kept going off, too, but every time I rang the bell for the nurses to check it, they would simply readjust the straps on the monitor and the alarm would stop. Each time, a nurse indicated that the baby was just moving around. It struck me as strange, though, because I could not feel him moving at all. Finally, a nurse gave me a button to push whenever the baby moved so that the machine would record it in relationship to the contractions. I never pressed the button because he never moved. What none of us knew at the time was that a knot in the umbilical cord was tightening with each contraction as he moved down the birth canal, a situation that would turn into an emergency as he moved closer and closer to delivery.

At about midnight, I was so worried that I asked the nurse to alert the OBGYN on call. A middle-aged woman in a white coat with several IDs dangling from a cord around her neck barged into the room without ceremony, followed by a gaggle of fledgling medical students who looked too young to drive let alone deliver a baby. She didn't introduce herself or any of them before she stuffed her hands inside me and scoured my insides with what could only have been a handful of steel wool. I clawed my way backwards up the bed. I had never felt more in danger in my life. I tried to escape, but she restrained me by sitting on one of my legs while ruthlessly scraping my insides out. She did not look me in the eyes, and she did not speak to me. When she finally extracted her hands, she snapped off her bloody gloves, tossed them in a bin, and stalked out of the room with her silent entourage in tow.

Breathless and confused, I replayed what happened. I felt like I had been violated. I was so stunned and it happened so fast that I started to wonder if it had really happened at all. Had I really just been treated like that? Recurring abdominal cramps and a pounding thump, thump, thump *in my chest told me that it was real. An expressionless nurse appeared and repositioned the fetal monitor belts, ignoring me altogether as I wept. Then she left. As the hours progressed, my anger mounted. Instead of sleeping or talking to my baby and coaching him through the transitions of birth, I ruminated. And, I cried. I had never felt so alone.*

Before my son's birth, I thought that women who had already given birth would naturally unite and support others who were in the process of the same, but the fact that other women were involved in stripping my dignity was a significant element of my negative experiences. I was (and, to some extent, still am) enraged. I felt betrayed by several of the nurses but most profoundly by the female OBGYN. She was a doctor and an educated woman who was serving as a role model to students about how to care for a labouring woman, and she acted inhumane. Her actions were morally injurious to me, and even now they evoke powerful feelings of indignation and disgust. She shattered my expectations about women supporting other women yet solidified in me a passionate commitment to helping others (both women and men) preserve their own dignity in the face of adversity. Reflecting on my own stories and trying to consider them as they related to my prior beliefs, the prevailing cultural norms, and prior research helped me to see that the process of crafting stories for the self can be complicated and take time for women who experienced trauma during delivery. To follow the redemptive storytelling sequence, I will conclude this section by commenting on self-transformation. I believe that crafting these stories for the self helped me resculpt my self-image and reclaim my life.

Stories for the Child

Although stories for the other and stories for the self both serve vital purposes, I consider the stories for the child to be of the greatest importance. This belief may reflect both my actual dedication to my children and my buying the notion that a good mother places the needs and welfare of the child above all else, including herself. I believe that starting a child's life narrative off with a powerful yet authentic story of origin plays an essential role in ongoing socio-emotional development. As a fundamental element in the developing stories of their own lives, children's stories of origin should reflect strength, curiosity, and engagement with the world, and they should highlight the beauty and allure of the human-to-human connections. As a mother, I tell stories about my children to them on a regular basis. When birthdays roll around on the calendar, the frequency with which stories of origin are presented or requested increases. These stories help frame the child's arrival and situate the child's understanding of his or her role within the larger family structure.

My son is the first born, the oldest child, and, regardless of age, the second man of the house. My daughter is the second-born child who arrived a bit early only because she was already strong and she was so excited to meet her brother. My son knows that my husband had to "talk to him" through my belly (after more than twenty hours of labour) because as such a happy and relaxed baby, my son appeared to be "content to linger around inside reading comic books by flashlight where he was all warm and cozy." My son laughs and co-narrates this story, describing how daddy cupped his hands as a megaphone to talk through my belly to tell him it was "time to be born already; there's a whole world waiting out here for you!" My daughter strikes a superhero pose during accounts of her story, with a clenched fist held high in the air. She co-narrates about how she punched her way out fist first so that she could go "get busy and play" with her brother and how daddy was lucky he didn't miss her daring debut while he was asleep on a hospital bench in the hall.

They also know their ties to foreign culture and that their passports reflect a different country of origin than mine or their father's. We celebrate the international connections inherently bound in their identities, and these stories situate not only their place in the family but their place in the world. We still have their first passports in the collection of artifacts that are associated with their stories of origin, along with other mementos, such as their keepsake pajamas and the hat they each wore on the drive home from the hospital. We get these things out from time to time and reminisce together as a family. I imagine that their stories will be restoried again and again as our children mature and ask new questions, but the core elements of warm parental welcoming, positive personality strengths, their place in the family, and connections to the larger world, at least for the foreseeable future, will likely remain.

Sharing birth stories is an important means of strengthening intergenerational bonds; however, the medicalization of the birth experience in the U.S. may have interrupted intergenerational sharing of stories and even silenced women who cannot recall birthing events due to anesthesia or other pain-reducing medications (Berhmann). Still, Robyn Fivush et al.'s work on maternal reminiscing underscores the value of maternal-child reminiscing as well as using an elaborative conversational style on many developmental outcomes for the child, including understanding of the self and others. McAdams and McLean suggest that parents who use an elaborative conversational style help "stimulate self-story telling skills in children" (235). As I write this story about crafting stories, I realize that my own mother used just such an elaborative conversational style.

My mother reminisced with each of her three children about many different events. The stories I heard from her about our births, though, all centred around how quickly my siblings and I each arrived. A time and date stamp of the exact moment of birth typically marked the end of each story. If there were any terrifying events that happened during the process, she never told me. Either my mother knew about the events and did not tell any of her children, or my parents were both complicit in secrecy. Alternatively, maybe she did not know about any such events (although a doctor might have known but never disclosed to her). My hope is that she never said anything negative because everything went perfectly fine. If she went through anything similar to me, then I am not sure I would want to know. Perhaps I would have benefited from knowing before my children were born, but if she purposely did not tell me negative things then I know it was because she wanted to protect me in some way.

However, now that I have two children of my own, my siblings' stories and even my own are somewhat difficult to recall. Here is what I do know. After very quick labour (three hours for my sister, who was the first, and even less for my brother, who was the second), one of them was born at "ten minutes to 9:00 a.m." and the other at "eight minutes to 8:00 a.m.," although I am not sure which stamp goes with which story. Length and weight were always included, and we all knew my brother would be tall because he was such a long baby. I know we later got a puppy named Jeremy because he was born on my sister's birthday, and my brother got his own fireworks every year for having arrived on the Fourth of July. The details of my own story have faded in recent years. I know the day, of course, but I cannot remember the time stamp or information about my size. The only details I recall are my mother saying that I had black hair and dark eyes and that the father of another baby that had been born the same day complimented her on my looks. I realize now that I do not include either the time and date stamps for my own children or size details in their stories, mostly because I have trouble remembering this information and because they both were tiny babies who were born at a very high altitude so I never wanted to place much emphasis on their sizes.

We have photos we show them, of course, but they are carefully chosen. Both photos that I consider to be their newborn pictures are ones where they are smiling. My son's photo was taken within the first few days of life when we caught him smiling in a fleeting moment. My daughter's newborn picture was taken when she was closer to three months old, when the last evidence of medical assistance for survival was removed. Of course, I have dozens of photos of her from before that moment of freedom, but they are quite difficult for me to view without becoming emotional. She knows that she needed supplemental oxygen to help her breathe for a while, and she has seen a few photos of herself with an oxygen cannula on her face. So far, though, she has never seen the very first photos we have of her, which were snapped in the NICU while she had so many wires and monitors attached to her that she resembled a human octopus. In fact, I have only looked at those photos a few times and have never shared them with anyone except my husband. They seem to represent (or perhaps misrepresent) a level of vulnerability that I could not protect her from when she was born. I hope that someday I will look upon them as reflecting her resilience instead, and perhaps that is when I will decide to share them with her. My favourite newborn photo of my (three-month-old) daughter shows her smiling while snuggled alongside a plushy toy that had a similar smile. The toy came from a promotion that our neighbourhood grocery store was doing on fruits and vegetables, and the plushy in the photo is some sort of onion or garlic. The crucial part of this photo is how it captures my daughter's amazing smile, one she showed all the time once she no longer had a cannula taped to the delicate skin of her nose or her cheeks.

Stories of Origin as a Starting Place

Much of my experience is consistent with research I found on sharing stories of origin with children. Julia Hayden et al. have indicated that as mothers share stories of origin with their children, they are communicating important information, such as feelings of love and bonding as well as family unity. By default, the story of origin begins as something biographical but morphs over time into a story that is increasingly autobiographical. Although I never received any coaching on how to share stories of origin with my children, there has been some work on doing so with children who have been adopted. Erin Krusiewicz and Julia Wood interviewed adoptive parents regarding the "entrance stories" they crafted for their adopted children and found that the stories often included themes of how fortune and misfortune coexist as well as how destiny, compelling connections, rescue, and legitimacy all factored into how a child entered the adoptive family. They acknowledge that once the stories are shared, they belong jointly to both the (adoptive) parents and the child. I believe the same is true for my stories for the child. I crafted them to provide my children each with a positive starting place for the rest of their lives.

Bridging the Gap

Although my own experience allows me to separate stories of origin into three different types, I recognize that other women may have significant overlap in their stories or may share their stories much differently than I have. Sarah Blainey and Pauline Slade conducted research that involved women sharing stories of traumatic birth experiences anonymously yet publicly by writing and publishing their stories online. These stories more closely approximate what I consider to be stories for the self, yet the authors shared them freely online for any other women who may want to read them. Blainey and Slade found that the women who wrote the stories reported various motivations for doing so but often included motives such as wanting to help others and trying to validate some of their feelings.

I also understand that cultural norms change over time and what might have been (or appeared to be) prevailing norms when I gave birth to my children may already have changed. Barbara Behrmann has called for women to reclaim their legacy stories and to find out more about their mothers' and grandmothers' experiences in order to increase their confidence and empowerment in birthing. In "Uncovering Your Own Birth History," Behrmann even provides a list of questions and coaching tips for women to use in how to interview female family members regarding these legacy stories. I support this approach and believe that deliberate sharing of more detailed stories of origin may serve useful purposes, including helping both the self and others. Indeed, someday I may find myself sharing my original stories for the self in some limited but specific way with my children as they approach parenthood. Jennifer Lilgendahl and Dan McAdams suggest that well-being in midlife is related to the ability to make growth-promoting interpretations of events and that this ability may become more sophisticated as people progress through adulthood, finally peaking in early old age. I would not be surprised if I find that as I age, my views on the utility and purpose that each type of story serves for various audiences may change, as they may focus less on who wants to know than on what greater good can come from sharing specific information.

Deciding what details to share and how to disclose them in a story of origin depends on many factors. Stories for the self, stories for the other, and stories for the child all serve important functions, although the specificity and style of story presentation may differ. Ultimately, any story of origin may exist in multiple versions and change over time, depending on who wants to know and to what extent the storyteller may have processed the events. As people say, having a baby will change your life, although the more complete and less frequently shared story would be that the act of having a baby may do the same.

Disclaimer: The opinions expressed in this chapter are the author's own and do not necessarily reflect the views of the United States Military Academy, the Department of the Army, or the United States Government.

Endnote

1. These story patterns, however, are applicable only in situations where the child was born healthy or alive, perhaps despite a horrific labor. Birth experiences that end in tragedy, heartbreak, and loss are likely storied in an entirely different way.

Works Cited

Ayers, Susan. "Delivery as a Traumatic Event: Prevalence, Risk Factors, and Treatment for Postnatal Posttraumatic Stress Disorder." *Clinical Obstetrics and Gynecology*, vol. 47, 2004, pp. 552-567.

Ayers, Susan. "Thoughts and Emotions During Traumatic Birth: A Qualitative Study." *Birth: Issues in Perinatal Care*, vol. 34, 2007, pp. 253-263.

Ayers, Susan, and Alan Pickering. "Do Women Get Posttraumatic Stress Disorder as a Result of Childbirth? A Prospective Study of Incidence." *Birth: Issues in Perinatal Care*, vol. 28, 2001, pp. 111-118.

Ayers, Susan, et al. "Narratives of Traumatic Birth: Quality and Changes Over Time." *Psychological Trauma: Theory, Research, Practice, and Policy*, vol. 7, no. 3, 2015, pp. 234-242.

Beck, Cheryl. "Pentadic Cartography: Mapping Birth Trauma Narratives." *Qualitative Health Research*, vol. 16, no. 4, 2006, pp. 453-466.

Behrmann, Barbara. "Uncovering Your Own Birth History." *The Journal of Perinatal Education*, vol. 12, no. 4, 2003, pp. vi-x.

Blainey, Sarah, and Pauline Slade. "Exploring the Process of Writing About and Sharing Traumatic Birth Experiences Online." *British Journal of Health Psychology*, vol. 20, 2015, pp. 243-260.

Ellis, Carolyn. *The Ethnographic I: A Methodological Novel about Autoethnography*. Altamira Press, 2004.

Fivush, Robyn, et al. "Elaborating on Elaborations: Role of Maternal Reminiscing Style in Cognitive and Socioemotional Development." *Child Development*, vol. 77, no. 6, 2006, pp. 1568-1588.

Grekin, Rebecca, and Michael O'Hara. "Prevalence and Risk Factors of Postpartum Posttraumatic Stress Disorder: A Meta-Analysis." *Clinical Psychology Review*, vol. 34, no. 5, 2014, pp. 389-401.

Hayden, Julia, et al. "The Transmission of Birth Stories from Mother to Daughter: Self-esteem and Mother-Daughter Attachment." *Sex Roles*, vol. 55, 2006, pp. 373-383.

Iovine, Vicki. *The Girlfriend's Guide to Pregnancy*. Pocket, 2007.

Krusiewicz, Erin, and Julia Wood. "'He was Our Child from the Moment We Walked in that Room': Entrance Stories of Adoptive

Parents." *Journal of Social and Personal Relationships*, vol. 18, no. 6, 2001, pp. 785-803.

Lilgendahl, Jennifer Pals. "Constructing the "Springboard Effect": Causal Connections, Self-Making, and Growth Within the Life Story." *Identity and Story: Creating Self in Narrative*, edited by Daniel McAdams et al., American Psychological Association, 2006, pp. 175-199.

Lilgendahl, Jennifer Pals, and Dan McAdams. "Constructing Stories of Self-Growth: How Individual Differences in Patterns of Autobiographical Reasoning Relate to Well-being in Midlife." *Journal of Personality*, vol. 79, no. 2, 2011, pp. 391-428.

Lothian, Judith, and Alyson Grauer. "Giving Birth: 'We Just Don't Talk About It.'" *The Journal of Perinatal Education*, vol. 21, no. 2, 2012, pp. 123-126.

McAdams, Dan, and Kate McLean. "Narrative Identity." *Current Direction in Psychological Science*, vol. 22, no. 3, 2013, pp. 233-238.

Murkoff, Heidi, and Sharon Mazel. *What to Expect When You're Expecting*. Workman Publishing, 2016.

Savage, Jane Staton. "Birth Stories: A Way of Knowing in Childbirth Education." *Journal of Perinatal Education*, vol. 10, no. 2, 2001, pp. 3-7.

Sternberg, Robert. "Love as a Story." *Journal of Social and Personal Relationships*, vol. 12, no. 4, 1995, pp. 541-546.

Thomson, Gill Margaret, and Soo Downe. "Changing the Future to Change the Past: Women's Experiences of a Positive Birth Following a Traumatic Birth Experience." *Journal of Reproductive and Infant Psychology*, vol. 28, no. 1, 2001, pp. 102-112.

Chapter Four

Single Mothers Storying the Absent Father and Values-Based Cartooning

Penelope Mendonça

An NHS nurse with a Spanish accent bursts in to the cubicle and delivers an unexpected question: "Where is the father?" I look at her with surprise. There is clearly no man here, so why is she asking me this? My body slowly melts into the hospital bed as the liquid morphine takes effect. "Spain?" I reply through the miscarriage hell I'm experiencing, "or maybe the sperm bank, or was it Wormwood Scrubs?" The thing is—it's none of her fucking business.

One year later, I am desperate to keep the next baby inside me. I gratefully cross each day off the calendar with a black, water-based marker. At 168 days, I spend too many long nights trying not to be in labour while on a labour ward. I hear it all: the cervical sweep, the pessaries, and the surrendering to painkillers when the tens machine proves totally useless. I am an unwilling witness to other women's raw, embodied experiences; I hear their relationships crack under the weight of the incoming baby. I quietly draw and paint entertaining cartoons under dimmed lighting and secretly list the top ten benefits of single pregnancy.

At 280 days, my belly bulges and hardens; strips of my skin stretch and strain around me like my dad's old bungee cords. I give the solo performance of a lifetime in my very own bloody, druggy drama. A midwife looks concerned and asks whether hubby is on his way. I have no idea who she is talking about. All that I am interested in is my baby's survival.

During "father-only" visiting time, I sit alone with my little girl *squeezed to my outrageously lopsided breasts. I watch as women are photographed with their babies by men bearing hand-crafted fresh flower arrangements. I look at the slightly pathetic bunch my mother and father left for me earlier and smile, everything is good as gold. "When is the daddy coming?" someone asks.*

As the autobiofictional (Barry) writing above suggests, single women may be required to negotiate well-meaning, intrusive, and/or morally loaded questions and comments about their child's origins—whether they be pregnant or mothering, whether they are trying to conceive or even miscarrying. Here, I am resisting the reader's desire to know where the father is or, indeed, why he is apparently absent. Whether any explanation concerning the whereabouts of the biological father or sperm donor is necessary in the first place is a matter for feminist debate. Family histories, family tree graphics and birth certificates all ask for the name of the father. They demand the filling of those spaces that may contain unanswered questions, secrets and spicy mysteries, and even as we check formal records for facts, our family stories dance shamelessly with whatever it was that people wanted us to believe. Throughout history single pregnant women and single mothers of babies have represented a challenge to dominant Western ideologies about family and parenting. They may have internalized and/or perhaps resisted moral judgement, defending single parenting as a valid, even preferable family form. They are likely to have had to negotiate questions and comments about their circumstances, at times with profound consequences (Mendonça "Fallen Woman"). Their stories, responses and actions reflect the significant levels of agency, emotional and social intelligence required of them. Despite changes in societal attitudes, single women who have babies continue to actively push the boundaries of gendered, age-related, religious, and cultural expectations.

This chapter will consider elements of an interdisciplinary, practice-based PhD undertaken from 2012 to 2018. In my associated research, I wished to answer the question of what a case study looking at single mothers storying the absent biological father or sperm donor could tell us about contemporary motherhood. I also considered what the new research method of values-based cartooning (Mendonça "Situating") would reveal when used in the study's methodology. Interviews and workshops included graphic facilitation and cartooning with twenty single women aged between sixteen and fifty-two Participants were all pregnant and expecting their first child or they were first-time mothers of babies. Their narratives and perspectives were filtered and condensed into creative nonfiction graphic narratives.

The area of interest (single motherhood) and practice (graphic facilitation and cartooning) were interconnected from the moment the research was conceived. As such, the art was neither subordinate to nor separate from the topic. The researcher was also the artist, and the research involved identifying problems and responding through practice. It was a hybrid and iterative methodology where analysis is "concurrent with data gathering/generation and is cyclical/iterative" (Gray and Malins 132). Through values-based cartooning, I wove together shared and at times sharply contrasting views and experiences while contributing to both the fields of motherhood studies and comics scholarship. The research generated alternative and nuanced visual and textual portrayals of contemporary mothering, which challenged assumptions, disrupted stereotypes, and subverted romanticised narratives of conception, pregnancy, and early motherhood. The aim was to access and represent multiple and diverse lived experiences and to move away from the tendency for autobiographical comics by female cartoonists to be based on what Chimamanda Ngozi Adichie describes as a "single story."

This chapter begins with an overview of the research, followed by an explanation on the topic of single mothers storying the absent father; it then looks at literature examining the stigma (and agency) associated with single pregnancy and early single motherhood. Next, the chapter explores the information and advice that single pregnant women and single first-time mothers may be required to navigate. And finally, a brief description of my research method is presented, followed by selected annotated examples of graphic narrative from the research.

Terms and Terminology

Many women embarking on motherhood outside of a relationship will already be labelled as, and/or self-identify as "single" (Lahad; DePaulo; Reynolds), they may consider their single status as a temporary or permanent state. However, some research participants who were over the age of thirty-five preferred to describe themselves as a "solo" rather than "single" mothers, suggesting that "solo" is associated with more positive pursuits, such as being an artist, a performer, or an aviator

(Engel), whereas "single" mother is more stigmatized in Britain. Cultural background and context are also relevant here, as "solo" mother arguably has negative connotations in my country of origin, New Zealand. "Lone mother" was described by one of my research participants as a "sad and negative" label.

"Donor" refers to known, private, or anonymous sperm donors, unless otherwise stated. It is worth noting that research participants had different understandings of sperm donation; some described it as a planned formal and/or legal process, whereas others had applied the term to biological fathers retrospectively, as it became clear that they would be entirely absent, with no responsibility for parenting, and no place on the birth certificate. In contrast, some younger participants referred to biological fathers as their "baby fathers," despite their physical absence. One younger participant referred to her absent ex-partner as the child's "donor dad." Many older participants sought to be clear about the limited role, responsibility, and legal status of the sperm donor by avoiding any reference to him as a "father" or "dad." This clarity around terminology is thought to help reduce confusion when talking to children and others about the nature of family and child origins (Montuschi). Participants who used double donors tended to integrate both egg and sperm donors into their narratives.

"Lone parent" is increasingly used instead of "single mother" in order to acknowledge one-parent households led by single fathers and to move away from reductionist gendered language. However, there is a "veneer of equality" in the more gender-neutral language of "parenting" (Thomson et al.), which risks masking gender inequalities (Motapanyane). Within heterosexual couple relationships women undertake the large majority of the labour associated with raising children (Asher), and 90 per cent of single parents in Britain are women (Gingerbread). In this study, I consider the experiences of those who identified as pregnant women and/or first-time mothers (see Reed and Surkan for a discussion on gender, identity, and LGBTQ parenting).

Stigma, Agency, and Single Pregnancy

Single motherhood is linked to economic disadvantage, lower levels of education, and young motherhood. With the trend towards mid-life mothering (Mantas and Peterson; Golombok) as well as separation and divorce between parents, single motherhood has also become associated with older, middle-class mothering. The idea of the "single mother" is likely conjure up images associated with perceptions of bad, or good, mothering—stereotypes that inevitably reveal attitudes toward social class, age, race, gender and sexuality, disability, and health. Research into single motherhood has tended to focus on negative aspects, with women's capacity for agency undermined and intersectional issues hidden; this is only now beginning to be challenged (Motapanyane; Ajandi; Golombok; Robinson et al). Given this relentless interest in the problems of single motherhood, it would appear that academic research, while turning a spotlight on the inequalities facing women, has inadvertently contributed to the enduring stereotyping and stigma associated with single motherhood. Jennifer Ajandi calls for: "an alternative discourse that does not make the struggles and challenges of single mothers invisible but highlights parts of their lives that are often not reported or not asked about in research studies" (411).

Data about single pregnancy and early single motherhood where the biological father or sperm donor has been absent since before birth reveals a complex picture. Research includes different definitions of single motherhood and has a tendency to categorize single mothers in to groups in order to understand their experiences. Golombok suggests that fifteen percent of babies in the UK are born into single-mother families, this figure comes from Kiernan's study from 2006 which included babies who had non-resident fathers (Kiernan quotation in Golombok, 2015). In Britain, unmarried mothers cannot include a father's name on the birth certificate unless he either attends the birth registration, completes a statutory declaration of parentage, or obtains a court order giving the father parental responsibility (Gov.uk, 2018). In 2016, just over five percent of live births were sole registered by the mother (ONS, 2018) this figure represents a decline in the proportion of sole registered births by the mother among all births over the past twenty years. First-time mothers made up forty-three percent of all births sole registered by the mother, which was just over two percent of all births registered in 2016 (ONS, 2018). Fifty-eight percent of first-time mothers who sole registered were under twenty-five, compared to only eighteen percent of all mothers. This suggests that women who sole register births are significantly younger than women who register with the father, or within a same-sex couple. The actual number of first-time mothers who sole registered over the age of forty was just five hundred and twelve. However, it is problematic to assume biological father absence where a birth has been sole registered. As the Office for National Statistics point out 'the Millennium Cohort Study by Kiernan and Smith, indicates that although lone parenthood is highly likely at the time of a sole registration, in a large minority of cases, just under a third, the father is likely to be closely involved or living with the mother' (ONS, 2016). Furthermore, it is possible that the biological father could be in fact be absent, where the birth has been registered by a married women, for example, following relationship breakdown.

As Rozsika Parker suggests, "the image of the child as a shared creative project is rooted deeply in the unconscious" (52); from the moment a single woman's pregnancy becomes known or visible (or perhaps earlier if her intention to become a parent while single is known), there may be questions (spoken and unspoken about the child's origins). Conception is widely understood to require a man's physical presence, and raising children within a heterosexual, nuclear family continues to be promoted as the ideal. The single pregnant woman presents a challenge as society's "couple centric conception of parenthood points to heteronormative ideology—standard heterosexual conception requires two people" (Descartes 193). It could be argued that the image of a heavily pregnant single woman, or a single mother with a baby, offers a kind of text, which tells as well as invites a story. And given that a reader or audience brings their understandings to a text (Barthes; Belsey), judgment as to whether an account is faithful, authentic, or morally acceptable will be dependent on individual subjectivities. The values, beliefs, experiences, and relationship statuses of those who demand child origin stories will, of course, affect the way they are understood.

Some single women mothering within specific contexts and cultures (including LGBTQ cultures), who have supportive family members, friendships, and networks (these may be local as well as social-media and web-based forums), find that their circumstances and intentions are largely understood and accepted—biological father or donor absence is not necessarily a stigmatized experience (see Russell on the experience of women in Denmark and Oyewumi on mothering within the Nigerian [Yoruba] culture). Single motherhood may represent a preferred family form, and may reflect how women themselves were raised, for example, within a matriarchal culture (Moore), with strong, single-parent role models, as described by Wanda Wyporska, a trustee of the single-parent organization Gingerbread (The Voice). Intentional single motherhood may be seen as a subversive and feminist statement, an example of self-determination, and as a bold challenge to the nuclear family (Szuchman) as well as to gender stereotyping and cultural norms. For some, single motherhood may offer a healthy and happy alternative to parenting within an unhealthy and/or unhappy couple relationship. In *The Father: Historical, Psychological and Cultural Perspectives*, Luigi Zoja, suggests the following: "It has been said that the father is becoming a luxury. His traditional psychological functions are exercised to an ever slighter degree. His material tasks are conferred to mothers or institutions. His erosion as a psychological figure is by now accompanied by physical absence" (225).

In their longitudinal study *Making Modern Mothers*, Rachel Thomson et al. suggest that while contemporary family life has changed, some single pregnant women and first-time single mothers may still be required to defend themselves against charges of selfishness. The criticism they may face can touch on multiple intersectional factors, including age, race, disability, gender and sexuality, as well as class and income. Moral stigmatization has long been associated with single mothering (Morris; McIntosh; Kaplan; Quirk), as has the stigmatized experience of being welfare dependent. Robin Jarrett's (1996) study of welfare-dependent African American single mothers made an important contribution to the recognition of intersectional concerns, as her study found that Black teenage mothers, the majority of whom were poor, had to "struggle against being considered morally deviant, underclass and unworthy" (Kaplan xxiii). She continues, "these girls were silenced by the insidious and insistent stereotyping of them as promiscuous and aberrant teenage girls" (10). In Susan Harkness and Amy Skipp's British study of single mothers, depression, and employment, all of the single mothers interviewed discussed the stigma associated with their family form coming from government and the media: "Lone mothers thought they were seen as a drain on society, something to be 'discouraged' and often depicted as 'scroungers,' regardless of whether or not they were in work" (Harkness and Skipp 15). Charges of selfishness may also relate to the perception that single women may be depriving a child of a father. In this case, the traditional nuclear family structure, which includes a biological father who is physically present, is considered ideal for both mother and child; whereas the concept of a "fatherless child" is assumed to be a form of deficit with negative consequences for both the child and society (McLanaham et al.). Yet Ann Mooney et al. argue for a more comprehensive analysis, suggesting that family function and poverty may be more significant than family structure when considering negative outcomes for children.

For women escaping intimate partner violence during pregnancy or early motherhood, single motherhood may be a way to keep themselves and their children safe. According to the National Health Service in the UK, one in three women experience domestic abuse (violent, psychological, or sexual) during pregnancy. Refuges that provide emergency temporary accommodation for women and children fleeing abuse estimate that 20 percent of women who access their services are pregnant or have recently given birth. Among migrant mother families in Germany who had escaped gender-based violence, Lydia Potts and Ulrike Lingen-Ali found that living within a one-parent family was seen as a "preferable—though not desirable—family form" (282). Furthermore, Melissa Holmes et al. recommend that discussions on unintended pregnancy need to acknowledge the possibility of rape-related pregnancy. The issue of abuse is also present within the underexamined area of informal and unregulated sperm donation (McQuoid); here, experiences of violence and abuse are likewise likely to complicate the storying of a sperm donor.

A single woman's route to conception, her experience of being or becoming single, and her perceived choices may also affect whether she is viewed as pioneering or irresponsible. Navjotpal Kaur and Rosemary Ricciardelli's study of the transition from being infertile to becoming mothers of multiples through assisted reproductive technologies (ART) found that women saw themselves in a socially disadvantaged position because of the stigma attached to the unnaturalness of ART, which is connected to the stigma of infertility. Interestingly, romantic comedies exploring single pregnancy tend to celebrate intentional single conception yet conclude with a loving relationship between biological parents (Mack). Tabloid newspapers highlight stories of women who conceive via sex outside of relationships and those using online sperm donor sites and frame them as irresponsible and manipulative (Brown) or vulnerable and perhaps to blame for abuse they may encounter (Taylor).

Navigating Information and Advice

As Thomson et al. assert, those embarking on motherhood "must encounter and navigate the accumulation of specialist knowledge about maternal and child well-being, including layers of moral injunction and pathology created by successive waves of expertise." (165). There is some literature on how to talk about a child origin story in which donors have been used. Many books and articles aimed at single women considering or embarking on motherhood speak to a middle-class audience, as they appear to conflate responsible single parenting with a high level of financial independence (Sloan; Morrissette; Hertz; Bock). Much of this assumes the use of anonymous sperm donors through licensed fertility clinics, yet substantially more sperm donors are registered on connection websites than with clinics (Freeman; Jadva, Tranfield and Golombok). It is worth noting that ARTs, which involve choosing and buying sperm from private clinics, require research, time (including availability at specific times) and significant personal finance.[1] Education, social class, and income levels all have a bearing on the so-called choices available to single women, yet women may be judged harshly for conceiving via unregulated or informal routes. Here, I include literature targeted towards specific groups (such as single mothers by choice (Mattes) and those using licensed fertility clinics), because of its potential relevance to single women outside of these groups. Regardless of the route to conception and the experience of being/becoming single, women are likely to negotiate how to talk to their child and others about someone who is biologically related to the child but not parenting them. The literature referenced here refers to experiences from a number of countries. The laws, practices, and societal attitudes associated with marriage, divorce, child custody, conception, pregnancy, miscarriage, sperm donation, donor anonymity, parental responsibility, and birth registration vary across these contexts. Likewise, they may vary across many of the cultures found within multicultural cities, such as London (Sharia Law, for example, is permitted in Britain so long as it adheres to British law). There are other global considerations, as women often migrate between countries, travel in order to conceive under different conditions, and choose informal routes to conception, such as purchasing sperm over the Internet. Because of the limited research into, and stories of, single conception, pregnancy, and motherhood, many single women access support, stories, and advice from international sources. Such information includes blogs, pregnancy guides, health professionals, fertility clinics, donor websites, motherhood memoirs or "mumoirs" (Dymond and Wiley), art, film, and fiction.

When single women are storying anonymous sperm donors, they are likely to draw on donor profiles and donor promotions, which have been constructed to help people select donors but also to promote sales. The UK fertility industry is estimated to be worth £320m with a growth rate of around 3 to 4.5 per cent per annum, and 70 percent of the market is privately funded (Risebrow). The London Women's Clinic (in partnership with the London Sperm Bank) specifically targets single women through advertising campaigns. They promote the legal and health benefits associated with accessing their donors and treatments, claiming to know about "donor personalities, interests, hobbies and those qualities which make them human" (London Women's Clinic). They story the donor (and sell his sperm) through online profiles. "Our Impression of Donor 1320 (£950) ... Sporty and fit, he enjoys cycling, travelling and going to live music gigs. Kind hearted, with hazel eyes, reddish-brown curly hair, high forehead, square jaw-line, tall, athletic built recruit is motivated by a keen sense of family and belonging" (London Sperm Bank). Sperm donor profiles are highly selective and subjective. They both influence and reflect societal attitudes about race, intelligence (Goodey), disability, appearance, gender, and sexuality as they promote the attributes apparently required in order to produce so-called healthy, attractive, and intelligent children. Note, in 2015, the London Sperm Bank was accused by campaigners of practicing eugenics by rejecting sperm donors who had neurological conditions, including dyslexia, attention deficit hyperactivity disorder (ADHD), and autism (Mortimer). Interestingly, information about the sexual orientation of sperm donors is often not collected by Human Fertilisation Embryology and Authority licensed fertility clinics, "while many openly recruit gay donors, others do not because of the perceived link between homosexuality and sexually transmitted diseases such as HIV" (Freeman et al. 2083).

In 2002, the UK-based Donor Conception Network (DCN), which advocates being open with children and others about a child's origins, published a picture book for single mothers to read to their children called *Our Story*. The book describes a woman going to a doctor to get inseminated and calls sperm donors "very kind" and "generous" (Baxter). Here, as with the description of Donor 1320 above, the implication is that the donor is altruistic. Yet the motivations of sperm donors vary (Freeman et al.) and are not necessarily always unproblematic. Through research, concerns have been raised about promoting unrealistic expectations among donor-conceived children (Zadeh). And within unregulated practices, some men may be motivated by a desire to have unprotected sex with women (see *Desperately Seeking Semen*). The DCN received feedback that more neutral wording was required regarding sperm donors (Engel), and the organization has since produced other children's books on the topic.

In their guide *Pregnant Pause: A Guide for Lesbians on How to Get Pregnant*, the organization Stonewall, in partnership with and sponsored by the London Women's Clinic, includes those lesbians who are also single. The guide warns those considering importing sperm from outside of licensed fertility clinics of the following: "There are significant risks regarding the safety of the semen. Many of the websites in use are also unreliable. First and foremost in your mind should be your health and your child's health.... Think about it. If having a child is that important to you, do you really want to take such a huge risk with your child's health?" Safety is of course, very important. The independent researcher and founder of the Donor Abuse Foundation, Claire McQuoid, suggests that the online sperm donor community is characterized by a "culture of gender-based violence and exploitation" (McQuoid). However, licensed fertility clinics, such as the London Women's Clinic, who advertise at the end of the Stonewall guide, also deal in other forms of risk; the degree to which they can guarantee either a healthy baby or that the sperm came from an "athletic" or a "kind-hearted" man is questionable.

Whereas the Stonewall guide helpfully acknowledges multiple

family forms and routes to conception, mainstream pregnancy guides often ignore alternative experiences. By way of example, *Emma's Diary*, the online and printed resource developed in association with the Royal College of General Practitioners, continues to assume couple parenting. In their section titled "Can You Afford To Have a Baby Without Breaking the Bank," the organization states the following: "One of you losing your job might actually not be as horrendous as you first think, especially if one parent would actually like to stay home for a while looking after the baby... Communication with your partner is essential." The nuclear family form and heteronormative parenting are assumed, often through visuals as well as text; the experiences of single women and single LGBTQ parents are often marginalized at a time when they may be in need of information, services, stories, and imagery they can identify with, potentially contributing to feelings of isolation and stigma.

In generic pregnancy guides, discussion about so-called intentional or unplanned pregnancies can appear over-simplistic and lacking in nuance; at times, the experience of single pregnancy appears to be conflated with escaping an abusive relationship (Mendonca "Bump"). Single lesbian motherhood is also largely absent, including within literature aimed at single women (Descartes).

Jane Mattes, psychotherapist and founder of the American organization Single Mothers by Choice, devotes a considerable amount of space in her 1994 book by the same name to helping women think about how they talk about their child's origins. She includes a range of routes to conception (Mattes explains that she herself "accidentally conceived with a lover") [xviii], which allows for a more open consideration of how to story the absent biological father or donor. She advocates single women making their own fictional picture book about a "single mother by choice" family. She suggests possible storylines, including "conception with a man who was not able to be a good father for whatever were his reasons" (133). Unlike numerous other guides, she touches on the possibility that the absent biological father or donor may not have been willing or able to be a good parent.

In *Mommies, Daddies, Donors, Surrogates; Answering Tough Questions and Building Strong Families*, Diane Ehrensaft, a developmental and clinical psychologist, offers strategies to those who use ARTS, including single women. Ehrensaft advocates being "open" with children about their origins very early on, not least to avoid being caught out by "leakage"—that is, others sharing information with the child before the parent does. Like Mattes, she promotes storytelling even when the child is a baby, as this provides them with a "preverbal experience of a verbal tale" (182). The UK-based *Donor Conception Network* supports this idea: "This is an ideal opportunity for parents to practice and become familiar with the language of donor conception. Babies will be forgiving of parents' stutters and stumbles over words as long as the tone generally communicates pride and love. A real bonus of talking with your baby in this way is that you will be freed from worry about when to start talking with your child" (Montuschi 8-9). Ehrensaft reassures parents that it is fine to "make mistakes as you tell the tale, then pick yourself up, correct yourself, and keep going ... you will all negotiate the terrain together, shaping a family narrative about your child's birth and making adjustments as you go" (179). These ideas may also be relevant for some single women who did not use a sperm donor but who have a different conception story regarding single parenting. In the context of my research, the initial audience for single pregnant women and single mothers of babies may in fact be themselves, as they reflect on their journey to single motherhood, perhaps speaking out loud to themselves or to an unborn child or a sleeping baby.

Family narratives are remembered, edited, told and retold well before a child is old enough to ask direct questions. Ehrensaft promotes a "model of tiered disclosure," (166) in which expectant parents agree on a plan about who, how, when, and whether to tell people about their child's origins; she calls for clear thinking, confidence, and an acceptance for how the family was made. However the nature of truth, memory, and subjectivity can mean that living up to Ehrensaft's guidance on the topic may be difficult. Although some may find it straightforward to be consistent and clear, others may be reckoning with a complex set of emotions: negative reactions from family members or friends as well as concerns about single mothering, money, miscarriage, and the newborn baby's health. Many will be undergoing significant life changes. Figure 1, *Coffee Morning*, shows three new mothers, all fictional, considering this topic; their appearances and expressions suggest they are mothering in contrasting circumstances.

Figure 1. *Coffee Morning*, original in colour, Mendonca, 2016.

All of the previously mentioned guides and research about child origin stories have a relatively serious tone, as they encourage thoughtful and consistent approaches to storying. Louise Sloane, who mined the membership of *Single Mother's by Choice* for quotes for her book *Knock Yourself Up: A Tell All Guide To Becoming a Single Mom*, also discusses issues of storying under the heading "Coming Out about Single Motherhood." Running through this guide is a tone of irreverence and humour. Single women described reacting to questions about their circumstances as single mothers with a silence, perhaps delivering sharp responses with outrage or wit, or even relishing the drama of the moment as they leave someone squirming, wondering what on earth to say. The Donor Conception Network suggests this book "is not the place to turn to if you want to think deeply about the moral issues raised by the process." However, I question the assumption that Sloane or indeed her participants had not considered the moral issues raised by single motherhood; throughout the course of this research, I was struck by the awareness of women of different ages and circumstances of the potential implications of their stories and what that may mean for their children in the future. Single women spoke of intentionally using shock and humour as a strategy for positioning and protecting themselves and their families, for maintaining dignity and privacy, as well as for expressing pride. As suggested above, women who are single and pregnant, or trying to get pregnant, or who are already single parents, negotiate high levels of complexity and subjectivity in relation to the storying of an absent biological father or sperm donor. Many may avoid, block, or deflect questions about father absence, or depending on the context, some may explain paternal absence in a way that satisfies (or dissatisfies or disrupts) the perceived needs of the questioner. In some ways, the accounts given in Sloan's book resonate with this research in that the participants reflected on the different selves they presented as well as on the variable nature of their responses during this period when women may be celebrating, worrying about money, sleep-deprived, working, grieving, experiencing moments of clarity and/or feelings of doubt. The creative, rigorous, and visual nature of values-based cartooning enabled me to engage with and seek to understand, rather than edit out, the humour and drama within women's accounts of their responses, and to consider how they attempted "to shift or trouble dominant discourses of motherhood in order to enable greater possibilities and more varied productions of culturally validated mother identities" (Reed 50).

Research Method

This research method was shaped by my background in social care, my career as a graphic facilitator (Mendonça "Graphic Facilitation"), and my work as a social issues cartoonist working across diverse communities and civil society organizations and institutions while accessing and representing contrasting experiences and perspectives. This includes work on the impact of austerity, the Windrush Crisis, disability rights, barriers facing women in academia (University of Birmingham), celebrating UK Black Pride, commemorating Partition (India 1947), and representing modern-day slavery (University of Nottingham). Within this type of work, values have a heightened significance; an iterative process is required involving careful listening, an understanding of context, and sensitivity towards consent and anonymity. The multiple decisions I make in these contexts are indeed influenced by my values and beliefs, which were informed by a childhood rich with frank (and at times humorous) international family narratives about parenting, mixed race and ethnicity, gender and sexuality, aging, mental health, and disability. Differing memories and experiences mean that stories (whether shared within a research interview or in a hospital ward) will forever be evolving depending on the storyteller and their audience. Linda Sandino and Matthew Partington suggest in *Oral History in the Visual Arts* that "life stories sit between autobiography and biography.... [They are] assisted narratives that are the product, or the co-product of interviewer and interviewee" (13). As the researcher-artist, the questions I ask, the lines I draw, the colours I select, and the texts I weave within images represent high levels of subjectivity.

Researching and communicating social issues are values-driven and potentially political activities. The history of cartooning is scattered with examples of empowering, entertaining, influential, and highly discriminatory works examining social concerns. Cartooning has been used for everything from Nazi war propaganda to health promotion, and more recently, it has been the center of passionate debate about free speech, following the killing of twelve people at the offices of the satirical comic *Charlie Hebdo* in Paris in 2015. There have been moments when cartoons, comics, graphic novels and graphics have each been criticized for promoting violence (Wertham), sexism (Robbins and Yronwode; Chute), racism (Ayaka and Hague; Howard and Jackson), ageism, and disablism (Whalen et al.). As such, cartooning is a practice that can be associated with negative values as well as those considered to be more positive, depending on individual perspectives.

Values-based cartooning is a mode of working in which an awareness and understanding of personal, professional, participant, cultural, and organizational values guides the way a cartoonist or visual practitioner works. This includes selecting topics of interest, purpose, role, process, and participation, as well as making decisions about the language used, the colour applied, and the line drawn. How, when, where, and whether the work is shared is also considered. It is a mode of working that requires constant awareness of, and an ability to negotiate, ethical concerns and conflicting agendas, along with multiple perspectives and powerful emotions.

Such cartooning is a social practice—it requires direct engagement with those who have lived experience of the issue under examination, even if the practitioner has personal experience. This includes seeking out those whose voices may not be present or listened to within dominant discourse and engaging with civil society organizations that claim to represent their interests. This differs from some examples of autobiographical cartooning, comics and visual recording practices, such as sketchnoting (Rohde), in which visuals may be dominated by the creator's perspective or by the need for a positive image of the organization commissioning the work.

Values-based cartooning is committed to accessing and representing diversity and intersectionality (Crenshaw), acknowledging inequalities, and promoting equality and inclusion. It is useful as a research method for supporting co-production (Ostrom) as well as for working with multiple stakeholders and with person-centred approaches (Pearpoint et al.), particularly where asset-based thinking (McKnight and Kretzmann) is important. It offers a way forward for those undertaking or commissioning visual approaches that need to align with ethical code, to engage with complex systems as well as a diversity of opinions, and move to beyond simplistic caricature or inaccurate representations.

Participants

This research included women who were single for different reasons and who had conceived in different ways (including through ARTs, informal arrangements, unprotected sex with ex-partners or lovers, as well as sperm donors). By including a broad age range and avoiding one single route to conception or one definition of a donor, I sought to disrupt some of the assumptions associated with so-called good and bad single motherhood.

All participants claimed to have experienced biological father or donor absence from pregnancy to early motherhood. They had, or were expecting to have, sole parental responsibility when their children were born (including financial). I sought to access what Rosanna Hertz describes as "consummate" mothers, in which there was "no other parent or romantic partner present, and they were technically responsible 24/7" (143).

Participants storied a range of routes to conception: intentional and unplanned conception via sexual intercourse while in a relationship or outside of a relationship; fertility treatment via a licensed fertility clinic;

and a mixture of donor arrangements, including anonymous, known, and double (egg and sperm) donations. Participants also described different journeys to single mothering, including trying to get pregnant while single, relationships ending following conception, and absence due to a prison sentence. Many participants spoke of relationships with different partners and donors, miscarriage and repeated attempts at conception over many years. The range of participant contributions suggested different understandings of the language around parenting and sperm donation. Some participant accounts appeared inconsistent. For this reason, it is unhelpful to provide an analysis of participant routes to conception and/or routes to single status.

Those who were single due to the death of a partner were not included in this study. Women who lost a parenting partner to death tend to be viewed more sympathetically, as they are seen to have ended up as single mothers through no fault of their own (Wallbank). Furthermore, those who were in a relationship but who saw themselves as single parents due to a current partner being absent for employment were also excluded from the criteria, as they did not have sole parental (or sole financial) responsibility for their child. Most of the research participants lived in London; three lived in other parts of England. They had diverse backgrounds in terms of age, income, class, race and ethnicity, gender and sexuality, and disability. Ten were aged between sixteen and twenty-three; three were aged between twenty-five and thirty-five, and seven were between forty and fifty-two. Five participants described themselves as being of mixed ethnicity, including African, Caribbean, and European. One participant identified as lesbian, one as bisexual, and one as gender fluid. (Note: Within workshop settings where participants assumed heterosexuality and promoted heteronormative and at times homophobic perspectives, some women may have chosen not to reveal their perspectives on gender and sexuality.)

None of the participants self-identified as disabled; however, many spoke of mental illness, having contact with the health, social care and criminal justice systems, and/or having special educational needs. My background in social care and advocacy leads me to suggest that women with learning disabilities and women with mental health needs were included within this study.

In *Mothering in Marginalized Contexts*, Caroline McDonald-Harker calls for research that considers abused women's mothering experiences from their perspective: "Only when we give abused mothers a voice, pay close attention to their subjective experiences, and shine a light on their everyday lived realities, are we able to begin to understand their unique mothering experiences, which have been silenced and neglected for far too long" (255-56). As such, one interview was held in a refuge for women and children; however, accounts of violence in which the perpetrator was the biological father were also given in other interviews and workshops.

Two interviews were undertaken with single-mother community leaders: Jane Mattes (Single Mothers by Choice) and Emily Engel (Donor Conception Network).

Calls for participation were placed on Internet forums for single women interested in parenting. Numerous women who had conceived via licensed fertility clinics came forward; they tended to be older, white, and middle class, and to network through support organizations. I had to work harder to access younger single women and experienced gate-keeping practices from some organizations that did not pass on information about my research to women whom they perceived to be too vulnerable to participate. Despite being visible and seeking support on online forums, single women who had not been expecting to be single when pregnant seemed to be more isolated. Their experiences appeared to be marginalized by some generic parenting organizations and some literature promoting intentional single motherhood.

Despite clearly advertised criteria for participation, four single women who were not pregnant but were thinking about having a child and/or currently trying to conceive attended one of the workshops I facilitated. This was in addition to single, pregnant women and single mothers. The level of interest in this research that came from those who were not currently pregnant, along with the long and complex accounts given within interviews and workshops, challenged assumptions that a child's origin story necessarily begins when it is biologically conceived.

Interviews and Workshops

Interviews were held in women's homes, in cafes, and on Skype. Two workshops were run at a local college where young mothers were attending a course that provided free childcare. One workshop was held at the Donor Conception Network's national conference. Written consent was obtained prior to each interview and workshop; participants were given the option of withdrawing from the research at any stage.

Younger participants requested to be involved through workshops rather than one-to-one interviews. Some inconsistency was noted in relation to stated ages and relationship status; some focused on their identity as young mothers rather than as single mothers, and appeared to view their single status as temporary. A small number said they expected their child's biological father to leave their current partners in the future and return to them.

Interviews and workshops involved values-based cartooning, which combined and adapted different approaches including graphic facilitation and cartooning. I visually recorded workshops and interviews (in addition to using a dictaphone), anonymized perspectives, facilitated collaborative character design, and encouraged participants to respond verbally, visually, and textually to pre-prepared examples of my graphics and cartoons.

Participants were not observed as in an ethnographic study; however, as a cartoonist and researcher, I was particularly aware of my senses. I noticed the smell of baby milk, the full nappy, the colour of once-white clothing, the gentle stroke of a swollen belly, and the latching of a crying baby. I also observed stark differences in social class, poverty and wealth, the way facial expressions or body language suddenly changed when money was discussed. Participants expressed both low and high aspirations for themselves and their children. Where interviews were undertaken in participants' homes, I was shown photographs of proud pregnant bodies, objects that held memories, donor profiles in files, online forum posts expressing loneliness and fears about having a child on their own. I also picked up unexpected details, such as the number of locks on the door of one mother's flat who feared for her safety, and the notice on a classroom door informing students that their college course with free childcare had just lost its funding. These visual clues and additional details exposed me to fragmented narratives and social contexts that consciously and subconsciously influenced creative practice.

Examples of Creative Practice

The following selection of graphic narratives generated during this research includes a graphic produced following a workshop about storying child origins; a fertility maze, which interviewees commented on; a fictional portrait referencing domestic violence; and a cartoon strip based on a participant's account of a taxi journey.

An early research activity involved participating in one of the Donor Conception Network's "Telling and Talking" workshops for pregnant and/or parenting lesbian couples and single women. It could be assumed that those attending used sperm donors; however, there was no way of knowing whether this was the case. Furthermore, some women had more than one child and had conceived them in different ways. The workshop proved to be informative and stimulating, but it also highlighted conflicting perspectives and triggered painful and mixed emotions for some participants. I was struck by the difference between the women who said that they did not want anyone to pity them or to think that a man had deserted them and those women who were openly grieving the loss of an intimate relationship (not necessarily with the biological father or sperm donor). At times, the combination of those mothering within lesbian relationships and single women seemed problematic due to significantly contrasting experiences of pregnancy and early parenting. The organizers did not grant permission for me to develop a graphic of the discussions in real time; instead, I produced a graphic summary (see Figure 2) following the event as a way to capture my reflections.

The image in Figure 2 includes quotes, questions, and key points covering a range of perspectives, and it makes reference to animation and children's books that are dominated by father figures. The central focus of the image is a white, middle-aged mother who appears to be sharing a family narrative with her child through a book; to her right are references to tabloid newspaper headlines raising concerns about single women having babies. Behind her is a dotted outline of mysterious figure titled "the donor," and directly to her left are suggestions that her past experiences and current relationships affect her feelings.

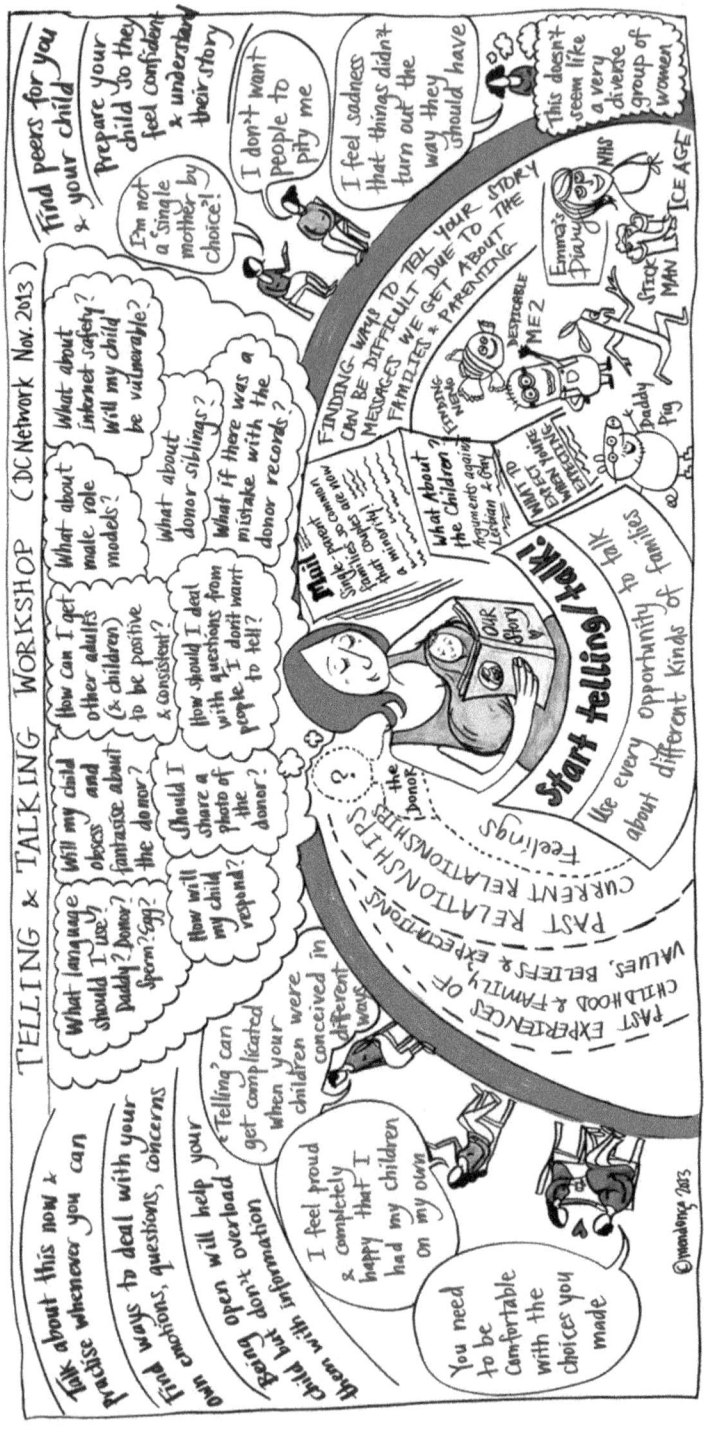

Figure 2. Graphic recording produced after the event (with no input from participants), original in colour, Mendonca, 2013.

Fertility Maze

Some participants' conception stories covered a long period of time and a number of potential donors and/or biological fathers. When asked about storying the absent biological father or sperm donor, one participant replied: "Which donor shall I tell you about?" Another asserted, "I am the father, as well as the mother."

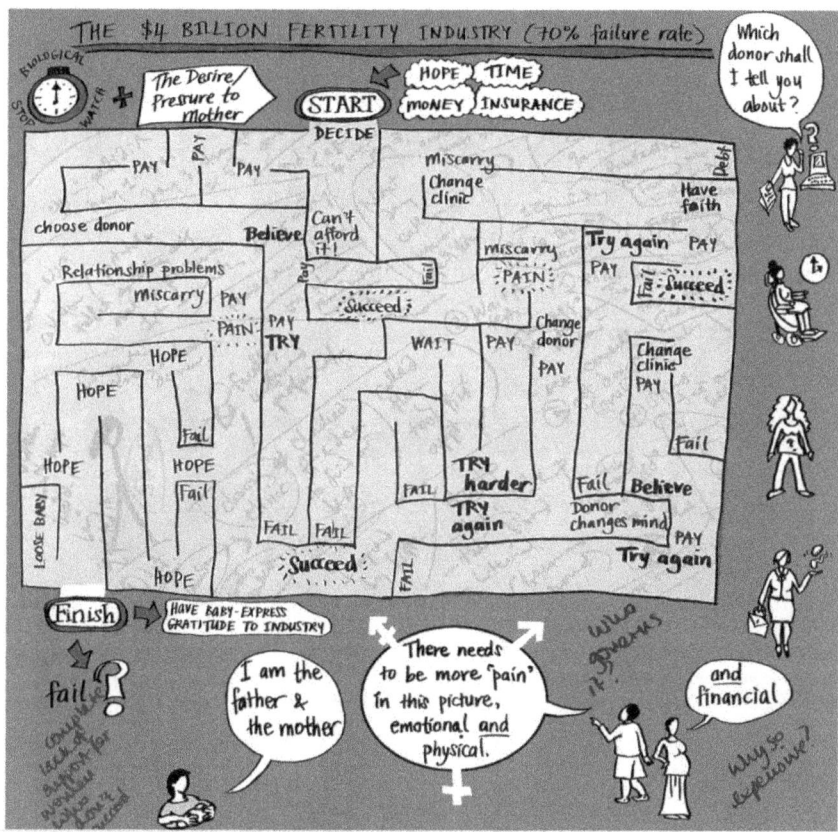

Figure 3. *Fertility Maze*, Mendonca 2017.

Figure 3, *Fertility Maze*, attempts to capture the complexity of storying when the individual had experienced multiple attempts at conception and pregnancy through licensed fertility clinics. The maze in the centre of the image was shown to a participant during an interview, and her quotes are included within a speech bubble: "There needs to be more pain in this picture (emotional and physical)." Included in her own handwriting are the phrases "complete lack of support for women who don't succeed," "why so expensive?" and "who governs it?" In a sense, she was annotating the graphic. Hand-drawn and hand-written details have also been added beneath the maze. This layer is one of my live graphic recordings of a participants' conception story; it includes graphic detail about her embodied and medicalized experience. Here, the comic form allows for the experience to be presented as is—a confusing and hastily recorded narrative, difficult to read and interpret.

A Pregnant Mother and Father with a Black Eye

On the left-hand side of Figure 4, titled "A Pregnant Mother and Father with a Black Eye," a woman with a black eye looks out at the audience in silence. The title invites the audience to look for the father, here, she is both the mother and the father.

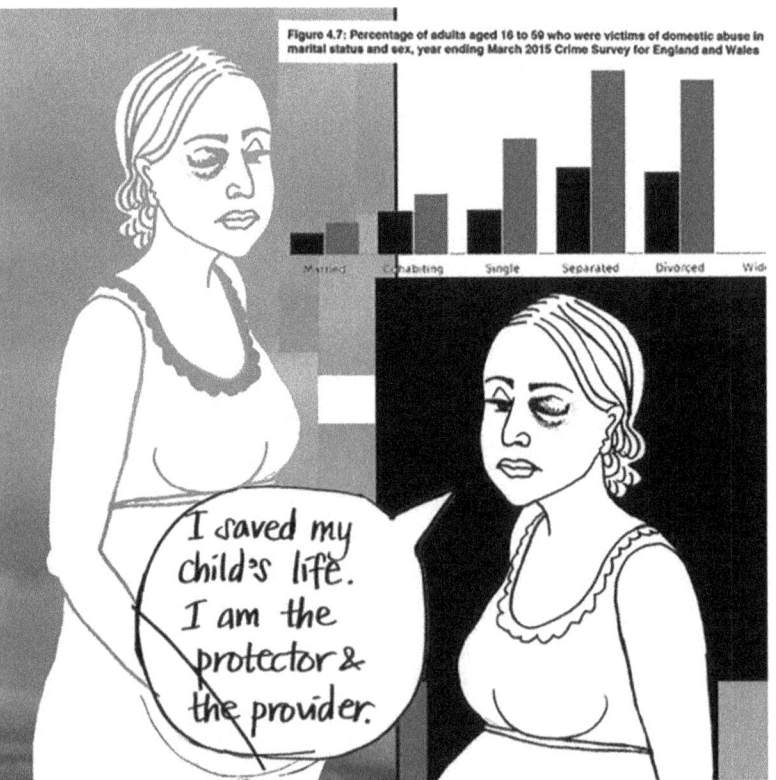

Figure 4. *A Pregnant Mother and Father with a Black Eye*, Mendonca, 2017.

On the right-hand side, she has a voice through a speech bubble which sits where her pregnant belly may be. In the background is part of a graphic from the Office for National Statistics, which shows that separated women have the highest prevalence of domestic abuse, more so than any other group of women, including single women. When a single woman has experienced violence, from a biological father, a donor or someone else and has separated herself from the perpetrator (or attempted to) during pregnancy, she has experienced multiple challenges and transitions, all within a short space of time. She may also have dealt with disbelief or criticism from loved ones, strangers, and/or professionals, or even rejection from family and friends who did not support her decision to remove herself from the relationship. All of these factors can affect the storying of an absent biological father. Through the image-text combination and the title, this character is presented as both a victim and survivor; she is positioned within a wider social context and is given the opportunity to argue that she is her unborn child's "protector and provider." This image is connected to a moment in a workshop when a single woman expressed frustration that social services still checked up on her when she was pregnant, even though she had removed herself from a relationship with a violent partner. She argued that social services should instead be checking up on the perpetrator of the violence, whom she felt presented further risk to women and children.

Taxi Driver: A Comic Strip

Figure 5 represents elements of a conversation one participant re-collected within an interview. She explained that on the way to register her child's birth, the taxi driver, whom she had never met, had asked her where the father of her baby was. The question and his subsequent questioning resulted in her constructing a fictional narrative and, within the comic strip above, she reflects on this experience. As the researcher and the artist, I faced multiple decisions about how to portray this participant's story on a blank, white piece of paper. What should the central character look like? Should she look like the participant? What would she be wearing? What should her facial expressions be like? What might my creative decisions suggest about the experience of single mothering when of a certain age, class, race and body shape? Should she break the fourth wall and address the audience? And what about the taxi driver? Am I to make assumptions about who he was? Would he appear quizzical? Suspicious? Aggressive? Distracted and only mildly interested? Would the comic strip be created and/or reproduced in black and white or in colour? What drawing style would be employed and how may that affect the tone of the piece or connect to the wider field of cartooning and comics? Here, values-based cartooning requires high levels of creative decision making, which affects the direction of the research, data generation and analysis, and dissemination.

In the end, only a central, fictionalized, and, therefore, anonymous character appears in this graphic narrative. Rather than reimagining and then drawing the story told, as if it were a reconstruction for a documentary, it remains clear that she is performing this story for us based on her memory of that moment. This allows the audience more space to imagine the taxi driver, the scene, and the atmosphere. It also means that the narrator could be shown holding her baby while storytelling, which reminds us she is talking about an absent biological father as an ever-present mother of a newborn baby, just as the participant had done within the interview. The inclusion of a baby being sick may be seen as humorous for some; for others it may be a welcome or an unnecessary reminder of the realities of everyday early parenting. Engaging with the abject is a common feature within autobiographical comic art, including work on motherhood, as Elisabeth El Refaie suggests, comics' artists "transgress the boundaries between self and non-self deliberately, offering explicit, shameless representations of bodily functions such as menstruation, sexual intercourse and miscarriage" (68).

Rather than the main character being presented here as a bumbling liar or as a lighthearted cartoon or caricature, she demonstrates an ability to process and reflect on what happened through her narration. This is an attempt to avoid a deficit approach by instead portraying her assets and skills (Henwood). The narration was integrated into the panels rather than separated as captions in an attempt to capture the sense of panic and confusion the participant expressed as she reflected on the encounter.

Figure 5. *Taxi Driver*, Mendonca, 2017.

In some ways the text stayed largely true to the interview transcript; however, it was still edited in the sense that it was positioned, drawn, and written intentionally and that the taxi driver's words were placed within sperm-shaped speech bubbles. This research has generated hundreds of images, ideas, and stories; some are incomplete, whereas others have developed into longer pieces. And as in all research, key themes and patterns have emerged. However, through values-based cartooning, a vocabulary of commonly used shapes, images, and words has also developed in relation to the topic examined. While the combination of graphic facilitation and cartooning means that outputs vary in terms of style, form, and length, there are some elements and underlying concepts that connect them. The themes here are visual as well as conceptual.

The participant who gave this account could have been a thirty-nine-year-old single mother with long-term mental health needs, who concerned about her declining fertility conceived via an anonymous donor sperm, or alternatively. Or she could have been a twenty-nine-year-old Eastern European single mother who had experienced domestic abuse during a casual sexual relationship. Or she could have been a nineteen-year-old Muslim mother who had separated from her fiancée during pregnancy. This kind of information is highly valued within psychological, sociological, and interdisciplinary studies, as it allows readers to undertake their own analysis of a visual representation. Clearly, Figure 5 does not provide a generic or neutral representation of a mother, and assumptions will be made about her, including her social class and level of education, given the fact that she can afford a taxi and the kind of language she uses. However, this research was a creative production project. The aim was never to draw conclusions about different single mother types and the way they story biological father or donor absence. Indeed, the limited size of the sample and the way storying father absence has been framed as a creative practice make generalizations problematic. Here, as in the other images, it is intentionally left to the audience to wonder about the character's backstory and perhaps to reflect on their own tendencies to make assumptions, to slip into stereotyping, or to expect answers. The audience is invited to consider what this desire for explanations concerning father absence may suggest about societal values.

Reflecting on Single Mother Types

This research sought to represent a more nuanced understanding of single women's lives—one that creates space for mixed emotions, changing circumstances and perspectives, as well as multiple identities and cultural contexts. Whereas some participants appeared to position themselves within the complex and loaded identities of single mothering types, others seemed to fiercely resist what they considered to be simplistic stereotypes. Including such a wide range of experiences within this research was at the expense of paying more attention to the common experiences of a specified age group or cultural context. Yet focusing solely on such clearly defined single mother types—that is, specific ages, routes to conception or experiences of being or becoming single—also risks missing those more complex experiences that may not neatly fit into academic, organizational, or popular definitions.

This broad and creative approach highlights the differences and similarities among single women. There were examples of both older and younger mothers who had faced a difficult decision—to stay in what they perceived to be a loving relationship without children or leave and have a baby on their own. Participants aged between sixteen and eighteen, who may not normally be identified as "single mothers by choice," spoke of planned pregnancies, sperm donation, and strategically timed intercourse. One woman in her late thirties, who was in receipt of welfare benefits, said that she sometimes felt she had more in common with teenage single mothers than older and middle-class single mothers. Whereas some participants who had used licensed fertility clinics were very clear that their journeys to parenting were entirely self-determined, others spoke of a time when they had hoped to become pregnant as a matter of course through sexual encounters both in and outside of relationships.

Conclusion

As they storied for the researcher and for others in the workshops, the participants' accounts were fluid, complex, emotional, humorous, and, at times, experimental. Their generous contributions allowed me, the researcher-artist, high levels of creative decision making, and with that came the risk of not remaining true to their accounts. Although the literature on this topic is diverse, there has been a tendency to categorize women, particularly in relation to their age and route to conception, which, in turn, may risk reinforcing assumptions about women's intentions, perspectives, and circumstances. This research included participants who appeared to resist being boxed into single mother types, and it was the research method of values-based cartooning that highlighted this. This method enabled me to create safe, accessible, and, at times, playful spaces for a diverse range of participants to explore and consider the topic of single mothers storying the absent biological father or sperm donor. It challenged me to negotiate the complex process of visual representation, both in collaboration with participants and in isolation from them. This research prompted memories and feelings about my own experience of pregnancy, childbirth, breast and bottle feeding, as well as becoming a mother and simultaneously becoming a single mother. It allowed me space to examine the way contemporary mothering is being portrayed and the privilege of determining how to represent single pregnant and mothering bodies and lives.

Endnote

1. At the time of writing, women aged under forty may be offered three cycles of IVF treatment from the National Health Service if they have been trying to get pregnant through regular unprotected sex for two years or if they have not been able to get pregnant after twelve cycles of artificial insemination.

Works Cited

Ajandi, Jennifer. "Single Mothers by Choice: Disrupting Dominant Discourses of the Family.

Through Social Justice Alternatives." *International Journal of Child, Youth and Family Studies*, vol. 3 and 4, 2011, pp. 410-31.

Asher, Rebecca. *Shattered; Modern Motherhood and the Illusion of Equality*. Harvill Secker, 2011.

Ayaka, Carolene and Ian Hague. *Representing Multiculturalism in Comics and Graphic Novels*. Routledge, 2014.

Barry, Lynda. *One Hundred Demons*. Sasquatch Books, 2002.

Barthes, Roland. *Image, Music, Text.* Fontana Press, 1977.

Baxter, Nicola. *Our Story—For Children Conceived through Sperm Donation in Solo Mum Families.* Donor Conception Network, 2002.

Belsey, Catherine. *Critical Practice (New Accents).* 2nd ed. Routledge, 2002.

Bock, Jane D. "Doing the Right Thing? Single Mothers by Choice and the Struggle for Legitimacy." *Gender and Society*, vol. 14, no. 1, 2000, pp. 62-86.

Brown, Larisa. "New Breed of Piranha Women Who Are Preying on Rich Men to Get Them Pregnant, Warns Lawyer." *Daily Mail*, 6 Feb. 2012, www.dailymail.co.uk/news/article-2097019/New-breed-piranha-women-preying-rich-men-pregnant.html. Accessed 12 Nov. 2019.

Chute, Hilary. *Graphic Women; Life Narrative and Contemporary Comics.* Columbia University Press, 2010.

Crenshaw, Kimberlé W. "Mapping the Margins: Intersectionality, Identity Politics, and Violence against Women of Color." *Stanford Law Review*, vol. 43, no. 6, 1991, pp. 1241-99.

DePaulo, B. *Singlism: What It Is, Why it Matters and How to Stop it.* DoubleDoor Books, 2011.

Descartes, Lara. "Lesbian Single Mothers." Motherhood and Lone-Single Parenting: A Twenty-First Century Perspective, edited by Maki Motapanyani, Demeter Press, 2016, pp. 193-204. Print.

Desperately Seeking Semen. BBC Three, 2017, www.bbc.co.uk/programmes/p05cg275. Accessed 01 August 2018.

Dymond, Justine, and Nicole Willey. *Motherhood Memoirs: Mothers Creating/Writing Lives.* Demeter Press, 2013.

Ehrensaft, Diane. *Mommies, Daddies, Donors, Surrogates; Answering Tough Questions and Building Strong Families.* The Guilford Press, 2005.

El Refaie, Elizabeth. *Autobiographical Comics: Life Writing in Pictures.* University Press of Mississippi, 2012.

Emma's Diary. "Can You Afford to Have a Baby Without Breaking the Bank". *www.emmasdiary.co.uk.* https://www.emmasdiary.co.uk/pregnancy-and-birth/preparing-for-baby. Date accessed 01 August 2018.

Engel, Emily. *Going it Alone: A Guide for Solo Mums in the UK.* Ingram Spark, 2019.

Engel, Emily. Personal interview. 15 Nov. 2013.

Freeman, Tabitha, et al. "Online Sperm Donation: A Survey of the Demographic Characteristics, Motivations, Preferences and Experiences of Sperm Donors on a Connection Website." *Human Reproduction*, vol. 31, no. 9, 2016, pp. 2082-89.

Gingerbread. "Single Parents Today". *Gingerbread*, www.gingerbread.org.uk/what-we-do/media-centre/single-parents-facts-figures/. Accessed 1 Nov. 2019.

Golombok, Susan. *Modern Families: Parents and Children in New Family Forms.* University of Cambridge, 2015.

Goodey, Christopher F. *Learning Disability and Inclusion Phobia: Past, Present, Future* Routledge, 2015.

Gray, Carole, and Julian Malins. *Visualising Research: A Guide to the Research Process in Art and Design.* Ashgate Publishing Limited, 2004.

Harkness, Susan and Amy Skipp. *Lone Mothers, Work and Depression*, Gingerbread, 2013, www.gingerbread.org.uk/wpcontent/uploads/2017/10/Lone-mothers-work-anddepression.pdf. Accessed 1 Aug. 2018.

Henwood, Melanie. "Skills Around the Person: Implementing Asset-Based Approaches in Adult Social Care and End of Life Care." *Skills for Care.* 2014, www.skillsforcare.org.uk/Document-library/NMDS-SC,-workforce-intelligence-and-innovation/community-skills/skills-around-the-person-web.pdf. Accessed, 1 Nov. 2019.

Hertz, Rosanna. *Single By Chance, Mothers by Choice; How Women Are Choosing Parenthood Without Marriage and Creating the New American Family.* Oxford University Press, 2006.

Holmes, Melisa M., et al. "Rape-Related Pregnancy: Estimates and Descriptive Characteristics From a National Sample of Women." *American Journal of Obstetrics and Gynecology*, vol. 175, no. 2, 1996, pp. 320-24.

Howard, C. Sheena, and Ronald L. Jackson II. *Black Comics: Politics of Race and Representation.* Bloomsbury Academic, 2013.

Jarrett, L. Robin. Welfare Stigma among Low-Income, African American Single Mothers. *Family Relations,* vol. 45, no. 4, 1996, pp. 368-74.

Kaplan, E. Ann. *Motherhood and Representation: The Mother in Popular Culture and Melodrama: Feminism, Psychoanalysis and the Material American Melodrama.* Routledge, 1992.

Kaur, Navjotpal, and Rosemary Ricciardelli. "'I Asked For It': How Women Experience Stigma in Their Transition from Being Infertile to Being Mothers of Multiples through Assisted Reproductive Technologies." *Journal of the Motherhood Initiative for Research and Community Involvement,* vol. 8, no. 1-2, 2017, pp. 232-248.

Knight, Paula. *The Facts of Life.* Myriad, 2017.

Lahad, Kinneret. *A Table for One: A Critical Reading of Singlehood, Gender and Time,* Manchester University Press, 2017.

London Sperm Bank. "Our Impression Donor 1320". London Spermbank, www.londonspermbank.com/catalogue/search/. Accessed 1 Aug. 2018.

Mack, Katherine. "Does Two a Family Make? Hollywood Engages Intentional Single Motherhood." *Motherhood and Lone-Single Parenting: A Twenty-First Century Perspective,* edited by Maki Motapanyani, Demeter Press, 2016, pp. 27-40. Print.

Mantas, Kathy, and Lorinda Peterson. *Middle Grounds: Essays on Midlife Mothering.* Demeter Press, 2018.

Mattes, Jane. *Single Mothers by Choice: A Guidebook For Single Women Who Are Considering or Have Chosen Motherhood.* Three Rivers Press, 1994.

McDonald-Harker, Caroline. *Mothering in Marginalized Contexts: Narratives of Women Who Mother In and through Domestic Violence.* Demeter Press, 2016.

McIntosh, Mary. "Social Anxieties About Lone Motherhood and Ideologies of the Family: Two Sides of the Same Coin." *Good Enough Mothering? Feminist Perspectives on Lone Motherhood,* edited by Elizabeth Silva, Routledge, 1996, pp. 148-157.

McKnight, John, and John Kretzmann. *Building Communities from the Inside Out: A Path Toward Finding and Mobilizing a Community's Assets.* ACTA Publications, 1993.

McLanaham, Sara, et al. "The Causal Effects of Father Absence." *Annual Review of Sociology* vol. 39, 2013, pp. 399-427.

McQuoid, Claire. "Too Many Women Are Assaulted By Their Sperm Donors." *Huffington Post*, 29 Sept., 2016. www.huffpost.com/entry/i-wanted-a-baby-but-i-was-raped-instead-sex-offenders_b_57dfd5cae4b053blccf29fa7. Accessed 12 Nov. 2019.

Mendonça, Penelope. "Review: Bump, How to Make, Grow and Birth a Baby, Kate Evans." *Studies in Comics*, vol. 5, no. 2, 2014, pp. 425-28.

Mendonça, Penelope. (2016). "The Fallen Woman, The Foundling Museum, London 25 September 2015–03 January 2016." *Studies in the Maternal*, vol. 8, nol, p 8. doi:10.16995/sim.213.

Mendonça, Penelope. "Situating Single Mothers through Values-Based Cartooning". *Women: A Cultural Review,* vol. 29, no. 1, 2018, pp. 19-38.

Montuschi, Olivia. *Telling and Talking; "Telling" and Talking about Donor Conception with 0-7 Years Olds: A Guide for Parents*. Donor Conception Network, 2006.

Mooney, Ann, et al. *Impact of Family Breakdown on Children's Wellbeing: Evidence Review. Research and Analysis*. Department of Health, 2009.

Moore, Henrietta. "Mothering and Social Responsibilities in a Cross Cultural Perspective." Good Enough Mothering? *Feminist Perspectives on Lone Motherhood*, edited by Elizabeth Silva. Routledge, 2013, pp. 58-75.

Mortimer, Caroline. "London Sperm Bank Turns Away Dyslexic Donors in Move Branded as 'Eugenics' by Campaigners." *The Independent*, 30 Dec. 2015, www.independent.co.uk/news/uk/home-news/london-sperm-bank-turns-away-dyslexic-donors-in-move-branded-as-eugenics-by-campaigners-a6790891.html. Accessed 12 Nov. 2019.

Morris, Jenny. *Alone Together: Voices of Single Mothers*. The Women's Press, 1992.

Morrissette, Mikki. *Choosing Single Motherhood: The Thinking Woman's Guide*. Houghton Mifflin Company, 2008.

Motapanyane M. *Motherhood and Lone/Single Parenting: A 21st Century Perspective*. Demeter Press, 2016.

Ngozi Adichie, C. "The Danger of a Single Story." *TEDGlobal*, 2009, www.ted.com/talks/chimamanda_adichie_the_danger_of_a_single_story. Accessed 12 Nov. 2019.

National Health Service. "Domestic Abuse in Pregnancy," *NHS*, 2018, www.nhs.uk. Accessed 12 Nov. 2019.

Office for National Statistics (England). "Intimate Personal Violence and Partner Abuse." *Office for National Statistics*, 11 Feb. 2016, www.ons.gov.uk/peoplepopulationandcommunity/crimeandjustice/compendium/focusonviolentcrimeandsexualoffences/yearendingmarch2015/chapter4intimatepersonalviolenceandpartnerabuse Accessed 1 Sept. 2017.

Office for National Statistics. Live Births, Sole Registered by the Mother and First Live-Born Child to the Mother, by Age of Mother, *Office for National Statistics*, 2016, www.ons.gov.uk/peoplepopulationandcommunity/birthsdeathsandmarriages/livebirths/ahocs/009054live birthssoleregistered by the motherandfirstlive born childtothemotherbyage ofmother, 2016. Accessed 1 Sept. 2017.

Ostrom, Elinor. "Crossing the Great Divide: Coproduction, Synergy and Development." *World Development*, vol. 24, no. 6, 1996, pp. 1073-87.

Oyewumi, Oyeronke. "Conceptualizing Gender: The Eurocentric Foundations of Feminist Concepts and the Challenge of Africa Epistemologies." *CODESRIA: Council for the Development of Social Science Research in Africa*. 21 Dec 2015, www.codesria.org › IMG › pdf › OYEWUMI. Accessed 12 Nov. 2019.

Parker, Rozsika. *Torn In Two: The Experience of Maternal Ambivalence*, Virago Press, 1995.

Pearpoint, Jack., Marsha Forest and Judith Snow. *The Inclusion Papers*. Inclusion Press, 1992.

Potts, Lydia, and Ulrike Lingen-Ali. "Escaping a Life in Violence? Migrant-Mother Families in Germany: Coping with Gender-Based Violence, Undermining Stereotypes, and Claiming Agency." *Motherhood and Lone-Single Parenting: A Twenty-First Century Perspective*, edited by Maki Motapanyani, Demeter Press, 2016, pp. 265-84.

Quirk, Christin. "Historicizing the Marginalization of Single Mothers: An Australian Perspective." *Motherhood and Lone/Single Parenting: A 21st Century Perspective*, edited by Maki Motapanyani, Demeter Press, 2016, pp. 207-224.

Reed, Elizabeth. "Lesbian, Bisexual and Queer Motherhood: Crafting Radical Narratives and representing Social Change through Cultural Representations." *Women: A Cultural Review,* vol. 29, no. 1, 2018, pp. 39-58.

Refuge. "Domestic Violence and Pregnancy. The Facts." *Refuge*, www.refuge.org. Accessed 12 Nov. 2019.

Reynolds, Jill. *The Single Woman: A Discursive Investigation.* Routledge, 2008.

Risebrow, Hugh. *In Vitro Fertilisation: UK Market Report.* Laing Buisson, 2018.

Robbins, Trina, and Catherine Yronwode. *Women and the Comics.* Eclipse Books, 1985.

Robinson, Laura D., et al. "Sole Mothers in the Workforce: A Systematic Review and Agenda for Future Work-Family Research." *Journal of Family Theory and Review,* vol. 10, no. 1, 2018, pp. 280-303.

Rohde, Mike. *The Sketchnote Handbook: The Illustrated Guide to Visual Note Taking.* Peachpit Press, 2013.

Russell, Helen. "'There's No Stigma': Why So Many Danish Women are Option to Become Single Mothers." *The Guardian*, Sept. 14 2015, www.theguardian.com/lifeandstyle/2015/sep/14/no-stigma-single-mothers-denmark-solomors. Accessed 12 Nov. 2019.

Sandino, Linda, and Matthew Partington. *Oral History in the Visual Arts.* Bloomsbury, 2013.

Sibbet, David. *Graphic Facilitation.* The Grove Consultants International, 2006.

Sloan, Louise. *Knock Yourself Up: A Tell-All Guide to Becoming a Single Mom.* Avery Trade, 2007.

Stonewall. "Pregnant Pause: A Guide for Lesbians on How to Get Pregnant." www.stonewall.org.uk/resources/pregnant-pause-guide-lesbians-how-get-pregnant. *www.stonewall.org.uk.* Date accessed 01 August, 2018.

Surkan, K. J. "That Fat Man is Giving Birth: Gender Identity and the Pregnant Body." *Natal Signs: Cultural Representations of Pregnancy, Birth and Parenting,* edited by Nadya Burton, Demeter Press, 2015, pp. 58-72.

Szuchman, Paula. "No Dad? No Problem. Meet the Moms Who Opt In Forever—and Aren't Complaining." *Single Mothers by Choice,* July 2014, www.singlemothersbychoice.org/2014/07/26/no-dad-no-problem-meet-the-moms-who-opt-in-forever-and-arent-complaining/. Accessed 12 Nov. 2019.

Taylor, Joshua. Health Warning for Would-Be Mums as Men Use Gumtree to Sell Black Market Sperm. Mirror December 15 2016: n. pag. Web. 01 Aug. 2018.

The Voice. "International Women's Day: We Celebrate Dr. W. Wyporska." *The Voice,* www.voice-online.co.uk/category/category/lifestyle/female?page=7&quicktabs_nodesblock=0. Accessed 1 Aug. 2018.

Thomson, Rachel, et al. *Making Modern Mothers.* The Policy Press, 2011.

Wallbank, Julie A. *Challenging Motherhood(s).* Prentice Hall, 2001.

Wertham, Fredrick. Seduction of the Innocent, Main Road Books, 1999.

Whalen, Zach, et al. *Disability in Comic Books and Graphic Narratives.* Palgrave MacMillan, 2016.

Zadeh, Sophie. "Disclosure of Donor Conception in the Era of Non-Anonymity: Safeguarding and Promoting the Interests of Donor-Conceived Individuals?" *Human Reproduction,* vol. 31, no. 11, 2016, pp. 2416-20.

Zoja, Luigi. *The Father; Historical, Psychological and Cultural Perspectives.* Brunner-Routledge, 2001.

Chapter Five

A Familial History of Alcoholism and Depression: An Imagined Interaction with my Daughters

Sarah LeBlanc

As I lie on the couch, my chin rubbing against the peach fuzz hair on top of Evangeline's head, I fight back the sting of tears threatening to fall from my eyes.

How could something so small, so fragile be prone to depression? I worry about this as Evangeline (Evi) and I lie there; her head is snuggled between my breasts as she sleeps soundly in the middle of the afternoon. Her eyes are tightly shut, and the smooth skin of her face reminds me of a doll, a doll with no worries in the world.

As I settle deeper into the couch cushion, conscious that the television is on and a pill commercial is running, I think about my daily medicine routine and how sometimes Caroline, my other child and a toddler, stands beside me staring as I take my pills.

Will either one or both of my daughters be required to take a combination of antianxiety and antidepression meds? If they experience depression, will they understand why they feel a certain way? Will they be able to deal with the symptoms? Will they turn to alcohol for help like others in our family have? I ponder all these questions, as my chin moves back and forth on the fuzzy hair of my daughter's five-month-old head.

My eyes begin to drift shut as Evi and I lie on the couch; my ears are on alert as I listen for the stirring of my two-year-old. While my body is telling me to nap with Evi, my conscious mind will not stop running, worrying about how I will know when or if my girls may need my help for depression or alcoholism. Caroline has already been through so much in her short lifetime: failure to thrive, asthma, and now glasses for farsightedness. I begin to worry if her mood swings, one minute giggling and the next minute a full out tantrum, are early signs that something is amiss. And perhaps I am overly concerned because of a family history with alcoholism and my history with depression.

I have struggled with mental health issues for almost twenty years. At present, I am under the care of a local psychiatrist and counsellor. I monitor how I am feeling throughout the day, such as if I am too sad or feel too angry. Monitoring my state of being is a habit I formed when I realized I need to report on how my medication is working. Given my family history of alcoholism and my mental health struggles with depression, I have real concerns about what inherited tendencies towards depression and alcoholism Caroline and Evangeline may have. As a family communication scholar, I know I want to have conversations with them about these possibilities. But not having been exposed to such a conversation myself, how will I go about preparing myself? What will I say?

When Alcoholism and Depression Came to Light

I grew up in a household where we did not talk about mental health, particularly not depression, or alcoholism. As I explored causes and symptoms of my depression, I became aware that depression did exist within my family and that lack of communication escalated the problem. For example, when I was ten or eleven years old, I was overheard on the playground saying, "I want to kill myself." The school called my mom, and that led to me having a conversation with my mom about why I said I was going to kill myself. While I remember the talk occurring, I do not recall the content, nor did my mom acknowledge or provide any information about a family history of depression during that conversation. We never discussed the incident again. Like most important events in my family, my suicide announcement was swept under the rug.

As I began to focus on my own physical health and recalled how we did not talk about mental health in our family, I vowed to communicate with my daughters about my struggles and how to handle illnesses, such as alcoholism and depression, even if the conversation did not go as planned or had to happen more than once. But I wanted to make sure I was equipped with the information, both historical family and research based, to prepare myself for the talks that would someday come.

When I began my exploration of familial depression in 2012, I did not set out to expose family skeletons or open and expose wounds. But in the process of organizing my ideas, exploring the literature, and writing my personal field notes about my depression, I realized that family skeletons and old wounds were where this exploration was taking me. It started when I came across a field note I took of a conversation Matt (my partner) and I had on our way home from a southeast conference (SEC) football game in 2012. This conversation was when we first vocalized our shared concerns about passing on certain genetic traits, such as depression and alcoholism, to our offspring:

"I want to have a baby," I muttered as Matt navigated the interstates around Charleston in an attempt to stay awake for the last twenty minutes of our commute.

"I worry about passing things on to a child," he countered.

"What do you mean?" I ask, startled as my exhausted body came to alert with Matt's statement.

"I mean alcoholism, depression, etc. It runs in my family," he informed me, not going into much detail but making his point just the same. This is not the first time he had mentioned this, but this time it stuck and gave me a jolt.

I replied: "I think it runs in mine, too. You know I have sought therapy for stuff, but I never received an official diagnosis. In fact, seeing a counsellor became a taboo subject that I couldn't discuss with my mom and dad because my mom would ask things like, 'Why are you seeing a counsellor? Why are you wasting your time?'" I recalled her words as I tried to explain this to Matt. I stopped for a moment to catch my breath before I went on: "If we had a child or children, I wouldn't want them to feel shame for seeking out help or feel they are doing something wrong, which may lead them keeping it a secret. I would want us to be open with them ... to help them and not make the problem worse."

Following this discussion, we decided that we would have children, and because of our families' histories of alcoholism and depression, we would not ignore the possibility of our children having a mental illness.

A Familial History

Families are where we learn to communicate (Harwood et al.). More specifically, mothers and daughters often have close relationships, which are considered one of the most significant relationships within the family system (Harrigan and Miller-Ott). I learned some of my communication skills from my mother, and my daughters will learn some of their communication skills from me. However, this closeness may make it difficult for mother-daughter pairs to communicate about sensitive issues, such as sexual issues (Coffelt) and health issues (Baiocchi-Wagner and Olson). Elizabeth Baiocchi-Wagner and Loreen Olson found that mothers are less likely to discuss health issues with their children as compared to other family issues. In an attempt to understand how widespread my familial alcoholism is and if it is something I should prepare to discuss with my daughters, I started digging into my family history shortly after my husband and I decided to have biological children.

I found that the tales of Charlie, my maternal grandfather, having the ability to hunt down alcohol were legendary in my family. The tales are legendary because Charlie was blind. Jennifer, my older sister, and the genealogist of the family, emailed to say: "That one time on the Admiral [a once landmark ship on the Mississippi River in St. Louis, Missouri], he found the onboard bar BLIND and came back with three buckets of beer. Mom [referring to my sister's and my mother] thought he fell overboard he was gone so long. And when we [our family] did tours of the Anheuser Busch factory, a beer factory and tourist destination in St. Louis, Missouri], he always skipped the tour and went straight to the tasting room."

I asked Jennifer to tell me the stories about Charlie drinking in the cornfield. She did not know about the cornfield but did provide some interesting information about his drinking: "Nana didn't like Dadt[1] [aka Charlie] drinking, so when they visited us on Long Island, Mom would hide the alcohol in the ice chest and Dadt knew it was there."

"Didn't he hide alcohol in the sunroom and the old kitchen at the farmhouse?" I replied back.

Jennifer immediately sent an email back: "Don't know. Would have to ask mom. But Charlie drank, Charles [Charlie's firstborn son and eldest brother of my mom] drank, Uncle Joe drank, Aunt Chris did drugs and drank, and Uncle Harold, drank although he is related by marriage and not blood."

"I already knew that Uncle Joe drank," I replied to Jennifer. "Aunt Dina explained how Joe would become mean and disappear when he had too much alcohol."

A more detailed account of Dina and Joe's relationship was provided to Matt after Uncle Joe's death and during our data gathering stage for the research. Matt's and my research, published in *Death Studies,* examined how mourners, family, and local press saw Uncle Joe. We reported that his bouts with alcohol made him angry, resulting in him fleeing, sometimes even from the country, such as to India (LeBlanc and LeBlanc).

I continued, "I know Aunt Chris also had a problem. She would disguise her early morning drinking by using a "juice cup" that we were asked not to touch. I always assumed it was apple juice but later learned it was beer. She had beer while our parents had coffee."

The more emails Jennifer and I exchanged, the more things started to come back to my memory. As a child I remember leaving an Easter celebration early because of excess drinking, and on the way home, my mom hung her head outside the passenger side window of the van in case she got sick as my dad drove us home, only to later get sick himself. Their excuse for this behaviour was that they were "allergic to Scotch."

As I recalled that memory, I felt my heart starting to pound faster. Then I recalled the pictures in family photo albums memorializing Dadt holding a beer as he sat on a bench in our backyard. My hands shook over the keyboard as I wracked my brain trying to think of one photo in the album without Dadt holding a drink. As I reread my words on the page, my heart pounded faster. The shaking of my hands continued and hovered over the keyboard as the realization finally hit: My family tree is filled with alcoholics, and silence surrounds this issue. While these realizations were fresh, I wrote them down; I stepped away from my computer and began walking, hoping to calm down and convince myself that I was wrong. The more I walked, the more the memories bombarded me and I began to dictate notes into my phone. With the first memory, I realized the following:

We are runners in our family. And I don't mean running as in the action, but rather when things get tough or we get too angry, we run. We leave. Mom took off for two days before Christmas once. No one knew the reason why she left. When she came back, she wouldn't speak with any of us. But like all the problems from the past, we swept the incident under the rug.

When we (my father, my mother, and I) closed on a house in North Carolina, Mom got upset because she perceived she was being treated as "a nobody." Again, alcohol was involved as my dad, my mom, and I celebrated getting a house on the shore. At some point, the ambiance of the room changed from celebratory to angry. Mom yelled at my dad and me, calling us names and slamming out of the apartment. I left the apartment and drove to a friend's house, vented about what was going on, just needing another body to listen. When I returned, Mom's anger was directed at me, as I had no business leaving to tell someone else our problems.

"Fine," I replied, slamming my bedroom door behind me after I made my way from the front door to my bedroom suite. I moved as far away from the door as possible, settling in the bathroom where I called Emily (another sister) to tell her I finally made it to the bottom rung of the ladder.[2]

At some point, I heard the front door slam and prepared myself for bed. I was on the bottom rung, a new place for me as I had never occupied it before. I went to sleep pondering what that would mean.

Mom spent the night in the backseat of her Honda Accord, but she wanted to run. It seemed to be a pattern with her: she ran when she was mad. But as she was familiar enough with the roads, she wound up just sleeping in her car in the parking lot. The next morning, she entered my room as I lay in my bed recalling the night before. She told me she had spent the night in the car; she didn't apologize and said that we should keep this among us. The night before was glossed over. Positive language was used, and the problem was, once again, swept under the rug. It took me a few years to figure out what this incident was about.

The memories overwhelmed me; my body fought back tears and a sick feeling in my stomach. The experience left me with questions. Are these family behaviours with alcohol related to undiagnosed depression? Is alcoholism really the culprit and depression the mask, or vice versa? Will I run when things get tough? Will I shut down on my daughters?

Alcohol, Depression, Families, and the Research

Loreen Olson et al. define the dark side of family communication as "harmful, morally suspect, and/or socially unacceptable messages ... that are causes of negative effects within the family system" (9). Some families may consider yelling and excessive drinking as socially acceptable, whereas others may deem these acts to be socially unacceptable. It is within the family system that parents are seen as the main vehicle from which children learn (Olson et al.).

Family silences or, in the absence of silence, yelling, as well as excessive drinking have been present my whole life, yet I did not acknowledge the true meaning behind these silences, broken by yelling and the drinking, until I began to explore familial alcoholism. In a mysterious way, I think these memories are why I have an interest in the dark side of family communication. I investigate the negatively tainted communication that occurs in families and explore the long-term effects this type of communication (or lack of communication) has within families and how family members communicate about the issues with others within the family as well as with nonfamily members. Some of these issues include alcoholism, but most of my research explores depression, which in my family, appears to be related to alcoholism.

Through a thorough analysis of literature from fields other than communication, Chris Segrin determines that illness, specifically depression, is learned and demonstrated through two behaviours: mimicking of behaviour and a breakdown in interpersonal communication. The yelling that was prevalent in my family is an example of a breakdown in interpersonal communication. As the recipient of some of the yelling, I mentally left during those encounters and never brought them up in future conversations. Jake Harwood et al. agree that children learn how to communicate from their parents. One way is through mimicking their parents' behaviours. Children internalize the behaviours of their parents, much like partners in close relationships (Duggan). The parent-child relationship can produce an overwhelming number of depressive symptoms for one person as a result of the other individual's depression (Segrin, "Mental Health"). For example, my mom was known to lock herself in her room, and I was often used as the pawn to try and coax her out. I thought locking herself away was a natural way of dealing with hurt and anger. As a young elementary-aged girl, therefore, I started locking myself into the bathroom or hiding in the closet as a way of punishing my sisters. I thought it was a natural act. Girls are known to mimic their mother's actions starting from, the age of five (Nichter), including drinking a beer or a glass of wine or copying depressive-type behaviours. If a mom has long lasting periods of anger, such as continuous yelling or using silence as punishment, a child will learn these behaviours and consequently find them to be socially acceptable. In my case, I have an awareness of this tendency to mimic behaviours; thus, I express my fear of yelling (like my mother) to my husband and often apologize for yelling when I raise my voice. He counters with "that wasn't yelling." When I break my rule and yell at my daughters, Caroline responds back with "don't yell at me." I immediately feel bad and fear that I don't have my depression and anxiety under control.

But then there are the times, I work hard not to yell. As a result of not wanting to yell like my mother did, I am particularly sensitive to this tendency. I have started taking a breath before saying something or reflecting, Matt says I shut down, showing no emotion and not talking. Is this behaviour any better? Is it any better not allowing myself to get angry?

I also notice that I will walk away and hide in the house when I need time to work through hurt or anger, something, again, that my mother did. Often, I hide out in the open like in the chair in the master bedroom reading a book. Sometimes, I just grab the iPad and go into the bathroom. Or sometimes I just start cleaning, using the scrubbing material as a way to release the tension inside.

What I don't seem to know is whether these behaviours are healthy. Will my daughters observe what is going and start to clean as well when they are angry? Will they not show emotion? Should I teach them to say something like "I am angry and I need some time by myself to work through this emotion?" At least then, I will know why they have walked away.

Segrin suggests a strong correlation between interpersonal rejection, such as silence or yelling, and relational distress ("Social Skills"). The victim of a yelling incident may start to fear the relationship or develop anxiousness in sharing news within the relationship. Yet the yelling and the silence demonstrate the ineffectiveness in interpersonal communication. Yelling affects the receiver's reception of the message as well as the communicator's. If a child is yelled at each day when they enter the home, the child will begin to fear going home or even encountering the yeller. When a parent communicates through silence, a child will see this as a sign of rejection—of the mom not loving the child enough to talk to them. However, a parent, and particularly a depressed parent, may not see or know these acts as harmful to their children, despite the fact that research suggests otherwise. I notice this behaviour as my husband and I continue to try and potty train Caroline. Matt tends to get upset with her and yells about her needing to tell us she needs to use the bathroom. When I notice she messed her pants, I get down on her level, ask if she likes the dirty pants, and ask her how she can tell us she needs to go. I have yelled some and that is when I notice Caroline regresses in her training. My memories of being yelled at keep me from yelling, whereas my brain is arguing that I should yell. But I fear if I yell during her potty training, she will fear the potty and the act of using the potty. When I am firm but polite, she advances.

Nicole Hurt has determined that the choices mothers make in handling their illnesses, such as depression or alcoholism, affect their children, which supports the notion that one individual's behaviour may affect the entire family (Olson et al.). My mother was a yeller, and I fear I will become a yeller, impacting the emotional health of my two daughters (Hurt). I came to this realization while in group therapy during my doctoral years. When I would get angry, I would stop myself from yelling because I would associate anger with yelling. Now as a mother, I continue to fight this feeling of needing to yell especially when I am cleaning poop off the floor from a potty training accident or when the whining aggravates my already frayed nerves. I know that yelling will not help my daughters or me, so I choose instead to take a deep breath and continue. I may even walk away, count to ten, and then return.

Since I don't want the yelling to occur, I consciously control how I handle communication with my daughters, as I see in my handling of Caroline's tantrums. I get down on my knees so that I am on her level. I take her little hands into my hands, look her straight in the eyes, and say "I can't help you if you are crying. Stop the tears and tell me what is wrong." If she starts coughing, I rub her back. There have been times when this experience is a different reality in my head, the identity of my childhood fighting against my identity as a mom. During Caroline's tantrums, my inner child hears screaming, the sound of a feminine voice filling the air with constant yelling as I stand in the hallway of the house crying. As a mom now, I know that how I behave in these moments will affect Caroline in the long term.

Nicole Ehlert has found that if one family member suffers from depression, the demand and withdraw pattern of communication is more likely to surface. The more one individual demands, the more the other withdraws. Often times, as Ehlert has determined, this pattern sets the foundation for the depressed individual to take steps to leave the relationship. For example, the more a mother yells at her children, the more the children are likely to leave the relationship, either physically or mentally. As I aged, I physically withdrew from the relationship by leaving the house, either to ride my bike, play in the backyard, or stay after school. I could not mentally leave the relationship though; instead, I adjusted my behaviour to prevent a future yelling attack. In more recent times, when my husband and I have disagreements, I continue to physically leave the situation, a behaviour I carried over from childhood.

In the course of recalling memories and searching the literature, I found that the breakdown in interpersonal communication within the family and mental or physical withdrawing could be signs of functioning alcoholism. It is the classic dilemma of the chicken or the egg, but in the case of my family, which comes first, the alcohol or the depression? Children of alcoholics—whether diagnosed or undiagnosed—are likely to face bouts of depression (Manning). My mom grew up in a household with a father who drank. I grew up in a household where both my parents drank. And while I thought my parents were social drinkers, sharing a six-pack of Miller Lite or some gin and tonics while we played in the backyard pool, I never thought that they were alcoholics. It took confronting the memories mentioned in this chapter for me to come to the realization that they were alcoholics. I recognize that this chapter focuses more on my mother's behaviour; to date, I am unable to fully acknowledge that my dad was an alcoholic, as I fear it may tarnish my memories of him.

Peter Anderson et al. have found that heavy alcohol use affects the family and that alcohol is a kind of drug. I learned my adult drinking habits from my parents. I drank because the drink was there or for liquid courage. I drank as an award for surviving to the end of the week. I drank to celebrate and to commiserate. I drank to hide the memories brought up in my various counselling sessions. Perry Pauley and Colin

Hesse argue that there is a connection between depression and alcohol consumption—hence, why I drank to commiserate. In fact, Pauley and Hesse find that individuals drank more as their level of perceived depression rose. The more I encountered rejection during my graduate program, the more alcoholic drinks I consumed on Friday night.

Sripriya Rangarajan and Lynne Kelly conclude that a substantial number of children within the U.S. are in families with at least one alcoholic parent. They argue that by having an alcoholic parent, children's self-esteem suffers and the family faces more family stressors, such as financial difficulties and spousal conflict. Children of alcoholics are more likely to become substance abusers themselves, but they also work to keep their parents' alcohol problem secret from others (Manning). Research suggests that part of my depression may be from keeping my parents' use and abuse of alcohol a secret (Haverfield and Theiss).

Imagined Interaction Theory

After exploring parts of my family history of alcoholism, I still wonder how I will share my story, my family story, with my daughters. How will I explain about the secrets that I kept, the secrets that I have, and even the stories shared with me? How will I explain to them about my drinking, or lack thereof, and that of my family members? In thinking about these things, I pulled my interpersonal communication theories book from the shelf and flipped to James Honeycutt's chapter on the imagined interaction theory. I see the relevance of the theory and how it relates to sharing my story with my daughters.

The imagined interaction theory refers to a "process of social cognition in which individuals imagine and therefore indirectly experience themselves in anticipated encounters with others" (77). Honeycutt proposes six functions of the theory: "maintaining relationships, linking or managing conflict, rehearsing messages, aiding people in self-understanding through clarifying thoughts and feelings, providing emotional catharsis by relieving tension, and compensating for lack of real interaction" (77). All six functions of the theory are relevant to the imagined story and the imagined interaction I will one day have with my daughters.

Telling my daughters about the history of family alcoholism and my depression is not a conversation I look forward to having, but it is one I promised my husband and myself I would have. While I imagine the conversation occurring in ten to twelve years, as the girls enter their teenage years, I acknowledge that parts of this story will come out earlier. When they ask questions, I will be honest; my answers will come from a place of truth, humility, and sometimes shame.

Through imagining what I will say later in their lives, I hope to release the built-up tension, emotions, and the worry that I carry about knowing one day I will have to explain the familial history of alcohol and depression. It is my hope that having the conversation will help us maintain open and healthy relationships.

My Imagined Interaction: Sharing my Story with My Daughters

I ask my two daughters, ages fifteen and thirteen, to sit on the sofa and to get comfortable. All electronics are on silent and put in the middle of the ottoman, only to be touched if Dad calls. I imagine that Matt is still at work, and the girls and I have a day home together. On the coffee table in front of us sits a box of soft tissues and three glasses of water. I want us to be comfortable, as I don't know how long this discussion, this revealing of my history, will take. I believe that the sharing of my past and my experiences will help the girls, especially as they transition into their teenage and young adult years (Koenig Kellas et al.).

I sense it is time to have the talk.

I sit them down, take a deep breath, and begin.

"You both have grown up watching me take daily medication. While you never ask why, I wonder if it is something you have questions about. When I was your age, my mom never sat me down and talked to me about drinking, sex, or anything else really. I just remember her threatening us with jail if we came home pregnant." I imagine that Evi appears restless as if we are about to have the birds and the bees talk again.

"Wait, Evi, this is not another sex talk. I want to talk to you about why I take that medication. I want to talk to you about my history with alcohol and depression and my family's history with alcohol. I am sure somewhere down the line, your dad will tell you about his own struggles and his family. His story is not mine to share."

"Before we decided to have children, your dad and I worried about you inheriting a tendency towards things such as alcoholism and depression. Your dad and I promised we would tell you about our families' histories with alcohol and depression, and the time has come for you to know my history. Depression is something your father and I worry about you inheriting because we both have been diagnosed with depression at various points in our life."

I think about various snippets of memories from my childhood.

There was the time I thought about committing suicide.

My mother would lock herself up and I would hide in the bathroom or closet.

I have photographic memories of my parents with drinks in their hands.

I hope these memories provide a context of my behaviours as I aged. I want my daughters to understand the pattern of dark behaviour, such as the alcohol and depression that flows from generation to generation. But more importantly, I want them to understand my journey, starting with my childhood, and how I ignored the different signs and symptoms that were there during that time. I also want them to see how my determination, my strength, and my resilience have given me the strength to stop the cycle. I started at the beginning.

"Growing up, I would often think about my mother's behaviour, 'Well that is just my mother's personality.' But when I was twenty years removed from my home situation, I realized it wasn't her personality; she was an alcoholic. Many of her actions were symptoms of the disease. It wasn't until I started studying and researching 'dark communication' that I finally saw her alcoholism."

I foresee the beginning of the evening passing in a blur, with me only recalling snippets of stories—memories that slowly come to the forefront of my mind as the words roll off my tongue and into my daughters' ears. While I find the memories to be important, I want my daughters to understand my experience. I start by recalling how I would cope during my elementary school years and into junior high.

During my childhood, I turned to food to help. So when I was unhappy, I would blame my weight for me feeling down. I would eat multiple bags of Gummi Bears in one day to squash that feeling that was overwhelming my body and my mind.

I couldn't share with others. I didn't want to be the sensitive younger sister. I didn't want to lose my friends. I acted as if I was the same as everyone else—happy—when inside it was something completely different.

I moved on to tell them about my first attempt at seeking help. "I saw my first counsellor during college as a result of snapping at and being mad at your Aunt Emily. I was attempting to see a guy who would only call in the middle of the night, which caused indefinable feelings in me. Rather than take these feelings out on him, I took it out on my sister, your Aunt Emily. She finally said something and asked why I was snapping at her all the time. I made an appointment with the student counseling office."

"'Why are you here?' was the first question I was met with."

"'I don't know why I am here, but I have sort of been seeing this guy, and he only contacts me in the middle of the night, and I get upset, but instead of dealing with my anger towards him, it leaks out and I snap at my sister,' I said in one long run-on sentence."

"The counsellor sat there in her comfortable chair directly across from me, staring at me through her big-rimmed glasses and her short, brown Mia-Farrow haircut. I don't remember the first conversation and only bits and pieces of the follow up appointments, probably because I was disappointed with the outcome. She asked the routine questions such as 'what is your relationship like with your parents?' and 'what was your childhood like?'"

"It was when I recall that she said 'it is all your mom's fault; your mom is an alcoholic' that I began to question if I was getting the help that I needed."

"'My mother is not an alcoholic,' I countered."

My mother is not an alcoholic. She is not an alcoholic.

"One appointment later, she began with "Sarah, I don't think I can help you anymore. I am referring you to see a psychiatrist who can help you further.' Of course, I did not take advantage of the psychiatrist because I was an undergraduate student taking fifteen hours in credit hours and didn't want my parents to discover through their insurance that I was seeing one."

"It wasn't easy for me to acknowledge that my mother was an alcoholic. It never has been. I always just focused on her yelling. It was later that I realized that the drinking was the medicine for numbing the internal pain and the yelling was a way of venting her internal frustration."

I imagine the girls staring at me with their big blue eyes, Caroline picking at her cuticles and Evi twirling her hair. After a few moments, the silence between us breaks when one says, "You just said you didn't think she was an alcoholic. What happened to change your mind?"

"It took me a long time to acknowledge that fact," I say, "but I think it was sometime around the time leading up to meeting your dad as well as sometimes afterwards." I continue: "During the summer of 2010, the summer before I met your dad, I drank heavily with my parents and I put on at least twenty pounds. I had to find a new maid of honour dress for Emily's wedding because the one I found at the beginning of the summer no longer fit."

My daughters look at me, as if encouraging me to continue.

"My parents' house was never without wine. Their pantry always had jellybeans, chocolate, and wine. The liquor cabinet was always full, and they often did big wine purchases from local box stores when running errands or, later, when visiting their adult children. Your Aunt Abby and I would often leave their house, after a visit, stocked up with Crème de Cassis. Drinking with my mom and dad always started off fine, but there were times when it didn't end well."

"Is that why you only drink at the end of the year?" Caroline asks, questioning my tradition of drinking Bailey's only during the holiday season.

"Yes, but you will also notice that I never drink in excess. When you were younger, I was afraid my depression would turn into anger towards you. I also feared what alcohol would do to me. I didn't want you hovering in your closet or staying outside until I calmed down or me being so angry I get in the car and drive off. I found that alcohol was empty calories. Plus, I wanted so badly to begin demonstrating a healthier lifestyle for you."

"But what about your sisters?" Evi asks.

"My sisters also demonstrated behaviours that they knew they needed help for. When your cousin Jake was four, your Aunt Jennifer became so upset with him that her first husband said she needed help. She sought out a counsellor and went on meds."

"So this is why you take those pills every morning?" Evi asks.

"Yes, and my dosage has ebbed and flowed during the years. But," I emphasize, "I never really wanted to take meds. I made that clear when I went back to counselling during my doctoral years."

Caroline sits there and then asks: "Why did you go back?"

"Mean roommates," I say somewhat in jest but somewhat seriously. "My living situation was not doing much to help my feelings of self-doubt or inadequacy at that time," I explain.

"In fact, it was during my counselling intake meeting when I told the counsellor that it was important she know that I refused to take medication. I was not there for a quick fix," I explain to Caroline and Evi. "I wanted to communicate my problems and not medicate them. Nor did I want a counsellor who was going to blame everything on my mom being an alcoholic. I was there because I wanted to feel better about myself, and I wanted to stop blaming myself for everything that went wrong."

"Why did you tell them you didn't want to take meds?" Evi asks.

"I believed that meds were a quick fix, but what I didn't know at the time was how I was using alcohol to help fight the depression symptoms instead of taking pills that would have helped me handle the depression symptoms in a more healthy way. I also didn't think that my student insurance would cover the medication. I didn't want to go further into debt."

"What do you mean?" Evi asks, wanting me to dig deeper, threatening my privacy boundary.

"I went back to counselling before I met your father and before the summer of 2010, so I had not cut back on the alcohol. In my second year of my doctoral program, a colleague and I started a happy-hour tradition. Once I met your dad, our significant others would join us, and we would do a weekly Friday Happy Hour. My drink of choice was a raspberry Long Island ice tea. It was perhaps the one day of the week that I would drink. I may have had wine in my apartment, but I only truly remembering drinking on Friday nights."

"We would start at 3:00 p.m., when happy hour began at our bar of choice, and sometimes we would go until 11:00 p.m. The bartenders knew us and would take care of us. I once drove home under the influence, white knuckling the steering wheel, praying I wouldn't get caught. Once I did get pulled over for doing a rolling stop at a stop sign. I didn't get a ticket, but it was a close call."

"After I met your father, Happy Hour became more about 3:00 to 7:00 p.m. And it was always Long Island ice teas for me and beer for your father."

"Wow," the girls say in unison.

"I didn't realize how much the happy hours, and the anticipation of the happy hours, helped me get through the week. But the shittier the week, the more I was likely to drink that weekend. I wasn't a mean drunk or a yeller like your grandmother. I became flirty and clingy. I also liked to 'drunk text,' a habit that your dad broke me of. I think I had my last Long Island tea in December of 2012 when your father and I returned for my graduation."

"And you could go cold turkey?" Evi asks.

"I wouldn't call it cold turkey per se. I didn't like beer. The smell of beer somehow made me think of Miller Lite, the beer of choice of my parents during my childhood. Then there was something about the taste that I just found disgusting. I wouldn't drink wine fast enough before it went bad in the refrigerator, and hard alcohol was expensive. Plus, I would never be able to figure out the recipe for those Long Island ice teas. Prior to getting pregnant with Caroline, I would drink hard cider, but I would not get drunk anymore. And for two years, after leaving Missouri, I used food as my medicine to fight depressive feelings more than alcohol. When we lived in South Carolina, I wasn't comfortable asking for help. Honestly, I didn't feel as if we had the money or the time for me to get help, although I did think about it quite a lot, especially since I was having anxiety attacks two nights a week." I continue to try to help them understand my association with alcohol.

"And then my mom got sick, congenital heart failure. I didn't want that to happen to me when I got older. I blamed her excessive drinking for her getting sick. I wasn't alone with this thinking, as some of my siblings also jumped to this conclusion. So between her getting sick, me being pregnant, and then me nursing, not drinking became easy."

"Then why did you go back to counselling after you moved to Indiana?" asks Evi.

"After Caroline was born in May 2014, I lost my job and spent the summer breastfeeding while filling out job applications. When Caroline's cries became overwhelming, I would begin crying. Your dad walked in one day and found me crying over the changing table, as Caroline wailed from the cushion as I fidgeted with changing her diaper."

"Step away from the table. I got this," your dad told me.

"I didn't acknowledge that I had postpartum depression [PPD] mainly because I didn't know it existed," I explain to Caroline and Evi. "Instead, I lived with it, thinking that how I was feeling was normal: no job and being a new mom would cause anyone to not be able to handle their emotions, right? I eventually got a job so that helped some with whatever was going on internally."

I continue. "Then in February 2015, Caroline, you were diagnosed with failure to thrive, and were hospitalized for six days. You were put on a feeding tube for nightly continuous feeds for six weeks and subjected to all sorts of medical tests. Less than two weeks after you were discharged from the hospital, my dad died at the age of seventy-three. I had work and Caroline's health to keep me occupied, but slowly my anxiety began building to the point where I was paralyzed from even checking email. I honestly could not log into my email account or if I did, I would only read emails that I thought contained good news. Those three events—PPD, Caroline's diagnosis, and my dad's death—I could handle separately, but the combination of all three in less than a year elevated my feelings of depression and anxiety."

"I needed help," I inform my daughters. "Instead of drinking, I was over caffeinating, and I was acting through life instead of living life. One afternoon, I texted your father to say 'I think I need to go back to counselling.'"

"He said I needed to do what I needed to do, but he hadn't realized things had gotten so bad," I tell them. "After my intake session, my counsellor referred me to a psychiatrist. When I saw him six weeks later, he diagnosed me with depression, anxiety, and attention deficit disorder [ADD]. I was put on a combination of medication to help me manage the symptoms. Between the drugs and my weekly sessions with my counsellor, I immediately began feeling better."

"What was different this time than the other times? Why did you decide to go on the drugs?" Caroline asks.

"Because my life wasn't just about me anymore," I reply. "I had a husband to love, a daughter to love and take care of, and I couldn't let my inner demons control my relationships with them. I had a job I loved. And I was tired of being tired. I was exhausted and acting through life. I wanted to smile and not force it. I wanted to know what it would feel like to be an adult Sarah and discover who I was without having to pretend. I wanted to fix myself, so I could be a good mom and so our family could grow. And I still kept my diagnosis from my mom. I think she found out eventually when she visited once when I had an appointment, but I never told her I was in counseling and on medication."

I didn't realize the impact medication would have until I feared I

A FAMILIAL HISTORY OF ALCOHOLISM AND DEPRESSION

would have to go off it. "When I was pregnant with you, Evi, I worked with my psychiatrist to make sure you would not have any side effects of the drugs. Low dose anxiety and antidepression drugs helped me through the pregnancy, but also afterwards I didn't exhibit the PPD symptoms I experienced after Caroline was born. I was able to work from home during the semester you were born, Evi, and not have crying fits. Even with job insecurity and fearing another failure to thrive baby, I was able to cope. I still saw my counsellor. I still had check-ins with my psychiatrist, but things were different postbirth with you than with your sister."

"Since that time, I guess you can say I am maintaining. I still see my counsellor and check in with a psychiatrist. And I do still slip, overeating things like Gummi Bears and Tootsie Rolls, instead of turning to alcohol," I say sheepishly with a smile.

"As I said at the beginning, I am not sharing this to scare you, make you love anyone less, or even treat me or each other differently. I want you to know this history so you are prepared if sometime you just don't feel normal. I am not saying that you will face depression or alcoholism, but I do want you to know that it does exist. And I want you to know that you can come talk to me, and if needed, I will help you help yourself. I want you to know that I will never question you or your feelings. I will never make you feel guilty for not feeling right or being on medication. But don't think I will look the other way if you start abusing drugs or turn to alcohol. I want us to break the cycle. I don't want you to continue to grow and mature and then fear talking with me. I don't want us to have an estranged relationship during your adult years. I want us to be real, to be us, who we are, and who we have and will always be: The LeBlanc Girls.

Conclusion

Back in the present, I continue to rub my chin against Evi's fuzzy head. I hear Caroline stir from her nap. I put Evi down on the blanket next to the couch, turn, and meet Caroline in the hallway. I pick her up, kiss her cheek, and ask if she had a good snooze.

After I prepare my daughters a mid-afternoon snack, I change the television to their afternoon cartoons, and listen to them giggling at each other. It is hard for me to imagine that these sweet innocent faces may one day know their familial history of alcoholism and depression. By exploring my family history—understanding it more through an exploration of the literature and medical information, and then imagining the conversation I will have with my daughters one day—I know I am better prepared for whatever comes our way.

Through this process, I realized that I am not my mother. I love and will always love my mother, but as I look at my daughters, comforting them when they are crying and watching them grow, I promise I will never put them in the position of not being able to come to me for help. I will never run away when things don't go my way. I am the carrier of the known pieces of my family history, just one of the messengers. I want to be able to share our familial history, both good and bad times, with my daughters. It is through imagining the difficult conversation one day with my daughters that I believe I will be able to strengthen our relationships and release the tension within.

Endnotes

1. "Dadt" is the result of my sister Jennifer realizing that she had a dad and our mom had a dad. So she started calling our grandfather "Dad Two," which was shortened to "Dadt." The term is used by the current generation of grandchildren to refer to my father, even posthumously.

2. My sisters and I used the metaphor of a ladder to discuss who Mom's favorite was at the moment (top rung). When Mom was mad at one of us, we were on the bottom rung. During other times, we were spread upon the other steps on the ladder. Each of us spent time on the bottom rung.

Works Cited

Anderson, Peter, et al. "Communication Alcohol Narratives: Creating a Healthier Relationship with Alcohol." *Journal of Health Communication*, vol. 16, no. 2, 2011, pp. 27-36.

Coffelt, Tina. "Is Sexual Communication Challenging Between Mothers and Daughters?" *Journal of Family Communication*, vol. 10, no. 2, 2010, pp. 116-30.

Duggan, Amy. "Sex Differences in Communicative Attempts to Curtail Depression: An Inconsistent Nurturing as Control Perspective." *Western Journal of Communication*, vol. 71, 2007, pp. 114-35.

Ehlert, Nicole M. *Couples' Depression Symptoms, Partners' Demand/Withdraw Communication, and Steps They Have Taken to End Their Relationship, within a Clinic Population.* Dissertation. University of Maryland, 2013.

Harigan, Meredith, and Aimee Miller-Ott. "The Multivocality of Meaning Making: An Exploration of the Discourses College-Aged Daughters Voice in Talk about Their Mothers." *Journal of Family Communication*, vol. 13, no. 2, 2013, pp. 114-31.

Harwood, Jake, et al. "Communication Accommodation Theory: An Intergroup Approach to Family Relationships." *Engaging Theories in Family Communication: Multiple Perspectives*, edited by Dawn Braithwaite and Leslie Baxter, Sage, 2006, pp. 19-34.

Haverfield, Marie, and Jennifer Theiss. "Parent's Alcoholism Severity and Family Topic Avoidance About Alcohol as Predictors of Perceived Stigma Among Adult Children of Alcoholics: Implications for Emotional and Psychological Resilience." *Health Communication*, vol. 35, no 5, 2015, pp. 1-11.

Holman Jones, Stacy, et al. *Handbook of Autoethnography.* Left Coast Press, 2013.

Honeycutt, James M. "Imagined Interaction: Mental Representations of Interpersonal Communication." *Engaging Interpersonal Communication: Multiple Perspectives*, edited by Dawn Braithwaite and Paul Schrodt. Sage, 2015, pp. 75-87.

Hurt, Nicole E. "Disciplining through Depression: An Analysis of Contemporary Discourse on Women and Depression." *Women's Studies in Communication*, vol. 30, no. 3, 2007, pp. 284-309.

Knobloch, Leanne, and Amy Delaney. "Themes of Relational Uncertainty and Interference From Partners in Depression." *Health Communication.* vol. 27, no. 8, 2012, pp. 750-56.

Koenig Kellas, Jody, et al. "The Benefits and Risks of Telling and Listening to Stories of Difficulty Over Time: Experimentally Testing the Expressive Writing Paradigm in the Context of Interpersonal Communication Between Friends." *Health Communication*, vol. 30, no. 9, 2015, pp. 1-25.

LeBlanc, Sarah S. "Good-bye Daddy: An Autoethnographic Journey Through the Grief and Mourning Process." *Journal of Loss and Trauma* 22, no. 2, 2017, pp. 110-19.

LeBlanc, Sarah S., and Matthew LeBlanc. "The Bright and Dark Side of Joseph Fenton. An Analysis of Narratives Describing the Man Known as Sudharman." *Death Studies*, vol. 40, 2016, pp. 445-53.

Manning, Jimmie. "Families Living in Closets: Talking About Alcoholism In and Out of Family Households.: *Contemporary Case Studies in Health Communication*, edited by Maria Brann, Kendall Hunt, 2015, pp. 161-73.

Nichter, Mimi. *Fat Talk: What Girls and Their Parents Say About Dieting*. Harvard, 2000.

Olson, Loreen, et al. *The Dark Side of Family Communication*. Polity Press, 2012.

Pauley, Perry M. and Colin Hesse. "The Effects of Social Support, Depression, and Stress on Drinking Behaviors in a College Student Sample." *Communication Studies,* vol. 60, no. 5, pp. 493-508.

Rangarajan, Sripriya, and Lynne Kelly. "Family Communication Patterns, Family Environment, and the Impact of Parental Alcoholism on Offspring Self-Esteem." *Journal of Social and Personal Relationships*, vol. 23, no. 4, 2007, pp. 655-70.

Segrin, Chris. "Mental Health." *The Routledge Handbook of Family Communication*. 2nd Ed., edited by Anita Vangelisti, Routledge, 2013, pp. 512-28.

Segrin, Chris. "Social Skills, Stressful Life Events, and the Development of Psychosocial Problems." *Journal of Social and Clinical Psychology*, vol. 18, no. 1, 1999, pp. 14-34.

Interlude

The Secrets of Your Conception

Noun | In-ter-lude: An intervening or interruptive period, space, or event.

Sagashus T. Levingston with
Kerri S. Kearney and B. Lee Murray

I, Kerri, love the bruised and battered. The ones who find themselves outside of the lines—society's lines, their family's lines, the lines of whoever is drawing them that day, week, year, generation—falling down, getting up, brushing off, and getting FIERCE. Like really FIERCE. I love people who own their stories and stand without shame and without excuses and demand a voice and a place in things. I love it when someone refuses to be painted in the false dichotomy of good or bad based upon her race or her upbringing or her family of origin or her choices. I love all this even more when that someone is a woman and most especially when she is a mother because there remains so much opportunity for harshly judging women and mothers. Even by other women. Sometimes especially by other women.

When Lee and I first received Sagashus T. Levingston's abstract for a proposed chapter in this book, we were excited because Sagashus wanted to write about how she told her children about their conceptions—conceptions that were outside of "respectability politics." An early note in my file on chapter authors for this book still says, "BINGO! This one seems just perfect," and when we received Sagashus's chapter draft, it was, indeed, everything we hoped for.

Through follow-up conversations with Sagashus, we decided that the three of us—Sagashus, Lee, and I—would work together to position this special piece. As I sat down to write, I decided to go to Sagashus's webpage (www.infamousmothers.com/) to learn more about her, and I discovered this media blurb for her book:

> We are teen moms, baby mamas, mothers who once sex worked and were addicted to crack. We're not your average good girls. We are survivors of domestic abuse and sexual trauma. But don't call us damsels in distress. We are women with moxie and grit—game changers and powerhouses. We did more than go through the belly of hell and survived, we brought something good back. Coming out on the other side as doctors, artists, nurse practitioners, homeowners, counselors, and so much more, we are 20 women who make a difference in this world. Read our stories and witness how. (Infamous Mothers)

I immediately ordered her book.

Sagashus's first book is about women and how they survive and even thrive through tough times. This current book about origin stories is about women, too, but as mothers. As mothers, we don't always end up being the only ones accountable for our choices; our children sometimes get in on that action, too. Even the simplest example will likely touch most of us. How many times has your child asked you a question about your past for which you attempted to avoid giving an answer? Maybe you softened the reality of the answer. Maybe you just said, "We'll talk about that when you're older." Heck, maybe you flat out lied about whether you smoked dope, drank at age twelve, went for joy rides in the family car, or had sex when you were fifteen. We've all been there—hoping our children will somehow make better choices in some area of growing up than what we did. Do we diminish ourselves and our own self-worth when we hide the lesser of our choices? With three teenagers now, there are many days I ask myself that question. And when one of those choices leads to the conception of one or more of a woman's children, what then?

Sagashus's raw, honest, and beautiful piece speaks to exactly this issue. I'm so honoured to position it as an interlude to the chapters—a chance to pause the action and process what you've been reading thus far.

INTERLUDE: THE SECRETS OF YOUR CONCEPTION

Introducing Sagashus T. Levingston . . .

"Teach your children that if they are stripped of everything, they are still worth something, and never tell them something they could throw in your face later." Realizing I was pregnant with my first child, a woman in my community gave me this advice on her way to work one day. The first piece she offered I understood and made it my sworn duty to carry out. But how do I do the second one, especially when most—if not all—of my children were born out of circumstances that could be thrown in my face.

I hate baby books. I homeschool four out of my six children, and one of our courses is family studies. For one of the units, we are working on creating a narrative and closing any gaps around their dads' lives and their relationships with their dads. To help frame those discussions, I purchased *Conversations with Dad*. It is something like a baby book, but instead of recording the early years of a child, it focuses on the life of a father. I hate the questions "Where did your parents meet?" "What was your first date?" "When did you get married?" and "How did you [the dad] feel about the news that you were going to be a father?" The bias screams at you. The questions assume you did everything the "right" why, or they imply that you should've. You met. You courted. You got engaged. You got married. You got pregnant. Nice and neat. I read over the questions, and I think to myself, "Wow, are you (*Mr. Conversations with Daddy* book) prepared for the answers I'm about to give? If you'd known the answers already, would you have framed them differently or asked different questions? I can't help but wonder. The reality is, though, that these are the questions. Some will just have to be left unexplored, whereas others, well, we'll just have to face."

...

"Hey girl, since you all in my car, check it out." I met your dad while walking down the street. At the time, I was dating a man who was clearly dating someone else. He told me he was going out of town. But I saw him driving through the streets of Chicago in a maroon Thunderbird, swapping out his normal ride (a blue Regal) for this unknown one. Intent on catching him speeding down my block, I watched for every maroon Thunderbird I could and stared into each one with laser-beamed focus. One night, while walking from the gas station with my friends, I spotted one with black-tinted windows. I froze, staring at the glass that seemed to repel me. It felt impenetrable, yet the barrier began to fall. On the other side of it, I found myself looking face to face with a chocolate-skinned, baby-faced, droopy-eyed man saying, "Since you all in my car, check it out." Clearly, he noticed me noticing him.

The meetings are always easy to recall and share. "I met your dad in church," I tell my oldest daughter. "I met your dad while buying jewelry at the university bookstore. He was a vendor"; that's what I tell my second daughter and oldest son. "I met your dad while walking down the street," I tell my second son and third daughter. "And I met your dad while shadowing a professor in a nonfiction creative writing course," I tell my third son, who is also my final child. The beginnings are always so innocent, so funny, and so respectable. It's the conception part that always brings about so much shame.

I got pregnant by a married man. Twice. It was hard telling my children that. I had a history of dating men who were attached to other women—this person's baby daddy (that was my first daughter's father) or that person's live-in boyfriend (that was my last child's dad). And somewhere in between, I managed to get pregnant by a man who was married. In my defense, I didn't know. He didn't tell me before I had fallen in love with the idea of him—his support, his companionship, and his ability to wipe away the stain of being a single mother. In his defense, he was separated. Already stressed from the trials and tribulations of all they experienced before ever setting eyes on me, their marriage had suffered so much. His decision to move out was as much about clearing his head and making sense of all they had gone through as much as it was about so many other things—things that I found out during and after my relationship with him. But this is not a story about him, and it is not my place to tell his tale. Suffice to say, when I met him (or maybe shortly after), I was visiting him at a place he shared with a friend of his. And it was there my daughter was conceived.

Shortly after, he took me to a family event to meet his mother, who looked at me with concern. In fact, the entire place looked at me with concern: his sister, aunts, and other people whose relationships to him were unclear to me. They were all staring. Finally, his mom sat me down and said in a way that sounded professional—she's a therapist and knows how to handle situations like this—"You do understand he is married." "Yes." Her look of concern remained. She was much more aware of the bigger picture and the bigger problem than I was. Soon after, we discovered that the wife was also pregnant. She wanted him to decide. He can either father her soon-to-be son or my soon-to-be daughter. He did not have the option to be both of their dads. He chose, and I went my separate way. He came back, and she went her way. The divorce happened. I birthed our second child. Through the months, there was so much chaos—a lot of arguing, a lot of lonely nights, and a lot of thoughts about suicide. And then we ended. There was so much guilt on both ends about the child he will never get to see and maybe a lot of resentment about the son that will never know him. These are your birthing stories, ones I am not proud to tell. But they are yours, as much as I can understand them.

I have three daughters, and I worry about them so much. In a world riddled with diseases (some of which are incurable), domestic violence, and sexual assault, I am frantic to keep them alive. I am desperate to protect them. But I am also poor and Black and female with a sketchy past with men. I made a series of bad choices: drug dealers, alcoholics, gamblers, abusers, etc. What's worse than the decisions I have made is that I cannot guarantee that I will never make them again. For now, all I have are my stories of failure—the ones that will make you laugh to keep from crying—like the story about how I got pregnant while sharing a bag of sunflower seeds, and then there are the ones that come with only cries and no laughs, like the time I was kicked down a flight of stairs, big and pregnant. The ones where we traded in date nights for violence.

How do I tell my children that while all of them were unplanned, most of them were unwanted? For one dad, it had taken a few weeks for the news to really sink in. After a very satisfying love-making session, he got on his knees and begged, "Please, get rid of this baby." There are different versions of this scenario across all my children's stories: "I gave you the chlamydia, but I didn't give you no baby." The dads always coupled their anger with good, sound advice: "Why don't you have babies with somebody that wants a baby with you?" and "You should get to know the people you are having children with before you have them." I tell my kids that "The common denominator wasn't you. It was me. The rejection was all mine. They didn't even know you then. You weren't even people yet. It was a life with me they wanted to abort." Even in the cases where it was really about the kid, why make a mortifying situation worse? It was always about me.

People whisper, and they talk. As I child, I listened to adults speak in hushes around me, judging my dad for his lifestyle and ultimately judging me for being his daughter. I did not know how to protect myself from all the stares, the gossip, and the dismissals. As a mother of my own children, people say things. They remember the chaos and confusion associated with the different pregnancies. They remember the men's denial and my depression, for instance. Just when I am laughing and happy about the life I have, they remind me of the life I had. I am more confident today. They test that confidence with stories of yesterday's rejection. My children are doing amazing things: going off to college, singing with a city-wide group, and excelling in sports. I imagined these things for them. I (and they) willed and worked for them to be. Part of building that will and doing that work meant letting them know their own histories, including how they were created and the circumstances around those creations.

I always tell my children that low self-esteem kills more people than heart disease, high blood pressure, HIV, and cancer. How can you protect a life you do not value? How can you properly manage something you cannot even look in the face? I explain to them that more times than not, I offered my body at a discounted rate to whichever stranger smiled at me. I lived on the clearance rack. I felt my vagina was as ugly as I thought the world saw me, so I gave it away for the slightest attention. It also did not help that I had a propensity for men who seemed broken, endangered, or misunderstood, or for anyone who needed to be saved in my eyes. It never dawned on me that if they were buying me for a penny, I was probably doing the same, or maybe it did. Maybe I did know, and maybe I felt that if I fixed them up, made them as good as knew, they would be soldered to me—their savior. I was mistaken.

Their insecurities played out differently. It made some gigolos, players, gamblers, and hustlers—people whose so-called businesses depended on exploiting women who loved to save. When this wasn't the case, it made them emotionally unavailable—people who were not interested in cuddling and loving. They depended on women to be receptacles, objects of their release. When this wasn't the case, it made them addicts, alcoholics, and abusers—people too numb, too angry, or too disconnected to maintain families. Whereas I was running to them

INTERLUDE: THE SECRETS OF YOUR CONCEPTION

to save and be saved, their insecurities, hurts, past disappointments, failures, and rejections devoured me as much as they devoured them. The idea of being saved was something that they either played on, they were infuriated by, or both. These were the waters I had chosen to swim in. This was the pool I decided to choose from. While the men I had children with certainly were not the worst of them, they were of them.

In one of my daughters, I see a nervousness about whether or not she too will be the kind of woman to save. I talk to all of them about how so much of that desire to save is about wanting to be saved. I explain to them that the irony of dating from that place is that they will always find themselves in relationships with people they will need to be saved from. If they are not careful, they will find themselves in relationships with men who will create scenarios from which they will look to my daughters, their partners, to rescue them from. And I warn them: Before you know it, you will be saving them from other relationships, jail, pills, binge drinking, etc. I know because this was the cycle that led to the conception of you, some of you anyway. I got pregnant while trying to save men from themselves and from other people. I thought that if I'd save them first, they would be obligated to save me. Rarely, did it ever work that way. Almost always, I had to become my own hero.

"That's the problem with patriarchy," I tell my daughters and sons. "At least, that's one of the problems. It socializes us to see the potential of men and to ignore the real value of women. It invites women to be perpetual damsels in distress and punishes them for saving their damn selves." I explain to them that the last child was born because the city would not leave me alone. As a single mother of five, I was an eye sore to the community we moved to. For many, watching me raise my children in Madison, WI—where I moved to for graduate school—was like watching a woman walk a tightrope in a circus act. There was so much anxiety about the fall or the possibility of it. What would it look like: starving my children, beating them, or leaving them alone for days? Surely, a woman with so many children, raising them alone, is an accident waiting to happen. The calls to child protection services started—not because of what I was doing or not doing but because of concerns about what could be going wrong in a house like mine. Never mind the fact that I was a kickass single mom and that I was right there, at one of the top schools in the country as a master's and PhD student. People struggled seeing me beyond their biases and stereotypes. I was the welfare queen, the baby mama, and the mugshot on the nightly news. I was the reason for poverty, the drain on tax dollars, etc. More times than I wanted to I heard condescending community members say, "Don't you feel lucky to be here?" Even feminists were not protected from their bias. One professor looked at my pregnant belly and screamed through the halls of our department, "You know there is a cure for that?" A colleague suggested I wear a wedding ring to look more respectable. A Black man sympathized with my "current situation," telling me how much he understood because his sister had five children, as a "crack head." Still today, I do not understand the connection. I do know, however, that this kind of emotional and psychological violence led me to a relationship I probably did not need to be in and the by-product was another child.

...

As a graduate student, I study the rhetoric of motherhood and maternal theory and criticism. I am learning that "women fake motherhood like we fake orgasms" and that for Black women, the "homeplace" is a site of resistance. I am learning about the roles that are assigned to women because of sexism. And I think that maybe telling my children the stories of how they began is about more than having the will and putting in the work to help them grow and develop. Maybe it is about resistance and being free. It is about slipping through the hands of people who would want to blackmail me with the truth of my life. But of course, no one can tell my story like I can. There is power in crafting your own narrative, so I tell my children their stories again, but this time, I do it slightly differently. The stories stay the same, but the reason for telling them changes.

Each time I tell stories of how they were born, I add a little more insight. I explain to them about what it meant for me to grow up feeling like I needed a man to activate my existence on the earth and all of the things that cost me. I talk to them about being too insecure to demand men to wear condoms, at what those choices cost me. I then go on to tell them that for whatever reasons the good Lord saw fit to make me their mother, and for better or worse, I am what they have, and I am committed to giving this thing my all. But I am not, nor will I ever be, a martyr—and they should not be one. Mothering is not about dying so that your children can live; it is about living so that your children can live. Part of doing that means owning your truth. So much of my parenting is about this.

...

> All women have personal stories as vast in scope and as powerful as the numen in fairy tales. But there is one kind of story in particular, which has to do with a woman's secrets, especially those associated with shame: those contain some of the most important stories a woman can give her time to unraveling. For most women, these secret stories are embedded, not like jewels in a crown, but like black gravel under the skin of the soul. (Clarissa Pinkola Estés 374-75)

Sagashus is a woman who "runs with the wolves" (Pinkola Estés), and I, Lee, am so moved by her story. It is raw, visceral, honest, and hopeful. And I would like to think that I am running in a pack beside her. I absorb her story, separate from it gradually, surface, and take a breath. And then I relate it to my own hard truths—the ones I have shared and the ones (the hardest ones) that I still hold close and undisclosed. Why are those hard truths about mothering so difficult to disclose? We all live with secrets, big and small, shameful and harmless, terrifying and humorous. Why do we choose to tell certain people and not others? What do we want to happen when we tell? Do we have a certain expected response that we want from others? Do secrets lose their power in the telling, or do they gain power? We all understand secrets to a certain degree because we have all, most likely, held a secret, told a secret and/or probed for the disclosure of a secret. Secrets give us power and also undermine our power. They can be oppressive, but they can also be mysterious and attractive. The telling of secrets can cause pain and destruction, but the telling can also give relief and healing. The holding of a secret can cause suffering, but it can also offer protection. Every mothering experience is another story. And stories bring possibility and hope. Stories break the silence and stories shed a light on secrets.

Here are some suggested reflection questions:

1. When you meet or hear about a wild woman, a fierce woman or a woman who runs with the wolves, what are your immediate reactions or feelings?

2. How does Sagashus's narrative pull forward your own stories? How does her narrative relate to your stories, even though they may be different?

3. What is your hardest truth to own, especially when it comes to your children? Why is it the hardest to tell or to share?

Work Cited

Pinkola Estés, Clarissa. *Women Who Run with the Wolves: Myths and Stories of the Wild Woman Archetype.* Random House, 1992.

Chapter Six

Magic Carpets and Baloney Boats: An Origin Story Told by Two Moms

B. Lee Murray

I sit at the keyboard, and I have never been so stuck in my life. Not a word is coming forth. I try to shut my eyes and go back to that moment to write in the first person, present tense, and I can't seem to get there. I smile as I think about that afternoon and perhaps that is the problem. Who smiles when they are writing autoethnography? I usually cry quietly while I write and become nostalgic, contemplative, retrospective, and sometimes enlightened. And I do laugh on occasion at the humour that sometimes comes with tragedy. Perhaps I am stuck because I have never really written a happy story from beginning to end before, and perhaps people do not really want to hear a happy story. I wonder what we can learn from happiness. But I press on.

Originally, I wanted to write a manuscript about our parallel lives—my life being a frightened pregnant teen while my baby (Dave) listens to Elvis Presley music in the womb and Betty's life (Dave's mom by adoption) struggling with not getting pregnant. I thought this parallel life continuum would unfold in an ongoing tale of struggle, disappointment, joy, growing up and getting older, and life developing on different yet connected trajectories. But it didn't happen that way. Our lives did evolve and we grew older, but life moved in different ways for all of us. And, of course, Betty and Dave were connected as mom and son, sharing similar experiences. As time passed, I was possibly given an occasional passing thought by Dave and his family, and perhaps we all thought about the "what if?" from time to time: "What if Dave had been adopted by another *family?"* or *"What if my parents had adopted Dave?"* *It didn't cross my mind to wonder "What if I raised him myself?" because that was never really an option. I wonder if Dave ever thought about that. The three of us have agreed to share a space to discuss and consider an origin story as told by all of us within this adoption triangle. But it is much more than an origin story; it is a time to connect, to reflect, and to get to know each other better. It is a surreal time, at least for me, and a time that is precious and worthy of appreciation. Dave is now in his forties, and we met for the first time 14 years ago.*

As I prepare for this day, I go to buy some new tapes and batteries for my tape recorder. I am informed that they do not have any tapes as my recorder has become obsolete. I am a bit surprised but ask the salesperson, "So then what do people do or use to record conversations for transcription?" I end up buying a Zoom stereo recorder and leave the store quite pleased with myself. I don't bother to read the instructions and just assume that all will go well on the day I need it. When the day finally arrives, I don't have a clue how to operate this thing. It is a good thing Dave is a little more tech savvy than me.

So here we are. Dave and his two moms, sitting around my dining room table after having lunch together. It seems a miracle in itself that we have been able to coordinate this shared time in three busy lives. I am trying to keep up in a demanding academic career. Dave is living a hectic life inside investment and finance, and Betty travels daily to care for her husband who now lives in a long-term care facility due to a devastating diagnosis of Lewy body dementia. But we are all here, and we all feel this is an important time to find the space to share. We have exchanged numerous emails trying to make this happen for almost a year and then suddenly Dave finds an opening, and Betty and I both do our best to accommodate this specific date, and it works. We are finally going to share a time to reminisce and tell an origin story.

And so we begin.

The following paragraphs provide extensive excerpts within major themes that arose from the conversation with Dave and his two moms.

Are Biological Children "Like Syrup on the Ice Cream"?: Biological Children vs. Adopted Children

Betty: We always knew we wanted kids, and I guess a year after we came back from the Bahamas [in the mid-1960s] was when this was supposed to start. It was month after month of not getting pregnant, sitting on the toilet crying, and then we went to Dr. S. and went on fertility drugs, which we called futility drugs, and after the second month of that, we just said the heck with this: let's just check about adoption. And one thing that made me think that adoption would be good is that a very good friend of mine got pregnant with her second baby. She was quite a bit younger than me, and when she was pregnant, I had trouble showing her that I was happy. I thought this is crazy. I can't be upset with my friends because they are going someplace that I can't go.

Lee: Yeah, so was adoption always an option for you?

Betty: I guess that's something that we never thought about until it became something that we were obviously going to have to do. But yeah, I had friends that were adopted, and a little girl made myself and another friend feel bad because she was chosen (because she was adopted) and we weren't. So adoption was always a good thing and nothing negative about it at all.

I am starting to wonder about my colleague, friend, and co-editor when I ask the next question, and Betty and Dave have both read her work (Murray and Kearney) so they know whom I am talking about.

Lee: Because for Kerri, adoption wasn't second best.

Betty: No, this was just a way for us.

Lee: So Kerri didn't go through this feeling really bad that she wasn't getting pregnant.

Betty: Oh I see. Okay.

Lee: So it was a big deal for you in terms of not getting pregnant?

Betty: I wanted children. I wasn't going to go through life without them.

Dave: I find it odd that Kerri would think it didn't matter because you would still want the child to be "of you" in a way. That would be your first choice. We just look at our two children and what they took from each us, and I find it hard to believe that someone would say that, you know, because it's the added pleasure. I get it, but you would think that someone would still want or be disappointed that they couldn't have that little extra, right? It's like the syrup on the ice cream. The ice cream is good but if you can put the syrup on that's a little added. Not that it's a negative.

Betty: I think Dave, once we realized that [pregnancy] was not going to happen, we considered adoption, and it wasn't a big deal.

Dave: For sure, I was talking about Kerri more, when she said that it didn't really matter. I would say that, well she has a child of her own now right, and she can kind of see that. But did she adopt before that?

Lee: Yes.

Dave: That's when I would say that sometimes you maybe talk yourself into that it didn't matter because that's your only choice. I'm not saying that she's wrong, I'm just saying that...

Lee: Yeah, it's surprising for you.

Dave: Adopting for me wouldn't be a big deal either, but you would always wonder, you know, what you would have in the other.

Betty: I would have never probably chosen adoption over having my own if I had the option, and other people need babies. If I could have my own, I would.

Dave: And people choose to do that sometimes. They have a health condition and they choose not to have children because it's dangerous. Now that I have met you Lee, I see how my son looks like your son (my half-brother).

Betty: Yes, had you not found Lee ... it is kind of fascinating.

I wish I would have explored this further at the time rather than rushing to the next question. It is an important concept to explore: Is adoption always a second choice? I know it is not the case for Kerri, and I decide to ask her to respond to this piece of the transcript and here is what she said:

> It is a topic that I think a lot of people (on both sides of the issue) struggle to understand.

One thing that stood out to me is the discrepancy in what you said and how Dave interpreted it. You said that I didn't feel badly that I didn't get pregnant and that adoption wasn't a second choice. Both are absolutely true statements, although probably I should clarify that I didn't feel badly. I was surprised that I didn't get pregnant in my first marriage, and I felt horrible for failing others and felt worse when I experienced their reactions, but their reactions weren't what I felt for me (and a secret I kept, see Kearney & Murray). But back to Dave—what he said (at least as I read it) is that biology vs. adoption didn't matter to me and that is not what you said or what I said. Of course, it matters. It is someone's life story—the child's and mine. And there are implications for both choices. I just don't see them as unequal choices.

I always knew I wanted to adopt. Like Betty, I was exposed to adoption as a child (through extended family), and I just thought it was a great way to build a family. My real ideal was to have a family that was of both adoption and biology. But I really only wanted one biological child and mostly because I just wanted to have the pregnancy experience one time (I didn't want to miss anything!), not because I was concerned about biological ties.

It sounds like Betty came to the option of adoption because she couldn't get pregnant, and that is an often-shared experience. And it sounds like she was sad she couldn't get pregnant as her first choice, also a commonly shared experience. These just weren't my experiences, and while I may be in the minority, I certainly don't think I am the only one who saw adoption as a first choice, an equal choice with getting pregnant. It sounds like, in the end, Betty also didn't see adoption as a second choice—just another avenue. But she came to that position differently from me.

Although I was fully aware of and attuned to options for getting pregnant as a single woman (and postdivorce, as I was not afraid to break the societal rules to do so), I had already decided on adopting before I met my husband. When he asked me to marry him, it was a specific topic of discussion (among other things). I didn't want to agree to marry him if adoption was not an option for him. It was a commitment I had already made, so it is definitely not something I talked myself into because I didn't have other options. Fortunately, my husband embraced it, although, I don't know how much of that was about supporting me and how much was about his own feelings. It was a new idea for him, though. He wanted to allow for the possibility of a biological child, and I did, too.

So Dave's comments that you want to know the child is "of you"—that is a completely valid perspective that many people share. And, of course, we do look at our biological child sometimes and shake our heads at what she has clearly biologically inherited from one of us. It is fun. But because we know our son's biological family, we frankly do the same thing with him. We don't know our daughter's family and that is harder just because genetics is a real thing. I think it is fascinating to see how our kids develop from three different genetic pools but one common environment, and I'm sad that not every parent gets to experience that diversity. So, that is just my perspective and both Dave's and mine are valid and valuable, though different. I really don't see biology as a first choice. I've never felt disappointed. I do not have (nor does my husband have) any condition or illness that prevents or discourages us from being biological parents. The syrup and cherry on top just come to us in other ways that I find equally valuable.

I, too, believe they are equally valuable, and I believe Dave would probably agree. Kerri's views are perhaps not the norm, but she is not alone in her thinking. Similarly, my story of giving my baby to another family to adopt and raise without feeling that I was relinquishing my child—that he was being taken away from me or that I surrendered him—is not the norm either, but I do not imagine that I am alone in feeling I made the best decision at the time for my child and myself. Kerri and I do not feel regret, and perhaps that is also not the norm or a particularly good fit with the normative discourse of the time, particularly in my case. And Dave, who said adoption is not a big deal for him, is perhaps not the norm either. And so, we think we may be an unusual bunch. And, perhaps, meeting my son when he was a young adult and a father of two children is the happy ending. Or is the happy ending still in the future as we come to know each other better and his children are better able to understand the circumstances surrounding their dad's origin story and how it may be different or similar to their own?

Where Are the Blankets and Clothes?: The Adoption Story

Betty: A lot of people who have adopted get upset with our story of Dave's adoption because there was no long wait period then to receive a child. We were told by our social worker to talk to both our sets of parents to check if there was going to be any objection we knew of ahead of time. We said it wouldn't make any difference; it was what we were doing. My mother said get it out of a cabbage patch and, if possible, a red-headed, freckle-faced little boy. We went to my mother-in-law, and she was all for it, so we came home and applied for adoption of a child. So that would've been maybe middle of April and we had Dave [our first son] by August 16 and back then I think there were as many babies as there were parents wanting babies, so it was a matter of just matching up the histories. And with our second son, we didn't want the baby to mess up our summer holidays. We wanted to take Dave fishing and what not, so we applied to adopt him towards the end of August, and got him November 2. Our daughter, our third child, was a little longer because they lost one of our references. But there wasn't that years-long wait that a lot of people now have. We just did it at the right time.

Lee: So, what was it like that day you got the phone call for Dave? Were you ready for it?

Betty: We were ready, yes. The crib and everything was all set up; a room was ready to go. But you don't sleep that first night. I thought I may as well have gone through the labor too. We went to a nearby city and were directed to the provincial government building. I guess it's where you get babies. So, just so you know, I was excited, but just until you have that baby in your arms, you just, it's not real. And then they tell you: you can leave. They hand you this little baby; they trust you with this little baby, and Dave peed all over his dad the first day. It took me a minute to realize you had to put the diaper on top … and you walk out of that building with this baby in your arms, and I kept looking behind me because I said we are walking out with a little human and somebody is going to say stop. But they never did.

Lee: So, what was it like, when you first saw him? He wasn't red haired and freckled.

Betty: Well, ok. No, he wasn't red haired and freckled, but he was the cutest little dude I ever saw. But I remember the back of his head was very flat. I guess he'd stayed in his little crib too long.

Lee: When you say Dave's head was flat, it makes me feel really sad because when I saw him in court about two months after his birth, it didn't look like him anymore. And Dave had kind of a rash on his face, and I wondered if anybody was looking after him.

Betty: Well, I think [while in foster care] he spent a lot of time in his little chair thing, or crib. I'm sure three weeks later it was better.

I feel better when I hear this. I have dwelt on the fact that Dave appeared uncared for when I saw him in court, and he did not have all the clothes and blankets I left at the hospital for him! But Betty is right. His head was probably better in three weeks, and he had a very good childhood and life has been good for him. Again, perhaps it is just reassurance that I made the right decision because I could or should have taken him back if he was not being cared for in foster care. I reassure myself that it wasn't that long.

Dave: I did okay, and I don't remember that, so everything is good.

Dave is trying to make me feel better, but he is right: I think everything is good. Again, I am reassuring myself that everything is okay and I made the right decision. Perhaps I was never completely sure of that until this moment.

Lee: He was about three months old when you got him?

Betty: He was two months and three weeks I think but cute as a bug's ear. I've always said adoption is the best way—"no fuss, no muss, and no bother."

Lee: It's funny because when you give birth to a baby, it's a whole different ballgame. You feel like you kind of get to know them before they're born because you've talked to them for so long.

Betty: Exactly. And we just get handed this baby and told to be on our way.

Lee: You don't get to do anything to prepare, do you?

Betty: No, and especially with Dave, I remember just turning around and looking and thinking, "Well isn't anybody even going to say goodbye?" And the social worker said, "Just take your time and when you are ready, you can go." So we just opened the door and walked out with a little human being.

Lee: And they never gave you a pile of clothes and blankets?

Betty: We got what he had on.

Lee: Yeah, it always makes me wonder, like it's not a big deal, but...

Not a big deal! How many times have I brought this up? Why is it such a big deal? I am actually feeling anger when I think about it. Dave was different. He was not a baby who was unwanted. He was not a baby that was relinquished or that I surrendered. It was a decision, a long and very hard decision to make. It was not my decision to put him in foster care, and no one told me that was the process. So I left those clothes for the other mother so she knew I loved him and cared for him and about him. They had no right to keep those clothes from Betty or Dave. I'm still angry and hurt. I feel deceived. No one told me he was going to foster care. I thought his new mom would come and get him, and the clothes and all those blankets would connect us and keep us all warm. But they didn't. I'm sad, hurt, and angry. I can't bear to think of Dave in ratty clothes lying on his back in a crib way too long. I had even picked out a special outfit for him to go home in.

Betty: What ever happened to those clothes and blankets? I would've been thrilled to think that his mother had given them to him and to me.

Lee: I can remember coming back up to the city [about two months after Dave's birth]. I left the hospital and then I had to come back up to identify you Dave—to give you away through the court system—and there was a judge there. And my dad was crying because he and mom really wanted to raise you. And I can remember seeing you and saying to the judge, "I don't know if that's him or not, and the judge getting really upset with me and saying, "Well you have to tell us yes or no, and I say, "Well he looks different to me; you know he doesn't look the same." Like I said, he had this rash and I said, "Where are his clothes?"

I had gotten you all kinds of clothes and blankets, and I said, "Where is his stuff?" You had a ragged little sleeper on, and I repeated, "Where are the clothes that I had gotten him?" And so the judge is getting more impatient, and I finally just say, "Well I guess this is him," and then we left, and I didn't think that I would ever see you again.

It was surreal and awful. And Egbert [pseudonym], the biological father and my boyfriend at the time, came to court with me that day. And I still remember my dad saying, "Why don't just you and I go" and that's when I said, "No, he's the father, and he should be able to come" and like trying to be fair both ways. And I remember him coming; it must've been awfully hard for my dad to have him there. My dad just wanted to be alone with me I think, and he had said it several times, "Couldn't just you and I go?"

Betty: Yeah, that had to be hard.

Lee: And then wanting you to be okay Dave. You know what I mean, and not being able to do anything. I still remember when I first met your dad, and Bob saying to me, "Oh I just cried when I read that story [Murray, "Secrets of Mothering"] because I never, ever thought about it from your perspective—from the little girl's perspective."

Betty: I probably thought about it a little more, because being the mother.

Lee: Yeah. He just said that he didn't understand it before.

Betty: And what you went through while we were so happy.

Lee: I mean it was sort of serendipitously happening already. I mean you were deciding already on adoption. You didn't know it would be Dave, but you knew it should be soon.

Betty: And back then, the social workers every five weeks had a conference—I think it is what they called it—and the social workers would bring the histories of the babies and the other social workers would bring the histories of the parents and match them up. And we didn't get a baby the first conference. And it would've been somebody other than Dave if we had.

Lee: Well, I know, and it's just the way things happened. It was no wonder that I got pregnant because I had no idea. You know, seriously, and I guess that's why I'm so adamant that kids have to know this stuff. They need to know correct names of body parts and girls need to know how to look after themselves, and boys do too. As you know, my research provides sexual health education to adolescents with developmental disabilities because of the experiences of my youngest son [Murray, "An Autoethnographic Story of Abuse"], and I feel very strongly about this. It is hard for me to believe just how naïve and really stupid I was. And then realizing, something was happening to my body and not even thinking that I could get pregnant, that's how naïve I was.

Betty: That must've been a shock.

Lee: It was. I think it was a shock to my family too, and I can remember telling my mom and dad, and my poor dad, he just cried and cried and cried. And, so, I cried and cried and cried. My mom and dad thought we should go see the biological father's parents, so we went to see them, and I was crying the whole time and they were like, "What are you crying about? you guys are having a baby." They were all excited and assumed that we would get married, and I think that Egbert assumed that we would get married, too. And I remember my dad—it was after church one Sunday—and he said, "Well, if you are going to get married, you are going to need a place to live," and he was renting this little place in town. So we went in there to see it, and Egbert came too, and he thought this was going to be a great idea, and I'm thinking, 'What the hell, I can't do this." I don't know if my dad knew what he was doing or what because my parents didn't like me dating Egbert, but they would've supported us. But their solution was that they would adopt you and that they would raise you and that's what they wanted to happen, but they left it up to me.

Dave: That was after you said that you wouldn't move in with him?

I am starting to realize that my relationship with the biological father is very interesting to Dave and also probably important for him to know. We have not talked about the biological father a lot, and part of that is maybe that I have not had contact with him in the last forty some years, and it is a relationship I rarely think about, or really want to think about. But I think back and try to remember the circumstances of that time because I know it is important for Dave to know.

Interest and Curiosity: What Was the Biological Father Like?

Lee: I said I did not want to get married at the time. When they knew that I wasn't going to get married, I remember mom coming into my bedroom. I was on the top bunk, and she said, "I just have one question to ask you." And I said, "What's that?" because I was kind of rebellious, for how naïve I was. I said, "Well, what do you want to know?" and she said, "Do you love him?" and I said, "What?" And she said, "I just want to know if you love him?" I think I said something smart-assed, but then I remember thinking about that and then thinking, "Well, do I?" But then there was all that shame then [in the 1960s] because why would you do that [have sex] with somebody you didn't love? I mean, now it's very different, but then, it was why you would do that then if you don't love him? Not from my parents but society, right. But then I thought, if my mom and dad were going to raise you [Dave], am I going to be like your big sister and go into nursing, and come home on the weekends to see you or how would that work? And then I thought that would mean that Egbert and I were forever connected, and I didn't want that to happen either. So it was a hard decision because it was left totally with me really.

Betty: Ultimately, it had to be.

Dave: So you had broken up by the time you decided [on adoption]?

Lee: No, we kept going out during my first year in nursing. I guess we had been through a lot together, and there was still a year after you were born that I could have taken you back. There was that whole idea that I could change my mind up until a certain period of time.

Betty: Almost a year.

Dave: No, really??

Lee: It was quite a long time.

Betty: We signed the final papers approximately a year later, and there were criteria, so many, like you could've had him back thirty days after you got out of the hospital—no questions asked. That is why they had foster parents I think. And then, I'm not sure what the criteria were, but it was approximately a year later when the final papers were signed.

We had plans to go to Africa or some place if you had wanted him back Lee because we sure weren't giving him back.

Lee: It wasn't that I didn't ever want him back; it was just, what would his future look like, right? And that was part of making that decision—what was best for Dave? I truly believed, at that time and now, that it was the best for you. I still believe that, and yet I always look for reassurance that it was the best decision. I guess there isn't really a best decision, just a different decision with different outcomes.

Betty: We always told our kids that their mommies loved them enough to give them to us and that Dave's mommy, from when she was a little girl, had wanted to be a nurse, and if she kept him, she wouldn't be able to do that. So, we were very happy to find out that you were a nurse.

Dave: The document from social services said that my biological mother was going to be a nurse.

Lee: So you had quite a bit of information about me, and I had nothing. I didn't know where you were. I didn't know if something happened to you. The last time I saw you, you looked not cared for. Nobody said to me, "He's adopted now and with a nice family."

Betty: We were told that the birthmother would be given information. How did they put that, "reassuring information." Dad [Bob] has a good job, and we plan on having other children and that's what they told us that the birthmother would get.

Lee: Not a word, not a peep.

Betty: That's not fair.

Lee: I never heard anything.

Betty: Because you may have been able to relax a little more if you had known.

Lee: Yeah, because I always wondered if you were okay, always ... probably until we met.

Betty: I'm sure it would be hard. I know my mother always thought about your mother, on Mother's Day and on Dave's birthday and she used to say a little prayer to the other [grand]mother, that she's okay, the other grandma. That's who she thought about.

Lee: Aww, how thoughtful. And I think it would've been good for all of us to know that you were okay, Dave, because I think my mom and dad thought about that too.

Betty: Yeah. He's there and he's gone.

Lee: But they didn't want to bring it up to me. I don't know. Maybe they thought it would upset me or bring up memories or something. It's something that we never really talked about.

Betty: Now maybe that's something that has to be changed with the system.

Lee: I think that now it's really changed because they have open adoptions.

Betty: Even in the closed adoptions, I wouldn't have worried at all about sending a yearly update, like he's doing good, he's a brat, he's whatever.

Dave: You wouldn't have worried, but I bet it could backfire.

Lee: Because they aren't going to tell you if something is wrong?

Betty: Yeah, probably not.

Dave: I think that you know. You might just create that memory for the person and they might just try and get them back, instead of out of sight, out of mind.

Dave was out of sight for a very long time, but I often worried about him, so he was never out of mind.

Betty: I just think it would've been awful nice for you to know that he made it.

Lee: It was [hard]. I wanted you to be happy, healthy, and safe, but I never knew for sure, and I did not want to cause you any hardship by taking you back if you were with a happy family. And I wanted to make sure that time period was up, and when it was, then Egbert and I went our separate ways.

Betty: I remember we were told that both the birthmother and birth father surrendered the baby.

There's that word "surrender" again. It was a product of the time and the culture of unwed mothers. I have written a counter-narrative to the presumptions that birthmothers are pressured to place their babies for adoption, and I have refuted terms such as relinquishment, surrender, anguish, loss, survival, and powerlessness applying to all birthmothers (Kearney and Murray).

Lee: Yes. He was in court that day, but he never said he wanted to keep you. I knew that he wouldn't be able to parent you. He wasn't that kind of guy that would want to do that. But I still hung in there because I had to go to the finish line, you know what I mean? I guess I needed to feel like I was more normal and was going to get married and keep my baby and be happy with this man, but it was all a façade.

I remember there was another young single girl. I think maybe they deliberately put us in the same hospital room. She was younger than me, and her mom and boyfriend came up to visit her all the time. She never told either one of them she was pregnant; she wore really tight jeans and so she went into labour really early, but the baby was fine. They were all sort of happy about it and going to get married, so I remember knowing that we weren't getting married, but pretending that we were. Do you know what I mean? So we would talk about these things back and forth, but I knew that I was giving Dave up for adoption, but I let on that everything was cool. But I knew that Egbert was dating or seeing somebody else when you were born. I forget where he was when you were born, but he did come back a day or so after you were born, and he did come to see me every day I was in the hospital. And he joined in the façade. Perhaps neither one of us could deal with the truth and all the emotions and the future. So we made up another future where we would be happy ever after with our new baby boy, just like my roommate.

Betty: It must've been hard.

Lee: Yeah. It was a lot of pretending. Pretending everything was ok. I remember the day I left the hospital, mom took me to a jewelry store and we went and bought a nurses' watch. I think that was her way of saying "move on to the next step now." And then my cousin was getting married shortly after and I remember going up there to the wedding, and so that would be like maybe two weeks after you were born or something, and they didn't give me any pills to stop the lactation and so I remember going out there and thinking, what's wrong? And it was so painful I couldn't stand it. So I went and talked to my mom, and she felt so bad that she didn't say something to them or didn't do something. So I remember going to the doctor there, and it was just unbearable, unbelievable.

Betty: After everything else you just went through.

Lee: I still remember that. And my mom felt so bad because she thought she should've known, you know, but she never thought of it or she just assumed that they would've given me something at the hospital, and maybe they did, but they didn't give me any pills to take home or any follow up. It's funny how just talking about it, the memories start coming back. The pretending continued on into nursing school. When I was in nursing, I never told anybody. And then I remember telling my best friend. I met her in nursing, and I told her and she said to me, "I always wondered why you were going out with Egbert." I remember her saying that because I explained to her that I was waiting the year, and she was like, "Oh, I wondered."

Betty: And everything falls into place.

Lee: I just remember in high school when I was going out with him, and I thought I was in love just like all my friends. I remember my aunt coming to visit and she left and went back to Ottawa, and she wrote me a letter saying how I shouldn't be going out with this guy anymore and sort of pointing out all these things about him and I was so mad, you know. And my mom was like "Oh you know your Aunt, she just wants the best for you," because I was like her favourite. And I was mad, even though I knew a lot of what she was saying was true. That's probably what made me mad.

Dave: You want to prove them wrong. Sometimes I wonder if I have seen him and not known it. Perhaps at an event or in a crowd or somewhere.

Betty: It was Kari [Dave's wife] who told me that she met some of your friends, Lee, at your daughter's wedding, and they said they knew Egbert and said Dave should go find him; Egbert's family would be happy to meet Dave, and I'd often wondered if those people at the wedding did tell the family.. So we sort of said, okay well now Egbert knows probably where Dave is. If Egbert wanted to get a hold of Dave he could, but not necessarily, but you think someone would tell him.

Dave: Or maybe he doesn't want to meet me.

Lee: I think he would probably want to meet you.

Dave: So is he tall? Big? Strong? Little?

Lee: He would be medium build I guess; he was taller than me at the time, but I might have grown a bit since then.

Betty: I think social services said the father was 5'10.

Lee: Yeah. I was going to say about 5'9, 5'10.

Dave: So exact same as me then.

Lee: Yeah.

Dave: I assumed so.

Lee: I mean, you sort of look like him. I think that's where you get your dark skin from, his family. But his sisters didn't have dark skin.

Dave: So what was his nationality?

Lee: German I think.

Betty: Yeah that's what they told me. German and Scottish.

Dave: Have you seen him at all?

Lee: No. I have not seen him in years. I have no idea where he is. And I would be very surprised to ever run into him. Have you contacted him?

Dave: No, I never. I mean, the funny thing is the letter that I got from social services when they contacted you finally is still the letter I diarize every year to see if I want to go see him. Like still through my paper diary at work and I just always think, "I'll put if off for another year because I could go any time," and it's not like I forget now, but it's just like, "I'll put if off for another year." I don't know if I should or shouldn't. I don't know. You give me advice on that.

Lee: It's totally up to you if you want to or you want to get information or anything. I don't know. I can't guess what may happen, and I shouldn't say one way or the other.

Dave: It's funny the need [to meet my birthfather] isn't there ... it's one of those things I always say, "To be fair to them I should be in touch because maybe he doesn't want to mess my life up," but I don't know. But I always thought that maybe you thought that maybe you didn't want to mess up my life, so I should maybe let you know that's how it all really started ... kind of. There was a point where I thought about my parents, not just you, but my parents and just wondered—I bet for a long time they were still together.

Lee: Oh, you thought we were together still?

Dave: Yeah, because in the [social services] letter to my parents when I was adopted, it says that you guys were together.

Betty: In the history.

Dave: It says it was a happy couple, so Kari and I thought that you still were a couple, that there were pretty good odds of that being the case.

I guess we pulled off the façade. We appeared to be real. We even fooled social services.

Betty: I think that was the romantic notion.

Dave: More memories are coming up now. I remember, too, the social worker said, "You never know you could have full brothers and sisters." She talked about that too: "That's another reason why you should do this [search for your birthparents] because if it does work out, you could have full brothers and sisters."

Lee: Yeah, like not half brothers and sisters right. That is so interesting. I never thought of that. I guess I just assumed that you would know or think that I was a single mom.

Dave: Kari always said, "What do your mom and dad think of that?" And you guys were more than assisting, mom.

Betty: I often said that if he wanted to find a new mother and get rid of me, I obviously hadn't been a good enough mother over the years so. But no, I was never worried about that, like the history and everything else. I was as curious and wondering, like everyone else.

Lee: But it's just that loss of time; that's what I think about. I guess it's not really a waste of time because we both had our lives, but lost time somehow. Not knowing each other until you were all grown up, but yet that would've been how it was anyway. There was no way I would've been able to meet you until you were eighteen. So the only time lost was eighteen to thirty-four years old. That's a while though.

Dave: When did we meet? The time has flown by. I would say I've only known you four years, but it has been a lot longer. Eleven years? And your dad died in 2004, right?

Lee: Yes, December 2004.

Dave: So I would've met you just after, so 2005, I would've met you. That's why you couldn't meet me the first time. I think your dad had passed away, and you had to cancel. And Mom, you actually said, "I know why she cancelled now," because she saw it in the paper.

Betty: Yeah, I read the obituary.

Dave: I knew that later because the social worker told me that later—that your father had passed away.

How and why would the social worker know that? Why would they be keeping track of that and making note of it? It just seems very odd to me and outside the role of a social worker.

Betty: I remember phoning you and saying do you want to read your grandfather's obituary?

Dave: That's right.

Lee: And we hadn't met yet or had we met once?

Dave: No.

Lee: We hadn't met yet. Yeah, I think that maybe it was that I had told Dad that we were going to meet and showed him the picture.

Dave: Yeah, that's really too bad.

Betty: But at least he saw the picture.

Lee: Yeah at least he saw that, and he knew that we were reconnected and that you were okay and married. And I remember him saying, "Married with two kids, where does time go Lee?"

Were We in the Same Place at the Same Time?: Connections and Degrees of Separation

Dave: I could have run into [my birthfather] because as we have discovered Lee, you and I know some of the same people, and we have identified times when we may have actually seen each other or been in the same place at the same time—so many connections that are sometimes hard to believe.

Lee: I find the most interesting one to be that one of your colleagues and a good friend was someone who grew up very close to my family, and if my parents would have adopted you, you would probably have been good friends anyway, being neighbours in a small community.

Dave: And your mom's good friend used to work with my dad.

Lee: I know. I find that so hard to believe. We never knew about that connection until I said your parents' names to her, and she was shocked and so happy at the same time. She thought so much of your dad [Bob], Dave, and she was such close friends with my parents. It was a connection that she felt immediately. I imagine she met you at some time, as she talked about socializing with your parents and having such a good time in their company.

Betty: And my good friend's brother married your first cousin Lee.

Lee: That is really amazing in some ways.

Dave: I still wonder about visiting their home and hanging around with my friend [Lee's cousin's son]. I used to go there a lot. So [Lee's cousin] would have people upstairs, quite a bit, while we hung out downstairs. So odds are you were one of them.

Lee: I mean, I could've been.

Dave: I would think probably because I was there a lot, so the odds of you being there with the people that were coming in and out that would know her. Unless she had a ton of good friends, you would've probably been one of them.

It is as if we want this to be true. We want to imagine that we were in the same place at the same time, and it is somehow comforting to know that we were in a shared space and had a degree of connection even though we were unaware of it at the time.

Lee: Oh yeah, and it's funny because my cousin was there when you were born. She worked on labour and delivery, and I remember I stayed at my aunt's house, and I remember waking up and I had this really sore back, and I was just walking around the house, just rubbing my back, rubbing my back. And I remember I was looking out the front window and I was looking out in the street, and I was like, "Whoa, I wonder if there is something going on here because my back." So I went and woke up my aunt and my aunt phoned my cousin because she was at work that night, and she said this is probably false labour, but if you want to bring her up, that's ok. And so I went up, and I can remember I was hanging onto the top of the bed because my back hurt; I couldn't lay down. And she was like, "You'll be ok." And she gave me a smoke; she was like, "Here, have a smoke." Can you imagine in labour and delivery? So anyway, and I was like, "No, I have to push," she said "Oh Lee, you'll be ok, just breathe," and I said 'I'm not kidding you!' Anyway, you were born, like it was a matter of minutes [see Murray, "Secrets of Mothering"].

Dave: Oh, is that right?

Lee: Yes, she was right there when you were born.

Dave: That almost seems surreal, as I saw her often when I hung out with my friend, and it probably never occurred to either of us that she was there when I was born or that I was Lee's son.

Lee: I know it is almost eerie in some ways.

Betty: I can remember the year Dave was one year old. My friend who married this same cousin of yours was home for the summer with his little girl that would've been a little bit older than Dave, and we went out to the lake, three or four times, and I don't remember if his wife, your cousin, was there. She certainly wouldn't have recognized that tiny little newborn baby a year later, but it could've happened.

Lee: Yeah, it would be more likely for her to think of it a year later if she knew the baby was adopted.

Betty: Perhaps, and that was probably never mentioned.

Lee: Probably not.

Betty: Yeah. It wouldn't have been like, "this is Betty, a close friend of mine, and this is her adopted child." I would've popped them anyway if they would've said that.

Lee: Exactly because that was your little boy, your son.

Betty: Yes, absolutely.

Lee: Yeah, it's funny. All these connections and degrees of separation.

Dave: Yeah.

Lee: I know. It is such a possibility that we may have met somewhere, and I think of that, Dave, particularly when you said that you used to come to the lake with a friend of yours, and it was the same little lake where I took my kids every summer. The funny part is we could probably look at each other and not even know because that is not what we would have been thinking about at that time.

We both seem to be searching for all the connections we could have had before we even met. It gives us a sense of that invisible thread that held us together that intuitively awakened our awareness of each other and by some coincidence, we did see each other, someplace at some time. And perhaps for brief moments we wondered if we had a glimpse of what could have been.

It Doesn't Matter: Learning You Are Adopted

Lee: So what's your first memory of being told you were adopted?

Dave: It's funny because there is no one "Aha" moment; there isn't one where you are told, like you see in books or you see on TV. It really wasn't a big deal. It's funny because we had these stupid books, those red books, and I remember this very dumb reproduction book, and I remember there were four [books] together right, you know, about body parts and that.

Betty: I didn't give you a book about adoption at that time.

Dave: No, but it was a little book like the others. I was probably like six.

Betty: Yeah, they were pretty simple books.

Dave: And you just said, "We couldn't have kids like in the book." That was my memory of finding out, clueing in, but it didn't matter. People thought more of it than I ever did, and still do; it doesn't really matter.

I note that Dave has said that quite often, "It doesn't matter." And he also perceived that Kerri meant adoption vs biological children doesn't matter either. I wonder what "doesn't matter" means exactly, and I wish I would have asked Dave that question. Because he was clear that having biological children does matter to him, but he himself being adopted doesn't matter. At least on the surface, it seems like a dichotomy that would be interesting to learn more about. In fact, as this manuscript goes to press, Dave and I are discussing this further, and it may be food for further thought and perhaps a publication as together we unpack the layers of meaning— perhaps some that have been unconscious. Dave has indicated that being adopted was never an issue for him. When it did matter to him was when he had two children, and he was interested in the medical history of his origin family, and once he had children, he also had a desire to meet his birthmother. He realized that if he persisted, there would be a good chance of us meeting at last. And I am so happy he did.

Betty: I remember when you would've been almost four because we adopted your sister in March before you were four. And you knew we were getting a baby sister, and we kicked you out of that room and Dad built the bunk beds for you and your brother.

Dave: I have no recollection of that. I remember her coming home a little bit. But I remember being three, spinning in the kitchen while you were on the phone, while you'd sit on the phone in that chair by the stove. And I wasn't in school yet, so I can remember being three, but I can't remember switching rooms. But I do remember when the beds were done. So it's funny.

Lee: You remember pieces of it.

Dave: I remember pieces of it, but I do remember the bunk beds.

Betty: Yes, you used to stand on the top and pee on your brother.

Dave: I remember that because they were staggered, right? That's how they were. But there is that lapse. I don't remember the day she came, but did you go to my aunt's afterwards?

Betty: You were at your aunt's.

Dave: Right.

Betty: You and your brother were there.

Dave: Right, and you went to get her. See, I remember that now.

Betty: And I came home with such a headache. I said, "Here" to your aunt and gave her the baby. I went and got a couple of aspirin and went and laid in her big chair because I had such a headache.

Dave: I remember that, and it was a big deal for everybody, but it wasn't really for me.

Betty: When I was setting up the crib in the baby's room, you came in, and I said "We were going to get a baby." You wanted to know why, and I told you that the other mommy couldn't keep her, but she loved her enough to want to give her to us.

Dave: And that was the norm; that's what I thought everybody did.

Betty: And I said, "Because the mommy didn't have as much money and couldn't look after her." And you asked, "Would she have a crib at that mommy's house?" I said, "No, no, she wouldn't have a crib." I remember you opening the drawers and saying, "Would she have diapers?" I said, "No, that mommy doesn't have any diapers for her or pretty clothes." "Well, she better come to our house then," you said. "She better be ours." I think is what you said.

Dave: And the funny thing is my perception. You were trying to explain so I would understand, and yet I thought that her mom wasn't able to look after her. And I think you wanted me to understand that you could give her a better life.

Betty: Yeah, but I didn't mean to imply that your mother would do better without you or that you would do better with us. I always tried to say, "Your mommy loved you enough to give you to us." Because the first time I knew about adoption was when my friend told me she was adopted, and she said that her parents chose her and our parents had to take what they got kind of a thing. And I was just like, "oh my goodness." And I knew I was supposed to be a boy.

Lee: So when you say it wasn't a big deal for you, Dave, do you have any other memories about thinking about adoption or just that it was, like you said, not a big deal?

Dave: No, and it's hard to explain. It's really something hard to explain and it really was a nonevent, and it's probably more an event now in my life because of you. It really was a nonevent. I didn't care that I didn't look like anyone else. I never thought of it. I never thought of the health aspect until I got married and was about to have my own kids. Then my wife said to me, "You might want to pursue that," which is something we'll talk about later because there's good stories about that too, but yeah, it's truly a nonevent, and I know with other people it's not; it's a big event, where they might have found out when they were nine or even older.

Lee: Or by accident somehow.

Dave: Or their parents weren't good to them, so they always wondered if their life could have been better with the other family. I mean we grew up without very much money, but I didn't know that. That's the other thing: you don't know what you don't have. To me, we were actually the rich family on the block.

Betty: Well, the rich family at school, Dave. Yeah, some of the kids you knew in school had difficult lives and dealt with poverty.

Dave: Yeah, because my dad worked hard, and he kept the house, and we had a little pool in the back and all my friends came over. That was probably the only bath they got, right, like you didn't realize that.

Betty: Yeah, they lived in subsidized housing, but we probably didn't tell you they lived in subsidized housing.

Dave: It's funny how you could tie adoption to that; it was the norm, so you would never question it. So fighting was the norm, or not having money was the norm, and being adopted or a foster kid was the norm. So those things were not a big deal; they didn't matter. I knew young that I was adopted. I don't ever remember not knowing. I don't remember ever not knowing. But does that even make sense to you?

Lee: Yes, that may be because your parents were so open about it.

Betty: When they were really young, we had birthday cake, and then we celebrated adoption day.

Lee: Oh, did you?

Dave: I don't remember that.

Betty: It was just a special dinner and then a cake or a pie, and saying, "This is the day we brought you home to us."

Lee: Because that would be the significant day for you, not his birthday.

Betty: Yes. For us, it was the adoption day.

Lee: The day you brought him home like everybody else.

Betty: Yeah, when you came to us. So that would probably be part of why it was such a normal thing because we certainly never ...we didn't proclaim it, but we certainly never hid it.

Dave: And that's just why, I don't say it's funny, but I say to the people when you finally find out, I still don't know why people care so much. But I can see their point, like it's just like all these years, I could've maybe looked. But to me, it's like life is good, life is good. But that's my perception, maybe sometimes life isn't so good [for me or others].

Betty: And that is one thing that I didn't want you guys to ever go through. There was one girl. She wasn't a good friend of mine, but I knew her and she was looking for something in the attic when she was seventeen, just before her graduation, and she found her adoption papers. I remember thinking about that and thinking they've got to know.

Lee: Oh yeah. I think it's devastating for people to find out by accident or their own way. A friend of mine's mom grew up thinking that her grandmother was her mother, but her older sister was really her mom.

Betty: That happened a lot I think.

Lee: And she would hear people talking, and when she walked in, everybody quit talking. She always knew something was wrong, and when she found out, she left home and lived with her big sister [mother]. But she had very significant issues around that.

Dave: That was almost the set up for me, had it gone that way. Like I wonder how that would've played out.

It Could Have Been a Train Wreck: Deciding on Adoption

Lee: I know. That could have been your situation.

Dave: Had your mom and dad said what they would be to me? Parents or grandparents?

Lee: I don't know for sure, but I think their idea was that they would be your parents, and I would be your big sister. And I would come home from nursing school on weekends or whenever and see you I guess. But I would have been your big sister, and my little sister Rae was only five years older than you, so you would have been her little brother. You would also have had three older brothers to boss you around. They were all good hockey players. Ha.

Betty: It could've worked.

Lee: Yeah, it could've worked, but I just don't know how exactly.

Dave: Yeah, it may not have gone well.

Lee: I don't know, because it was a small town, and everybody knew everybody, and everybody knew everyone's business. The community would have known who your biological mother and father were. And you would have had a lot of relatives around that you may have not known were your relatives. I don't know how that would have played out.

Dave: It could've been a train wreck really.

Lee: You may be right. I really never thought of it that way. There would have been a time though that you would have found out or been told I was your mother, not your sister. You know it really could've been a train wreck, but I don't know. No one knows; we can just imagine. And perhaps part of that is reassuring ourselves that I made the right decision.

Dave: It could've been, yeah. Maybe it would've worked, but it could've been a train wreck.

Lee: I was really young to make that decision on my own. But I look back and think I made the right decision.

So even now, after our time together and feeling better about my decision than I ever had, I still enjoy that reassurance. Perhaps now I can let it go.

Betty: A wise decision for a seventeen year old.

Lee: I was also stubborn. But as troubling as it all was, for some reason, I had a plan, and I sort of stuck with it. But probably it was the hardest for my dad because I still remember meeting mom and dad for brunch at Earl's, about fourteen years ago now, and you had just gotten in touch with me, and we were going to get together. I had told dad and showed him the picture of your family that you had sent and your son Tag was just a newborn. I showed Dad the picture, and he was looking at Tag and thinking it was you. He thought the little baby was you with the family that adopted you. I said, "No Dad, that's Dave with his wife and children." He said, "Oh" and started crying. I'm probably going to start to cry telling you this story. And he said, "I've always dreamt of this day and meeting him." So in a lot of ways he probably thought about you as much as I did.

Dave: If not more.

Lee: If not more.

Dave is very disappointed he did not meet my dad, and he has regrets about not pushing the process to move a little quicker to make that happen, and I have the same regrets. I often marvel at the connection Dave feels with my dad, his grandfather, despite the limited amount of information he has received and the limited stories he has heard. There are probably many more stories I could tell him. I loved my dad and admired his energy, his tenacity, his generosity, his love, his dedication to his family, and his commitment to his community and broader social and political issues. He was truly a Good Samaritan. He was also a socialist (a political lefty) and raised five children to follow in his footsteps. He was a true believer, supporter, and organizer for the cooperative movement, the Wheat Pool, and the Farmers Union. My dad cared, and he was always thinking of ways to make the world a better place and life better for others. I think Dave has a sense of that, and he wanted the opportunity to embrace his grandfather and spend time with him. Dave also knew how important it would have been for my dad to meet him, and that is Dave's biggest regret. In some ways he is a lot like my dad.

Dave: Would I have been his first grandkid?

Lee: Yes, for sure. You were his first grandchild. I can't imagine how hard that must have been for him now that I have my own grandchildren, and I am so attached to them.

Dave: Things could have been so different if you didn't give me up for adoption. I guess I probably would have played hockey, but my life circumstances and experiences would have been very different growing up in a small town with my grandparents acting as my parents.

I smile and think that perhaps Dave would have been raised a socialist, too.

Lee: Yes, I think that is very true but for sure; you would have played hockey. It was a big sport in my family and still is.

I have so many thoughts and feelings about Dave being adopted by my parents and how that might have played out. My parents were great, but I think there definitely would have been challenges from a rural upbringing perspective and an aging parent perspective. My parents would have been in their late forties when Dave was born. So again, I wonder but will never know if it would or could have been a train wreck after all. But I do know that Dave's life story so far has not been a train wreck. Dave has been very successful in his career in banking and investments; he is happily married and has a very comfortable and loving relationship with his children and his wife. He says that life is good, and I think that is obvious from my observations and my interactions with Dave and his family. And, of course, that is very comforting for me to know and absorb after so many years of worry about the unknown. But throughout all the happiness, I guess he still wondered about me, which is also very comforting.

It Was None of Her Business: Wrestling with the Social Services Person

Betty: You were about twelve years old when you asked if you could find your birth mom. I said, "Not yet because we have to go through social services and you have to be eighteen years old."

Lee: Do you remember, was there something that happened, or you were just curious.

Dave: I don't remember doing it.

Betty: You said, "Do you know where my mother is?" or "Do you know anything about my mother?" And I said, "Not yet." But I said, "When you're eighteen, we'll go to social services together, and we'll look into [it] then." But you never, ever mentioned it again.

Lee: And what happened when you were eighteen? Did you think of it again or were you just so busy?

Dave: I think I started to talk about it more but it was never that you could do anything about it, so I can't even remember, believe it or not, what made me do the first step. I remember my wife, Kari, saying health wise, but I don't ever remember saying, "I'm going to find my birth mom now."

Betty: There was somebody I think at work that had found her birthmother and she gave you the number.

Dave: You are right. That's what it was.

Betty: And you carried that number around for years.

Dave: The funny thing was as hard and as complicated as it was, I just didn't want to explain to somebody what I wanted to do, but as soon as I phoned that number, they knew exactly what I wanted, and I was put through to a social worker, and within probably a month, she was sitting in my office at my workplace, and she interviewed me and she said, "Well you have to do this."

[But then the social worker contacted you, Lee, and] got back to me and said, "Well I'm having troubles with this, Dave, I'm having troubles because she's questioning it and I think she's [a] little bit put-back because she's a little bit rude to me on the phone." I remember that.

Lee: She was so snoopy, and I said, "This is none of your business. Dave and I'll talk about this when I meet him." She seemed so curious and nosey; she wanted to know so many private things and I said, "That's none of your business; I'll tell Dave those things if I decide to do that, when I meet him." I teach communication skills at the university level now, and on reflection, I think her skills were quite poor. Mine probably were too. Ha.

Dave: And she was like, "I was trying to get some information but I'm not getting everything that I need so that I can move on." So I said, "What's the next step?" And she said, "You've got to write a letter."

Betty: I remember that.

Dave: And she said, "You can't disclose certain aspects so that she'd be able to find you." She was like, "Be careful, because as much as I like to quiz them up to know they're good people for you, to warn you, I couldn't get as much as I thought I needed out of her to give you that heads up."

Lee: That's unbelievable, that's not her job. She really got on my nerves. She was asking me weird questions and I said, "Is it really your job to find out if I'm a good enough person that I can meet my son?" Because by then, I was pissed off. She would ask me all kinds of questions, and I would tell her that I would discuss those things with you when I met you. She wanted us to meet in her office, and I said, "Dave and I will decide where we meet, and we do not need anyone else there. I am sure we can manage on our own." I think she was really snoopy and wanted to get in on the action.

Betty: Yeah, I remember you [Dave] said you weren't sure if [Lee] wanted to meet you but that was probably because the social worker was putting her off.

Lee: I really did want to meet you. And it's unfortunate she was giving you distorted information because that slowed the process down.

Dave: Yeah, the biggest regret I have of the whole process is that it took so long that I didn't get to meet your dad, my grandfather.

Lee: Yeah, and it was so close, so close.

Dave: And that's my biggest regret out of all of it ... your dad, just because you say that it was important to him. And as a dad now, I can see how that's important; at the time, I didn't. But the things that you would want to do, like to sit and have a talk. I bet a million bucks we could sit up have a drink at 9:00 p.m. and still be up at 4:00 a.m. because he seems like he's that kind of a guy that he would want to know everything.

Lee: Oh, he was; he was a super guy. You would have loved him. I sure did.

Dave: But I had to let it be for a while because [the social worker] was of the opinion that you weren't ready yet; you weren't sure. She basically said that she didn't have the information to legally tick off all the boxes before we met, but she encouraged me to write a letter but to be very careful about what I said.

Lee: When I got that letter, I don't think I told anybody. And I can remember I thought it was something else when I got that letter the first time and saw where it was from. I didn't think, "Oh my goodness, this is Dave or my baby or anything," but I still remember going up the stairs and putting it in my jewelry box after I read it and thinking, "Yeah, I need to deal with this later" because it wasn't what I had expected. It had gone on a long time too; it was like the first four to five years of wondering everyday if you were okay but then having to sort of sit on that. It was so surreal when I received your letter. I just wasn't expecting it.

Dave: I wish I would've kept track of that part, now that we're here. I wish I would've kept track of that more because there was lots of discussion between Kari and I about where it's at, and I thought that you probably didn't want to meet me.

Lee: Were you okay with that?

Dave: Totally. Like I told the social worker, "At least I made the effort." And I said, "Well, if she doesn't want to meet me, that's okay because, really, my main goal in this is to find out my past health history for my kids in case something is really wrong." So if she could just write a list of things that maybe were in the family that there was whatever, you know, diabetes or something and that was my biggest concern, [not] somebody that didn't want to meet me.

Betty: I remember when you said that, and I said, "Medical information is terrific, but if she wants to meet you, you have to because you opened the can of worms."

Dave: Yes. You made sure I was going to go through with it.

Lee: So the reason I was laughing when you said that was because I think the social worker told me you were just interested in the medical history and I was like, "He doesn't want to meet me anymore?"

I remember that communication and being somewhat surprised and hurt that perhaps Dave was not that interested in meeting me after all. The social worker had been less than supportive, but I knew I needed to be a bigger person and realize that meeting my son was what really mattered regardless of the social worker being so intrusive. She definitely put me off, but I must admit I was also a bit nervous about what our differences may be in how we viewed the world and life in general. As it turns out, we are probably not on the exact same page when it comes to politics for example, but neither are we at opposite ends of the spectrum, and overall we appreciate the importance and power of relationship and so in some ways our world views are very close. I have always loved Dave as a son but as I get to know him, I realize I really like him and I guess I will always feel gratitude to both Betty and Bob for raising our son to be such a good person, with such a great sense of humor, which may be partly nature, but it is evident it is probably nurture to a great degree. Dave and his family have a very similar sense of humor to my family. Dave looks a lot like my brother and also has the same dry wit. And Dave's parents also have a very optimistic and almost joyful and humorous approach to life and its circumstances. Dave is a very thoughtful and generous man, and I recognize some of the same values we share as a family. There is no clear and defining line between nature vs nurture, only a never-ending circle of all those biological and social factors that make us who we are.

Dave: I never thought of you [Lee] as what you really are because you always think of the worst, right. You would never think of somebody who is so accomplished. You could've been the prime minister of Canada, but I would not have thought there was that possibility.

Lee: But you were told or had thought that she's somebody that couldn't get a crib, so you probably thought like, down and out perhaps?

Betty: But with Dave, we did say that his mother wanted to be nurse, that you always dreamt of being a nurse. So I think that you guys always sort of hoped that had come true.

Dave: And it's not that [I] thought that [you] were down and out. [I] just never thought you had your life together because I was the initiator. I asked the social worker, "Could she ask to meet me?' and she said, "No". At the time, you could've asked, but if I wasn't registered as wanting to know, they wouldn't have contacted me.

Lee: That's unbelievable. They wouldn't have phoned you and said, "Would you like to meet your mom because she has been inquiring about you?"

Dave: No, they wouldn't.

Lee: I thought things had changed.

Dave: It's a little different now. But then, that's what she said, that was my initial contact, so I said, "Do you want me to register so that if she registers we could be matched up?' and she said, "Actually, if you initiate it, I can make a call to see if she's up to going to the next step."

And that's where it started, but you couldn't have made the first contact. So when she said that you could only inquire, I asked if you had, and she said you hadn't. So that was something for me to think about because had you not registered the thought, you obviously didn't want to inquire or meet me, so should I open that can? So the discussion with Kari and I was, do you open the can? And then it was more of a health thing when you didn't respond and that's really how it started; then [I] thought more of it and I thought less of it, then I thought more of it again.

Lee: So you were kind of back and forth a little bit.

Betty: I don't think you wanted to push it.

Dave: It was important to me, but I didn't want to push it. I wasn't going to make it to the point where I was disappointed. But I also don't think I could've gotten myself to be disappointed. I would be more disappointed now, knowing what I would've missed out on had I not forced the social worker because I kind of waited quite a while.

It Wasn't Me Who Was Smoking: Finally Meeting

Dave: I remember being in the hotel lobby waiting to meet you for the first time, and Kari was with me for the start of it, waiting. And I had no idea who was coming, and it's funny because we saw this lady, who meets your description, circling the block smoking like crazy, and we thought, "Well, that's got to be her. I can tell because she's looking for me, and she's not ready to come in." And then she never came around again. So Kari said, "Well, I'll just leave you be." So I went inside and waited. And then I went and looked at the TV and kept walking back to check if you were there and that's when you walked up. You were totally not what I expected, after I had seen the lady chain smoking. I still expected her to come through the door.

Betty: That's funny. I didn't ever know about the lady smoking.

Lee: That is too funny. What a good story.

Dave: Yeah, like just circling and talking and yelling and like kind of pissed off, like probably a normal person but pissed off because she couldn't make a decision or something.

Lee: Probably because she was trying to pick somebody up, and they weren't there.

Betty: It was good you finally met.

We have talked about this first meeting several times and I have also written about it in more detail (see Murray, "Secrets of Mothering"; "Secrets of an 'Illegitimate Mom'"), and we have always laughed about the circumstances and have usually learned about something new that happened each time we tell it. And today, I learned about the woman circling the block and now we refer to her as the "lady smoking,"—a family story in a way.

Lee: So that first meeting, I remember, I didn't feel awkward.

Dave: No, no, it didn't feel awkward. It felt just casual. I remember coming around the corner in the lobby to see if I could see you and then going back to check the hockey score on the TV down the hallway. And I remember you coming up and saying something to me.

Lee: Oh yeah, I remember saying, "Are you Dave?" You peeked around the corner, and I thought you were going to leave.

Dave: Yeah, I'd go around the corner, and I would look out to see if I could see anybody because I could see the seating area. I said I would meet you in the lobby so I could see from around the corner if anybody was sitting there. There was a couple times a person was sitting there and looking out the window, and I didn't know if that was you or not. So I would casually come up, look, and then go back. And you probably walked in as I went back down the hallway.

Lee: Maybe because I had just sat in the chair and then I saw you peek out once, and then when you peeked out again, I got up and walked towards you and said, "Are you Dave?" And then you said, "I was just the checking the hockey scores" or something. I don't remember where we went, but I remember we talked for a long time and then we met your wife Kari and your children, Hope and Tag, and went out for supper.

Dave: That's right, too, I had forgotten about that, because I had phoned Kari and said, "Are you alright with that?" Because I was fine, you were fine, but you had to remember, she wasn't in on the meeting, so she wasn't sure what to expect.

Betty: But I think if you were inviting her, she knew that it was going to be okay.

Lee: And there's that curiosity piece too, right?

Dave: At first, I wondered if you were even "all in" because you didn't say much, but you were listening. But my other thought was I might be failing here because if Kari was here she could talk to anybody about anything and then I could fill in the gaps. That's always been the way with us and part of it is socially. After I've been at work all day talking to people and talking on the phone, I love to sit and listen but I don't need to engage. So I maybe have a bad skill, but that's the way I am. But that's what I thought, and I knew that she was as interested as I was or more, and I don't want to take away from how interested I was to meet you, because that's right up Kari's alley—to learn about people—and it was her kids too that she was finding out about. Because I know when we went out for supper, it shifted more from you and me talking to you and her talking because she was able to ask those questions that were maybe awkward for me to ask, and she was also a mom.

Lee: And then when it was over. I just didn't want it be over because I wondered if I would see you again because I was always connected to you, whereas you weren't connected to me so much. I had been connected to you for a significant part of my life, and at the end of the visit, I didn't want to let you go. I wanted to put my arms around you and not let you go. It may be hard for you to realize that I really want to be with you as an adult and your family, but you are still that baby I left behind. And your children have grown up so quickly. I thought we had lots of time because Tag was just a baby, and I did not have other grandkids at the time.

Dave: But you met them at the right time because you aren't a stranger to them, which is weird because they will always be connected. Tag still thinks your son Jordan is a hero. Tag is thirteen now, but Jordan is still the dude. I still remember riding the motorcycle in the parking lot at Fuddruckers because he had his motorcycle there and hanging together and doing stuff together. Couldn't have met at a more perfect age for my kids. Hope has the memories, and Tag has the experiences that created the memories for him and then of course, Tag went and played at a hockey tournament and you and McLeay's [Lee's other son] family came to all the games. It was like really being their nephew and your grandson.

It was a day to be cherished, and I wonder if we will do it again sometime. It was so nice to be together. There were lots of laughs, stories, and connections made and we were just one big happy family for that weekend. It seems surreal now. I was there with two of my sons, Dave and McLeay, and their families (poor Jordan was away and missed all the fun), and my two sons talked about sports and jobs, my two daughters-in-laws chatted, and my four grandchildren played together as cousins, the older two entertaining the younger two. It felt very casual and relaxed and appeared to be a frequent occurrence, but once we returned to our homes and lives, it seemed different again—an odd sort of line to walk. Dave is my son, but the relationship I have with him is different than the relationships I have with my sons McLeay and Jordan. It is not less than, just different.

Happy Endings: Or New Beginnings?

Dave: Does it seem like fourteen years since we met?

Lee: No. It's gone way too fast for me.

Dave: I almost feel bad that we don't get together more when you say fourteen years. We don't get together enough. We have gotten together quite a few times, but we have to do better. We are just so busy.

Lee: I know because we are all too busy.

Dave: It's like today. I didn't know if I could've booked today off to come do this. I should though, and that's part of why I hired somebody to do more at work for me, an assistant.

Lee: But that's true because I remember thinking I was so excited about being a grandma because I was so busy as a mom and I was so excited about being a grandma. And I can remember thinking, "Wow, I really have two grandkids [Dave's kids], and we'll really get to know each other so well." But you don't because you don't see each other enough, you know.

Dave: And its actually silly people don't, you know.

Betty: Well I don't see enough of you, since Papa's been in the home. I don't go and look after your kids any more.

Lee: If Bob was here today, like this, what do you think he'd say? I guess there is someone else missing from this conversation.

Betty: He'd be all ready for it; he'd be very happy.

Dave: He would be prepared; he'd have notes.

Betty: Yeah, the old Bob would.

Dave: He would say if you were taking the time to do this, you deserve the best out of him. He wouldn't want to forget one thing because if he would've gone home and there was one thing that he'd forgotten, he would immediately pick up the phone and fill in the blanks. He was a perfectionist that way, building boats, building anything.

Betty: He'd be all for it and he would probably have some strange memories that you and I don't think about; he would've lapped this up, and thought it was a wonderful idea. Even just the reminiscing and that.

Dave: And one of the good, fun memories for me, even though it was so quick, was the Leaf game.

Lee: That was so much fun! We still all talk about that. I was with all my kids. It was great! And you made it happen, getting the tickets and everything—also, the weddings, hockey, and rugby games, convocations, and the occasional barbeque.

Dave: And [my] kids had so much fun.

Lee: I remember Hope being so shy, like such a shy little girl. And she really liked my daughter Eve I remember. But it's hard to think about them as [my] grandkids. Do you know what I mean?

Betty: I can imagine it would be, yeah. They are somebody very special, but who are they?

Lee: Yeah, but it's a different relationship because you know what kind of relationship you have as a grandma with your grandkids; it's very different than that. Because [I'm] Lee, not Grandma Lee like I am with Kori, Blake, and Britton [Lee's grandchildren].

Betty: Oh another story fitting into this one here today. A relative of ours had a baby, and he decided he could not marry the girl and that was quite a bastardly thing to do at the time. And his girlfriend gave the baby up for adoption. But they have met their child, and he has told them that they made the right decision, as he had a good life and loved his family.

Lee: That's good. So there are happy stories out there, whereas the literature leads us to believe that the moms in particular who give away their babies have many difficulties in life as a result. But I guess it was because they didn't have any free will in doing that or didn't want to.

Betty: Or were probably told they had to.

Lee: And *Philomena*, you know that movie, have you seen it? That brought all those stories out again about people getting their babies taken away and the consequences and trauma they endured.

Dave: But you only hear the bad stories because that's the one that puts the flag up; we never promote the good stories like yourself; you would just say, "Those are my kids."

Betty: Yeah, I wouldn't say, "And by the way they're adopted."

Dave: I think the good experiences probably outweigh the bad. When you think about how many people are adopted out there. How many do you actually know? And there are probably lots, like people that are really close to you, and you still don't know. It's because I don't put the flag up. I don't say, "Oh did you know I'm adopted?" Because to me, it's not part of my life, and had it not been for meeting you, it would come up way less because you wouldn't bring it up. There would be no need.

Betty: My nail tech that I've been going to for a good two years, maybe three now, I told her that I needed my nails done because I couldn't go to Saskatoon with what I had, and she said, "why are you going to Saskatoon?" And I said, "To see my son's birthmother" and she said, "What do you mean?" And I said, "All my kids are adopted." And she said, "Really, why didn't you tell me that before?" And I said, "Well I didn't really think it was important."

Lee: Because they are just your kids; yeah, that's just the way it is.

Betty: Yeah, so it came up because of today, but otherwise I would never have brought it up.

Lee: So do your children, Hope and Tag, ever say anything about you being adopted or about me or how that all fits together?

Dave: Yeah. Actually Tag is quite the comedian about that. He teases me about being adopted, and his mom always reminds him that he is from me, so his history or lineage is adopted, too. It's a topic that they would probably talk about as much as I do, just because they wonder and have lots of questions, and Tag always wants to know about Jordan and what he is doing.

Betty: Probably with your kids because it happened when they were fairly young. It's just like part of the woodwork sort of thing.

Lee: And same with you, like it happened when he was really young. So it's just been normal.

Dave: Yeah.

Lee: It sure is funny because like you said, there are lots of stories when it's not a happy experience or happy ending, but it sure is hard to find stories when it is. I know that we have all had our struggles, but our story around Dave's adoption and life story have been quite positive. Don't you think?

Betty: Yeah.

Dave: Yes, for sure.

Lee: But really, it's a pretty happy story I think for everybody.

No one could predict this happy ending or beginning. This time of sharing has given us all perspective and understanding of what it has been like for all of us within this adoption triangle, and Dave has come to understand more about his origin story and the thoughts, experiences, and feelings of his two moms. And as we end this portion of the conversation and prepare to go for dinner, the subject comes back to hockey once again.

Dave: I wish I played more. I love watching it too. I remember Miracle on Ice, the Olympics in 1980. I remember it because I sat in the basement with my dad and watched it sitting on the magic carpets. We didn't have much money so we went and got carpet samples and we kept getting more carpet samples and then put them all together. Who sewed them together?

Betty: I think we glued them.

Dave: Yeah, so we glued them down and that was our carpet in the basement—all carpet samples.

Betty: All different colours; it was lovely.

Dave: Yeah, but people thought it was kind of cool.

Betty: And we had baloney boats; it was getting towards pay day one time, and the kids loved baloney, so I was going to make fried baloney and Kraft Dinner for supper, with a slice of tomato, and it would be just perfect. So I had the baloney in my big frying pan, and I wasn't watching them carefully, and I didn't slit them, so they curled up. I put one on each kid's plate and filled them with macaroni and called them baloney boats. Well they loved it. They said, "Can we have baloney boats again mom?" I don't know if I ever perfected it.

I wish someone would have told me my baby grew up with magic carpets and baloney boats; perhaps I wouldn't have worried about him so much.

Works Cited

Murray, B. Lee. "An Autoethnographic Story of Abuse: Healing and Finding Hope Through a Sexual Health Promotion Project for Adolescents with Developmental Disabilities." *Journal of Forensic Nursing*, vol. 12, no. 4, 2016, pp. 203-07.

Murray, B. Lee. "Secrets of an 'Illegitimate Mom.'" *Journal of the Motherhood Initiative*, vol. 1, no. 2, 2011, pp. 137-47.

Murray, B. Lee. "Secrets of Mothering." Dissertation. University of Saskatchewan, 2010.

Murray, B. Lee., and Kerri Kearney. "Twice Shamed and Twice Blamed: Assumptions, Myths and Stereotypes about "Giving up a Child" and "Taking in a Child."" *The Mother-Blame Game*, edited by Vanessa Reimer and Sarah Sahagian, Demeter Press, 2015, pp. 237-55.

Chapter Seven

Three Mothers of a *Metis*: (Re)Creating Complex Origin Narratives

Michael Howard

While all origin stories contain a certain amount of narrative ambiguity, some lend themselves to the possibility of more involved and complex storylines. This is especially true in the case of people who are what Malea Powell terms as *metis*, those of mixed backgrounds. My oldest son, Justice, certainly reflects this term from multiple perspectives. Biologically, he reflects the American melting pot; his genetic composition is in roughly equal portions: Native Alaskan, African American, Caucasian, and Hispanic. Additionally, he is adopted, which leads to a different type of *metis* experience. This chapter explores the roles of the different mothers of my son (biological, state, and my wife) in shaping his origin story. The origin story of a *metis* can be incredibly rich because of the diverse possibilities forming their early chapters, especially in the case of someone with a broad background of multiplicity such as my son, which can, in turn, create the foundation for an intricate and beautiful life narrative. However, multiple entities may battle for control over the narrative threads of a *metis*, each having its own agenda and seeing the *metis* as a vehicle to fulfill that agenda. This chapter shows how the complexity of my son's experiences in forming his origin story became an empowering experience for him, as a *metis*, resulting in agency and self-control rather than disempowerment and loss.

When speaking of someone's origin story, it is tempting to treat it as a monolithic and linear singularity. A story, after all, is told within a chronological matrix (even if it is a fractured one or uses such things as analepsis and prolepsis) that has a beginning, a middle, and an end, and contains a narrative that is (usually) intended to be understood by an audience. The narrator (again, usually) provides reliable information, which the audience can trust to guide them in comprehending the events occurring within the narrative. Thus, a story is told that the audience comprehends, interprets, and forms opinions about. They may then debate its interpretation over half-caf, light-foam, hazelnut cappuccinos.

However, origin stories rarely comply with the formative efforts of such simplistic interpretive acts. Origin stories are usually messy and complex. Unreliable narrators provide misinformation, and they disguise facts of a given origin for their own causes. They hide guilt, disguise pain, run in fear, or engage in numerous other emotional or legal factors that create haze around the details (or even the main narrative) of an origin story. Information is lost, misplaced, or misinterpreted. Eventually, reality recedes to a mist of misinformation, rumour, and half-truth.

And that can be for just an average origin story.

Some origins are more complex: lineage is confused, multiple entities insert themselves (wanted or not) into the narrative, geography distances people from their origins, cultures vie for supremacy, and politics, laws, and traditions attempt to dictate the correct version of an origin. This chapter reflects my perceptions of the mothering tactics and strategies utilized by the three mothers of my son. Three mothers—or rather, three entities—functioned in some capacities as a mother in the life of my son, Justice. Specifically, I explore the roles they played in shaping, forming, and/or disguising his origin story.

Early on in our relationship, my wife Tammy and I determined that we wanted to adopt—not because we had fertility issues but because we recognized that numerous children in the foster care system needed forever homes. Also, we decided that we wanted to adopt before having biological children; we felt that coming into a preexisting family and attempting to establish themselves within that family could be difficult for a child. By adopting first and making that child the oldest sibling, we hoped to provide them a clear role within the family structure.

In 1999, we completed the preadoption process and were actively working with an agency to find a child. We experienced several near misses. For example, one night we received a phone call asking us if we wanted twin newborns, and if so, we needed to be at the hospital within the hour, since the biological mother was about to complete her labour. As we hurriedly rushed out the door, we received a second phone call saying that a family member had stepped up at the last second to take custody of the babies.

One morning, I awoke with the urge to go house hunting. Although we couldn't afford a home at that point in our lives (as Tammy insistently pointed out), my impulse was strong enough that we went ahead and scheduled some homes to view. At one of the homes, the current owner was still there, managing her family, during our house visit. As we browsed through the halls, we noticed the pictures hanging on the walls of her with several children, many of whom were not present. We inquired about them, and she commented that she was both a foster and adoptive parent. We then told her that we were currently foster licensed as part of our preadoption process and that we were actively seeking a child. Her eyes narrowed, and she quickly asked, "How old?" We replied that we were fairly open, but we were considering a range from newborn to six years olds.

Smiling, the homeowner said that her mother, Delores, was also a foster and adoptive parent. Currently, her mother had a one-year-old boy in her custody for whom she was seeking a permanent placement. She also had custody of his older brother who as a result of injuries suffered while in the custody of his biological parents had shaken baby syndrome. Because of Delores's age (she was in her early sixties), the older brother was going to be a lifelong commitment for her. Unfortunately, he would never be able to live independently due to the severity of his injuries; his brain damage resulted in numerous symptoms, such as severe developmental delays, difficulty walking, and intermittent spontaneous blindness. She took custody of the younger brother only after the foster family with whom he was placed had neglected him, leaving him in the crib all day without interaction and feeding him watered down formula. After several months of this neglect, he was diagnosed with failure to thrive. Delores agreed to care for him temporarily to rescue him from the situation he was in, but she was not in a position to maintain permanent custody.

Two days later, we met the one-year-old child. The bond between us was instantaneous. That day, he took his first steps—to my wife. We spent the next few weeks building bonds, and a few weeks later, we brought him home on Halloween. He's been our little treat (and trick) ever since.

Adoption brings several different entities into play who can, to varying extents, claim some portion of the role of "mother." All of them, to some degree, jockey for position to frame the child's origin story from their perspective. For purposes of this story, I focus on three individuals or entities that fulfill parts of this role for my son: his adoptive mother, his biological mother, and the state of Washington. Under this last category, I include all agencies and representatives who worked on the state of Washington's behalf, in this case including but not limited to, social workers, foster parents, state-paid doctors and therapists, lawyers, and the entire bureaucracy that goes into creating and sustaining the foster and adoption system. While I recognize that these various subentities may have their own, often conflicting, interests, within their larger context, they are unified enough for purposes of this text to be referred to as a singular unit.

When we gained custody of our son Justice, we received mountains of information; literally thousands of pages of documents were delivered to us. These ranged from analyses by psychologists on the biological parents to pre- and postnatal reports by paediatricians to observations by the drivers who brought him to visits with his biological mother. This compilation of documents provided the state-as-mother's version, or at least part of its version, of his origin story. This compilation, much like a book, formed a narrative, albeit a fractured one, which framed a particular and peculiar morphology of his identity up to that point.

However, much like with other narratives, there were counter-narratives formed and subsequently disseminated to us; in many cases, these were not conveyed through the written word but transmitted to us orally. These conversations occurred with social workers, foster parents, lawyers, and others who interacted either with him or with his biological parents; these verbal narratives were conveyed to us under a wide variety of circumstances, both formal and informal. Often, the verbal narratives ran contrary to those transmitted in the written documents, even though some were written by the same people. These contrary voices created a type of parent, in this case the state of

Washington, who seemed to suffer from dissociative disorder. As a mother, she was fragmented into numerous voices and personalities; all claimed to have the best interest of the child at heart, but not all shared the same opinion as to what that was or how to go about fulfilling that need even when they did agree.

These various voices spoke in different tones and volumes—some loudly and often, and others in whispers, barely intelligible. For example, at one end of the spectrum, there were dozens of pages written by the supervisory worker who brought my son to the meetings with his biological mother. These were carefully detailed observations of his physical, mental, and emotional state; his foster parents' attitudes; and descriptions of the events of the visit, including analyses of the biological mother and her live-in boyfriend's mental state. This was a loud, clear voice, which spoke frequently and with authority. At the other extreme, there was a single two-page report from a psychologist, who performed an analysis on the biological mother. This brief note was one of the few pieces of documentation of narrative elements that contained an overt warning about her mental health.

Verbally, many of the narratives we received portrayed the biological mother as a victim. According to these, she had suffered at the hands of her husband and had survived tough times, but she was trying her best to get her life together. Much of the documentation concurred with this assessment; she was flawed but conscientiously working towards improving herself. This narrative was used as a basis for suggesting an open adoption agreement with her, which we agreed to. We were told that having some kind of connection to the biological parents via an open adoption would help alleviate potential identity issues as my son grew up as well as provide us access to potentially important genetic information. This proved to be true, but it also opened the door for a horrific and damaging visit with his biological mother during his early teen years because of a lack of appropriate information about her. If we had received more accurate and less conflicting information from the dissociative state of Washington "mother," we could have made better decisions on behalf of our son. As new adoptive parents, we were inclined to trust a system we believed was designed with the best interest of the child in mind. We did not (although we probably should have) assume selfish motivation on the part of the state of Washington "mother." The fractured and frequently self-serving story from this one mother, the state of Washington (charged by public policy to encourage open adoption agreements) led to an incomplete narrative—one that disguised or even omitted certain elements contradictory to a pro-open adoption narrative.

Another narrative that the physical documentation and the verbal narrative from the state told us was about our son's ethnic heritage. The paperwork stated his biological mother was a mixture of white and Native Alaskan heritage, which she confirmed during preadoption conversations. It also stated that her husband was Puerto Rican, which she also confirmed. This mixed ethnic background qualified him as what Malea Powell terms as a *metis*—that is, one who is a hybrid or of mixed blood, although it literally translates as "son of the translator" (8). Powell describes the *metis* as a trickster figure, although in the positive sense. A *metis* has the ability to move among various groups with the right to claim agency in each of them. However, the *metis* is also a figure of ambiguity, moving among and through various groups without full incorporation into any of them. Powell claims the following: "the tricks reveal the deep irony that is always present in whatever way we chose to construct reality Trickster discourse ... exposes the lies we tell ourselves and, at the same time, exposes the necessity of those lies to our daily material existence. The trickster asks us to be fully conscious to the simple inconsistencies that inhabit our reality" (9). Our son, a *metis*, is a trickster. He fights against the inconsistencies of his origin story, points out the flaws, and moves among groups, sometimes freely and with a smile, sometimes with a tear. Ultimately, however, we believe that his story is his to tell.

Early on, all three mothers were involved in Justice's daily life and making decisions on his behalf. Because of his Native Alaskan heritage, his previous foster mother and his social worker informed us that we were required to keep his hair long and only trim his bangs. We complied, and by the time he was three, his hair grew past the midpoint of his back in long, luxuriant curls. One day, his daycare called us in a panic. He had taken a pair of scissors and cut off all of the length of his hair on the left side, making him look horribly out of balance.

We were dismayed. We worried that we may have violated some super-secret clause in our foster agreement that could jeopardize finalizing the adoption, since the adoption process was stretching out much longer than expected. We feared this could be regarded as negligence on our part in ensuring that tribal customs were upheld. Would the tribe now intervene? In a panic, we called the biological mother and nervously told her what had happened. We let her know that we would probably have to cut off the other side so that he would be balanced, but if she felt strongly about it, we would refrain from doing so and try to make it work. Laughing, she told us that it wasn't a big deal and that, quite frankly, she was relieved. In the tribe to which she belonged, men did not wear their hair long, and she hated the fact that his hair was down his back. The woman who fostered Justice prior to us was Sioux, and men of Sioux heritage often wear their hair long. Our relief was palpable as we finally exhaled our stress and felt relief that nobody was going to come knocking on our door to try to reclaim our son, nor were we going to be perceived as not upholding tribal customs.

Ironically, neither the social worker nor the foster mother, of Native American ancestry herself, had bothered to privilege the actual cultural heritage of this particular child; they knew what his background was but either did not know or care about Aleut traditions. Instead, they lumped all Native Americans together into a singular, undifferentiated mass, and assumed that he should have long hair because of his Native heritage. We were frustrated that they failed to recognize that many Native Alaskan tribes do not wear their hair long. While we were aware of this (I grew up in Alaska), we had received specific instructions regarding his hair care. Because men in Delores's tribe wore their hair long, his foster mother either assumed that all Native men must do so or she felt justified in imposing her cultural traditions on members of another tribe. My wife and I, unfortunately, assumed that they had done their due diligence and were correctly informing us about the specific traditions that we were legally obligated to uphold.

As "mother," the state representatives for our son did not recognize the relevance of his actual ethnic heritage as a pertinent factor in their treatment of him. Children in foster care are supposed to have exposure to their native heritage; however, as long as the exposure that he received would be recognized by the larger citizenry as native, then the details of such exposure were largely considered immaterial by the state mother. (In this case, "state mother" refers specifically to the state of Washington in its role as mother, although it could refer to any government body functioning in this capacity.) The state's primary concern was adhering to the prescribed formula to which it was held accountable. The actuality of the needs of the child seemed to be subsumed by the need of the state mother to legitimize herself in the eyes of those watching her.

This was not the only occasion that the state mother misled us in ways that were not in the best interests of our son. As we were attempting to finalize his adoption, I decided that I wanted to return to school to get my master's and doctoral degrees. We were living in the Seattle metro area, and the plan was to move to the Portland area where my parents lived so we could have some support while I attended classes. At this point, we were close friends with Justice's previous foster mother, who still had custody of Justice's brother. A rather controlling woman, she informed us that if we attempted to move, she would contact his tribe and get them involved to prevent us from moving. Additionally, she indicated that despite the documented information provided to us by other representatives of the state that stated Justice's biological father was full Puerto Rican, she knew that he was, in fact, also Apache and that she would bring representatives from the Apache tribe into play. At this point, we were unfamiliar with tribal politics and laws, and the threat of losing our son justifiably scared us. The verbal information delivered in a threatening format by a representative of the state mother overrode the physical documentation provided by other voices; the immediacy of the vocal information trumped the passivity of words on paper. While we thought we should win if she pressed the case, the chance of losing him was too much of a risk. Of the multiplicity of voices from the state mother, the one that threatened our son was the one we felt we had to listen to. The threat to him because of his *metis* status, not the reality of it, was used against us, and we did not understand how to work in his best interest at this point.

Unfortunately, this was not the only area in which the cacophony of contradictory voices ended up being problematic, both for us and for our son. As previously mentioned, we were informed that his biological mother's heritage consisted of Native Alaskan and Scottish ancestry, whereas her husband was Puerto Rican. As such, we attempted to expose Justice to cultural experiences from his ethnic background, including attending events, purchasing books, and getting decorations for his room associated with his heritage. We embraced his status as *metis* and wanted him to feel comfortable and accepted in all aspects of his heritage. As part of our adoption agreement, exposing him to his Native culture was a requirement, one which we fully supported and worked hard to fulfill.

Our adoption was finalized when Justice was four; this was a significant joy and relief for us, as it legalized our lived experience as a family. When he was nine, our home was seized by the local government using eminent domain laws. We lived off the main road that connected our town to the major artery of the Seattle metro area, and after the construction was complete, the road was going to go from being thirty-eight feet away from our house to approximately two to three feet from our front door. Needless to say, we needed to move. At this point, due to the previous threats by his foster mother, our relationship with her had become strained, and we did not see her often. We also felt confident that any attempt to disrupt our family would fail, since the adoption had been finalized for over half a decade and the previous foster mother had at one point considered moving to Arizona. As such, we decided to use the money from the sale of the house for me to begin my graduate work, which would entail relocation.

The problem we ran into was the timing of the sale, as it happened relatively quickly during the summer. Most graduate programs require application by January for the following fall. This would mean over a year before I could begin graduate studies in most circumstances. However, upon investigation, we learned that the University of Alaska Anchorage (UAA) had a rolling enrollment program that would allow me to apply in the summer to begin that fall.

A move to Alaska would have multiple benefits from our perspective. I grew up in Alaska, so we saw this as an opportunity to share some of my childhood experiences with our children (we now had another son and a daughter). Also, Justice was about nine years old at this point, and we viewed this as a wonderful chance to expose him to Native Alaskan culture and traditions in person.

The years we spent in Alaska were quite good for Justice. He had friends who were Native Alaskan, and he attended cultural events and museums. Rather than hearing about Native Alaskan culture, he was able to actively participate. His mother (my wife), Tammy, sought opportunities for him to interact with Native Alaskan culture. Although she was not Native Alaskan herself, she recognized and valued his Native Alaskan heritage, and she wanted him to value that part of himself as well. Unlike the state mother—to whom his specific heritage was irrelevant—Tammy felt that exposure to his Native Alaskan heritage was worth moving to Alaska. While this was not the only factor in our decision, it was certainly a prominent one.

The value that Tammy placed on this aspect of his heritage as well as the positive exposure that he received by being around Native Alaskan culture resulted in him having a positive attitude about this aspect of himself. He took pride in his Native Alaskan heritage. He self-identified as Native Alaskan when asked. This became a critical part of his claimed identity. Although he recognized his Puerto Rican ancestry, he did not as strongly identify with it. His exposure was only secondary (books, articles, etc.) as opposed to the primary exposure to Native Alaskan culture he received while living in Alaska. His prior foster mother's attempt to associate the man we believed was his biological father with the Apache had been exposed as a ruse over the period of about a year. As such, we had never attempted to build the Apache into his identity.

Additionally, Justice avoided association with his Puerto Rican heritage, since as he explained, it came from his biological mother's husband (whom we all believed to be his biological father), who was currently incarcerated for the sexual abuse of our son's half-sister and two other young girls. The social workers on his case also indicated their belief that this man caused Justice's brother's shaken baby syndrome. As such, our son attempted to mentally distance himself from this part of his heritage—not wanting to associate his identity with someone he perceived as a horrible person. As far as he was concerned, his *metis* status worked against him at this point in his life, which led him to embrace one part of his heritage while rejecting another.

After I completed my master's degree, I was accepted into a doctoral program in Tennessee. Remaining in Alaska for my doctorate was not an option, as there were no doctoral programs available in my area. The options to work with professors in the area I was interested in were limited, as I wanted to work in a relatively small niche: cyborg theory. Of the schools I applied to, Middle Tennessee State University in Murfreesboro not only was the best option for us financially, but it also offered multiple professors who could guide my research. The area we ended up living in was on the outskirts of a college town, so the school district we were assigned to was fairly rural. Unfortunately, rural Tennessee is not as progressive as the Pacific Northwest. Justice had not encountered racism up to this point. However, three days into attending his new middle school (sixth grade), he asked us what a "wetback" was. With a sigh, we explained the origins of the term: the derogatory expression for an undocumented Mexican immigrant who swam across the Rio Grande. He looked extremely puzzled, asking why anybody would call him that, since he was not Mexican. This discussion resulted in a more general conversation on racism—a concept that was largely unfamiliar to him, as he had never experienced it firsthand.

Unfortunately, this was far from Justice's last encounter with racism; much of it was directed at him because he was perceived as Mexican. He received insults such as being told to go back home and comments from his baseball teammates in clear hearing of his coach that he should retrieve the foul balls, since he was good at jumping over walls. We kept reminding him that the attempt to label him as Mexican, especially with the derogatory connotations, was not only inaccurate (although even if it were accurate, it would not impact his value as a person), but it was also a mark of ignorance and/or willful maliciousness. These comments were both misguided and hurtful, and we pointed to their ignorance by showing that the people making the offensive remarks were unaware of his actual heritage, as they focused not on what his apparent heritage was but only that it was not white. Ironically, the largest blood quantum he possesses is, in fact, white, but this is not reflected in his physical appearance, which is all that these children cared about. His *metis* status was irrelevant to them; however, we encouraged him to continue embracing it, as his unique background was actually a blessing. It allowed him the opportunity to draw on a variety of viewpoints and cultures to shape his identity.

A few years later when Justice was fifteen, his biological mother told us that she had developed stage-3 cancer (although we later discovered that she was lying about her condition). Realizing that he might not have a chance to see her again (depending on her prognosis), we made arrangements for her to come to Tennessee. We believed this would give him a chance to visit with her and possibly get some closure if she did not survive. When she arrived, we discussed her family medical history, as we wanted to get an idea of what genetic issues may run in her family, especially since she suffered not only from cancer but also from lupus.

She shared various issues faced by her family, and we then asked if she had any knowledge of her ex-husband's family's medical history; that information would be useful as we tried to put together a medical profile for our son.

She looked at us curiously, and then cautiously asked us if we knew that her former husband was not Justice's biological father. Although this was vaguely hinted at by his previous foster mother, we were a little taken aback. There were literally hundreds of pages in Justice's file which referred to her ex-husband as "the presumed father"; none that we could remember identified anyone else as even a remote possibility. Justice's birthmother told us that during the time she conceived Justice, she and her husband were never intimate, but she was having an affair with a younger man. He was in no position to be a father, as he was exceptionally young and had no real financial prospects. At the time, she was also in the process of losing custody of her older two children for failure to protect them, as her husband had sexually abused Justice's half-sister and physically abused his brother. Eventually, she divorced her husband. Since she was married to her husband at the time of conception and delivery, the state of Washington required that he be listed as Justice's presumed father even though she told the workers that he was not the father. This measure ensures that there is a financially responsible party for the child, other than the mother, for the government to pursue for remuneration of expenses related to the child's upkeep. As such, the vast majority of the paperwork from the state mother reflected this legal position. Upon further review, we were only able to locate a single document that suggested that a different man could be Justice's father: a note from a therapist indicating that his birthmother hinted in one session that another man could have possibly been the father. This lone slip of paper was the only suggestion by the state mother that the identity of the man presumed to be the biological father of our son was in doubt.

A core cause of this rather apathetic reaction towards identifying his actual biological father seemed to lay in the state mother's self-preservation instinct. Economically, the ability to designate financial liability for the child on an individual removes such accountability from the state mother, consigning it instead to the presumed father. This paradigm eliminates the necessity of establishing actual paternity, as the law voids this requirement. The supposed relationship between the purported father and the child is subsumed by the relationship between the husband and the mother; the child's relationship with the presumed father is established through a shirttail relationship, flowing through the mother. Despite the lack of a proven relationship, the supposed paternal connection is treated as equitable to that of the child with the mother, unless there is a genetic test that proves a different father.

Additionally, labeling somebody as "father" satisfies society's need to establish a familial unit. Whether or not there is an actual genetic bond between the child and the presumed biological father, the establishment of a legal relationship creates the impression of a nuclear family. This satisfies the social need for a so-called normal family unit. The social order demands a complete family, especially for those in vulnerable positions. This law satisfies the social compulsion through the illusion of a complete family without the necessity of one actually existing.

The state mother's slapdash approach poses the potential to create difficult identity issues for children under its care. Important components of our son's identity were built around the information provided by the state mother. For over a decade, he believed his biological father was also the man who sexually abused his half-sister and supposedly physically abused his brother to the point that he had shaken baby syndrome. This connection to a person who was so abusive created difficulties for our son; the fact that he was connected to him at all was a sore point for him. Although he embraced his Native Alaskan heritage, any attempts on our part to help him connect to Puerto Rican culture was met with resistance or dismissiveness. As it turned out, the man who was his biological father was not Puerto Rican; his heritage was an equitable mix of African American and Mexican. We discovered that his biological mother's husband was not his father and that his ethnic heritage was vastly different than he had previously thought. His biological brother was suddenly his half-brother. The abusive man with whom he associated his own biology no longer held any connection to him except through the damage he had done to Justice's other relatives.

While Justice's lack of biological affiliation to his originally presumed father was a significant relief to all of us, his actual biological father was small improvement. Our son made an initial contact with him through Facebook, which led to various phone conversations; from these, he learned that he had several more half-siblings. In addition, his birthfather admitted to being a gang enforcer, hinting that he may have committed multiple murders in service to his gang. Unfortunately, our son's initial hope for improvement in this area of his origin story was swiftly dashed. His biological mother's revelation of this aspect of his history, intended to be a kindness, was really just a transfer of issues; he moved from one monstrous biological father to another. This did little to help him positively embrace himself as *metis*, but it caused him yet again to reject part of his biological heritage.

Additionally, Justice's visit with his biological mother was disastrous in ways that I will not elaborate upon here; it caused him to reject her and, by extension, the biological aspects of himself that he associated with her. As parents, we struggled to find ways for him to reconcile not with her but with himself. This has been a process that is on-going to this day. We hurt along with him and try to find a way to assuage his damage. The conflicting information—or perhaps more accurately not enough counter-narratives to the main victim narrative about her mental health—provided by the state mother caused us to put more trust in her than we should have. The characterization of her as victim within the narrative was supplanted during this visit by one of cunning manipulator and predator. He subsequently struggled with an identity crisis, as he now rejected the biological mother as well as father and tried desperately to locate himself within this biological cataclysm.

Tammy was exceptionally supportive of Justice during this period. She pointed out his ability to control his narrative; his origin story was irrevocably linked to biology, but it also included choices. While this was something she previously emphasized, rethinking his biological father's identity and eliminating all contact with his biological mother opened a new thought process, permitting him more control over his own origin story grounded less in biological connectivity and more in chosen relationships. During this time period, the fact that we chose him became more significant to him than his genetic connections. This approach provided him more control over who he wanted to be. Decisions became the formative factor in controlling not only who he wanted to be but who he was.

His newfound diversity also reemphasized his *metis* status. Coming to an understanding of what his heritage was not and then coming to an understanding of what his actual heritage was allowed him to come to grips with his *metis* identity. With support from both of us, but especially his mother, he was able to accept his genetic heritage without associating them with his biological parents. He now enjoys bragging about *metis* nature, joking that when he fills out a form, he gets to check every box.

As captain of his rugby team, Justice uses his position as *metis* to associate freely and easily with players from a variety of backgrounds. During one practice, some of the Hispanic kids were joking about being Mexican, and he joined them. When some of the African American kids made rejoinders about being black, he said that he was Black too. I was coaching, and both groups looked at me questioningly. I just nodded affirmatively. He uses his *metis* status to move easily between these groups and help forge links not only with himself but among various members of the team. He no longer views his diverse background as something to be ashamed of; he takes pride in being able to move between different groups of people and help them communicate. Despite a circuitous journey, he has come into his own self-determined identity.

The only way Justice was able to accomplish this level of control over, and comfort with, his identity was through the encouragement of his mother to write his own origin story. In his case, it would have been easy to allow the state mother or the biological mother to dictate that narrative, and to varying extents, they did for a number of years. For that matter, it would have been equally easy for my wife to attempt to control it—whitewashing all traces of his biological mother and state mother from his narrative and pretending that they were not factors in his origin story. However, by empowering him to determine to what extent they are featured in his narrative, he was granted agency to understand the roles they played in his early chapters and also how to manage them as he writes the rest of his story. He is no longer merely the subject of his story; he is its author.

I write this chapter as someone who is biologically male and identifies as strongly masculine. I am a former Marine, a current hard-charging rugby coach, and a type-A personality. I am also a feminist scholar, relatively empathetic, and have been known to quietly shed a tear at odd moments while watching Disney cartoons. However, I am neither biologically nor temperamentally a mother. This chapter is written from the perspective of an outsider to that role. As my son has gotten older, learning to support him in his choices while still guiding him is challenging. He is *metis*, a position with which I have no lived experience. He experiences difficulties at times in this role, sometimes embracing negative stereotypes portrayed in the media or struggling to fit in with different groups. And because I have not had the same experiences, I occasionally lack clear direction in guiding him. Because of Tammy's empathetic qualities as his mother, she often has more success in providing counsel than my frequently blunt and direct instructions. I am often directive rather than supportive (although I have improved over time in this regard), and while this assertive role can have positive functions in the family dynamic, in the case of a *metis*, such as our son, this role often does not permit the kind of self-directed narrative creation that allowed my son to take full agency in his own tale. I learned from my wife how to, at times, become more supportive and less directive.

As Justice continues to mature, he increasingly controls both his own origin story and the chapters that follow it. Any narration is simply the selection of specific elements from innumerable possibilities; those elements selected by the author could have just as easily been any number of other possibilities. For example, rather than telling the story from Harry Potter's perspective, Rowling could have chosen Hermoine's vantage point. *Star Wars: A New Hope* did not tell the story of the Bothan spies; eventually, *Rogue One* told that story. These elements selected tell a specific story; had other elements been selected, they would have told a different story taking place in the same world. For a *metis*, the possibilities for selecting narrative elements to tell their origin story are multiplied. As parents, our roles become that of helping Justice select the narrative elements from the numerous possibilities available to him and to discard others that he determines are not the ones upon which he wants to build; we all do this. We remember certain experiences and identities, deemphasize others, forget some, and latch on to the ones that we decide matter. For a *metis*, and in particular for my son, this process involves sifting through significantly more options, many of which may seemingly contradict or collide with others at first glance. The child must eventually resolve these apparent contradictions to create a unified narrative, and the mother can be an important part of helping the child select the narrative strands and bring them together into a cohesive story. Tammy empowered Justice to select his own narrative strands and from them weave his own increasingly complex origin story. Through active listening, embracing him for his choices, and accepting his *metis* nature, she became both a guide and companion on his road to agency.

All stories begin with early chapters and become more complex as new narrative elements are introduced. As a mother, my wife has empowered Justice to select the narrative elements he will utilize from his early years to open his tale; he will build upon these early narrative chapters to tell the remainder of his story. His options for telling these early chapters are more voluminous than others because of his *metis* status, and there is no formulaic methodology to synthesize the narrative elements he selects as there often is with non-*metis* stories. This means that his tale will not fall into a traditional narrative pattern, but so what? He gets to tell a story that is more unique and do it in his own way. After all, it is his story to tell.

Works Cited

Powell, Malea. "Blood and Scholarship: One Mixed-Blood's Story." *Race, Rhetoric, and Composition*, edited by Keith Gilyard, Boynton/Cook, 1999, pp. 1-16.

Chapter Eight

Once Upon a Time: Storytelling Origin Stories

Kerri S. Kearney

When my husband and I started the process for adopting our first child sixteen years ago, I voraciously read the literature that was available at the time. Of particular interest to me were open and closed adoptions and all of the various possibilities in between. Whatever the agreement we made with the biological parents, I was sure about one thing: I would be honest with my child about his or her origins. I very much wanted my child to know we could (and that I would) talk honestly about the hard things. After all, life does tend to serve up a variety of challenges.

Our first child was a boy, for whom at least initially we had an open adoption agreement with his biological parents. It wasn't always comfortable or easy, but it was something I felt committed to and that I believed was in the best interests of my son. Because I never wanted his adoption to be a surprise to him, I thought deeply about how to begin to introduce his origin story in ways that made sense for his age. I gathered and set aside numerous ideas.

Likely because I am a writer and reader myself, I finally chose to write a child's book, appropriate for a young toddler, which told his story in simple terms. His book, *All about Me*, used scrapbook type figures and decorations to represent key people who were a part of his origin story. Only a simple sentence or two appeared on each page. I had the story and pictures bound into a hardback book. My son loved seeing his book and often pulled it off the shelf where it sat with all of his other books. Because of my son's excitement about having a book that was about him, I later wrote another book, also hardbound, about him and his favourite stuffed animal, "Mr. Cow." He had great fun posing with Mr. Cow for real photos for this book. And, again, it became a favourite on his shelf—really it was even more of a favourite than the first book because he recognized himself and Mr. Cow in the photos.

When our second child was born, a daughter who was also adopted, I felt more confident that embedding her origin story into a children's book was the right initial communication step for our family. Based upon her biological mother's requirements, her adoption was closed. At age two, my daughter became captivated by fairies and fairy families, so I used the facts of her origin story to create a book about a fairy that I called *Little Faerie Princess*. Her origin story was less straight forward than my son's, so I wrote a more complex story suitable for an older toddler or young child. Based upon my son's reactions to his book with actual photos, I inquired about a student artist with the art teacher at the high school I graduated from. I hired a young woman, Kira, who was a senior at the time and a very talented artist. I provided her with pictures of our family to guide her illustrations and the children's story I wrote for my daughter. I also described my daughter's biological mother, whom I met only one time. I can't even possibly explain how amazed I was with the beautiful illustrations Kira created. Each was on its own art board and, after digitally scanning them for my daughter's book, I carefully packed and stored them in a safety deposit box at the bank so that my daughter would later have the original artwork.

Again, I had my daughter's book bound with a hard cover and placed it among all the kids' books. Like my son, my daughter was openly captivated by her book. She loved to have it read to her, but I would also sometimes find her sitting cross-legged with her book in her lap, just looking at the beautiful illustrations.

For the purposes of further discussing this practice of embedding my children's origin stories in children's book, I have chosen to share the actual story and illustrations from my daughter's more complex book (with her name changed). While it saddens me to print these beautiful illustrations in black and white, I hope that readers will still enjoy them as they imagine them full of colour and in the hands of a small child.

Little Faerie Princess

By
Mommy

Illustrated by
Kira Holzer

2006

For my precious girl.

I'm sure that someday you will ask
"But what makes a real mother?"
Is it biology?
Is it love?

And you will search for the answers you need
Without realizing that you are holding my whole heart
In your hands.

So in case I find myself unable to speak then
I will try my best to explain to you now
That it is a love and a tie that defies description
By any words
By any person.

I can only say to you, my precious girl,
That when you laugh,
My whole world brightens.

And when you cry, my heart breaks too.
When you hold my hand, I feel strong enough to take on
Anything and anyone,
For you.

It is in becoming a mother
That I finally understand the true significance of the words
"I would die for you"
Without hesitation, without a thought.

There will always be things in life
That are difficult to understand.

But one thing you can always count on
Is that I am,
And will be,
Here for you always.

Because
I am,
And will always be,
Your mother.

Once upon a time, there was a faerie named Katherine. She lived under a big green leaf in a beautiful field of flowers near an enchanted forest.

And, like most faeries, she loved to sing and dance.

One night under a full yellow moon, Katherine went for a walk, weaving around the fluffy toadstools and stopping to smell the flowers. She came upon a gathering of her friends and joined in their dancing and singing, swooping delicately here and about on her wings of gossamer, red hair flying out behind her.

Soon she caught the attention of a young faerie boy, a stranger who was just passing by. He was mesmerized by her, and soon he joined her in dance.

As the evening deepened into nighttime, the other faeries
silently faded away leaving just the faerie Katherine and the dark faerie
boy. Together they danced the night away.

And by morning, he was gone . . . leaving nothing behind,
not even his full name.

Weeks later, Katherine felt the delicate flutter of little faerie wings deep inside of her. And she knew immediately that in that one night with the dark faerie boy, they made a little faerie princess.

But Katherine was betrothed to another, and so she believed she must choose between the future she wanted and the baby she had made.

As the days passed by, Katherine made her choice. She would continue with her life as she had planned . . . without the faerie princess. By then, Katherine had grown heavy with the baby and no longer could dance gracefully with the other faeries. And so she worried and waited.

She did not know who would raise and love the little faerie princess.

One night under a full moon, Katherine sat watching her friends gracefully dance. And she cried tears of regret.

She knew not what to do.

Soon she looked up to find that a wizened old faerie had silently appeared beside her. He smiled gently and sat down. "I come with the knowledge of the destiny for the little faerie princess you carry," he said.

And Katherine's breath caught in her throat as she waited.

The wise, old faerie man continued, "There is a house not
far from here that is filled with light and love, where the mother and
father are searching for the daughter they
know is theirs. They know not where and they know
not when but still they search, and the mother's heart calls out for
her baby, every night without fail. Listen carefully
and you will hear her."

And Katherine listened but she heard nothing.

She opened her mouth to speak and the wizened faerie man hushed her and said, "Patience, my dear. You cannot listen with your ears, you must listen with your heart."

And so Katherine fell still and silent and she felt the gossamer wings of the baby move restlessly inside her. And then she heard the sad notes of singing, filled with the longing of a mother, that were carried to her with the wind.

And deep within her, Katherine felt the baby faerie princess
grow quiet and peaceful.

And she knew with certainty that the faerie princess had quieted to the
sound of her mother's singing. And she knew it was up to her to
take the faerie princess home.

Sunrise the next morning found Katherine with the wizened little faerie traveling forth from the forest to find the mother and father of the faerie princess baby. As evening fell, the wizened little faerie led her to a neat little house and settled gently upon the window sill.

Katherine looked at him with surprise. "Mortals?" she asked with no small amount of dismay. "Not a faerie family?"

"Just look inside," said the wise little faerie man.

So, Katherine peeked inside the window where she saw a cheery fire burning and a mommy and a daddy playing with a small, blond little boy. And as she watched, she could see the love that hovered around them, lots of love—more than enough for another child.

"It is still your choice, my dear," said the faerie man. "You will choose the future of the faerie princess you made. You may insist that she remain a little faerie or you may be brave enough to guide her to her true destiny, to the family that waits and longs especially for her, to a family who will give her all their love."

Katherine, confused and unsure, watched the family most
of the night . . . through the dinner they ate together,
through the kisses and warm hugs, until the little blond
boy was tucked deep into his bed. And then she heard the sweet, sad
notes of longing for her daughter but, when she looked closely, the
mother's mouth was still.

She turned in confusion to the wise little face beside her. "It is not
her. She is not singing."

"Ahhhh, but she is," the old faerie man assured her with a soothing smile, "A mother does not become a mother with her voice or because of her body, she does so with her heart."

"And if you will but listen with your own heart, you will see that it is this mother's heart that calls out, again and again, for her daughter."

And, as Katherine turned back to the woman, her heart did hear. And she knew with absolute certainly that this was faerie princess' real home. Katherine smiled in peace, knowing she would do what had to be done to give the little faerie princess her family . . . her destiny.

When she turned back to the wizened faerie, the space was empty. He was gone.

And there came upon the wind a trilling of trumpets and the tinkling of
piano keys and, when Katherine looked down, she
saw that her body had become mortal.

She glanced frantically behind her but the beautiful gossamer wings were
gone and long red, mortal hair curled around her shoulders.
And as panic set upon her, she felt the joyful dancing of little hands and
feet inside of her, and she calmed with knowing that
this was the path that she must take.

It was only a few weeks later that a baby girl was born. With hair threaded with red and gold and with eyes of blue, the beautiful little girl was placed in the waiting arms of her mommy and daddy, who called her Ava.

And her mother thought she saw a bit of gold dust fall from the flutter of the baby's eyelashes but, then she blinked, and it was gone.

The next morning, and only after many requests, Katherine agreed to see
the mother and the sweet baby girl . . . but just this once.

In the quiet, soft light of her room, Katherine could see that the mother
and the little faerie princess were surrounded by a gold
glow of love. And she was reassured that her journey had brought
Ava to the place she was meant to be.

Katherine heard the soft, lilting chorus of three hearts rising to the ceiling of the room, notes of peace and joy. And finally she lightly touched the soft head of the faerie princess and wished her Godspeed and great love in her life ahead.

By noon Katherine's room stood empty, and the little faerie princess was on her way home to begin her life with her mommy, daddy, and big brother.

As Ava grew into a little girl, sometimes she's sure she hears a particular set of musical notes sung by a delicate voice.

And sometimes she thinks she sees just a small flash of gold light beside her but, when she turns around, nothing is there.

And her mommy and daddy just smile, pat her little back as she drifts off to sleep, and send her into sweet dreams of fairies dancing and singing.

Ava is safe; she is secure; she is loved; she is their precious little faerie princess.

As my daughter's story closes, it seems an appropriate time to consider some of the implications of writing children's books based upon factual, and sometimes difficult, origin stories. For example, it may be that some readers, who are familiar with the adoption literature, are concerned that children who were adopted are often known to struggle with idealizing or fantasizing about their biological family members. The practice or mode of storytelling through a printed children's book, arguably, could enhance this tendency.

I shared this concern when I wrote the first book for my son. I felt even deeper concern when I actually did write a fairy tale for my daughter. I admit it was a calculated risk—one for which I weighed out what I believed to be the potential strengths and challenges. I was never sure, as a mother, how to begin to share some of the difficult facts of my beloved children's origin stories. I strongly believed that the facts of their origin stories, as best I knew them, were rightfully theirs. I believed that the stories I wrote for them, which were deeply threaded with these facts, could create conversation that over time and with age and maturity would lead to the open communication that I believed was in the best interests of my children. And there were times as an older child that my daughter did ask questions about what was real in the book, and I always answered those as clearly and honestly as I had the information for while also considering her age.

In addition, I want to be careful not to present myself as some sort of ideal mother who adopted and never had a twinge of resentment or fear about the ties that my children had to other parent figures. I absolutely had those concerns, even some jealousy sometimes that other women did things for my children that I did not—that they have certain types of ties to my children that I will never have. There were times when I wanted to scream, "No, these children are mine, and no one else gets to have any claim to them!" And I sometimes imagined future fears when my children may want to know their biological family members. When my son was young and problems in the lives of his biological parents began to arise, I once insisted that we install a full security system that included all of his bedroom windows. For some reason, during that period of time, I dreamed that his biological parents stole him in the night, despite having no real foundation for my fears.

So in addition to laying the groundwork for open discussion about their origin stories, the writing of the stories was also a type of accountability system for me to assure that my children's stories about other central figures in their origin stories were told. As I reread their stories now, however, I recognize that some threads of my fears still entered the stories. For example, in my daughter's book, the mother-child relationship is presented as preordained, as if her birthmother's only real job was finding her child's real mother. And this, indeed, is a common reassurance given to children who were adopted, and, I admit, it is also reassuring for me—a mother who does believe that these exact children were intended for me.

After our third child was born, a biological daughter, I again wrote a children's story using real photos. But this time, I wrote a story that featured all three children and about how real families get made in all of their myriad ways. Again, it was also a teaching book intended for children. And, again, all three children loved their book, which was on the shelf with all of their other books. We would read it together or, as they grew older, they would read it and point at the pictures and laugh together in moments of sibling bonding that, as their mother, I wholly treasured. It was their shared story. By this point, I was feeling relatively confident that this pathway of using children's stories had served the purpose I hoped for it.

However, when my third child was about three, she informed me of her dissatisfaction with not having her own book—one that was just her story like her brother and sister had. And she was right. I let my original intent for the book to lay the foundation for telling difficult origin stories for my children who were adopted cloud my thinking about the importance of origin stories for all of us. My third child also had an origin story quite worthy of a children's book. So I set about writing her story too, and it was illustrated, hardbound, and happily embraced by the child it was written for, and shelved with all of our other children's books. Based upon her childhood nickname, it was called *Our Precious Little Bella Boo*.

Each of my children, regardless of the complexities and details of their origin stories, seems to treasure their books even as early teenagers. Each now has his or her copy stored in a baby box of treasured items from childhood. But some extra copies are still on our shelves. For my son and older daughter, conversations about their biological family members and origin stories ebb and flow, depending upon their interest and/or questions at any given time. My third child also asks about her origin story almost as often. Each of my children, like every individual, has their own unique entry story into this world—each of them worthy of a book.

As I was writing the first draft for this chapter, my older daughter, now age thirteen, wandered into my office. I asked her if she remembers ever thinking that she really was a fairy. Just the mention of her book caused her face to light up and a big smile. She said that she did once think she really was a fairy, but as she grew older, she realized that it wasn't real because fairies aren't real. I asked her if she ever felt hurt or concerned about how I initially positioned her story—as a fairy tale. She just smiled and said never. As she grew and learned more about the facts of her origin story, she recognized the ties to her book. Her origin story, even the hard parts, has always been familiar, not strange, and never hidden. Her origin story is just a part of her. And that was the point all along.

As I reflect on the roles and reactions of each of my children to their story books, I recognize that each of them has responded quite differently. As noted, my older daughter, who was adopted and is now a teen, is overtly positive about her book and knows where her copy is. She is a child who almost never refers to her adoption and, even when information is offered, rarely chooses to receive the information. It seems that the story in her book and early clarifications of it have provided her with all of the information she wants for now. Hers is a story she holds closely to her and about which she is very private.

My son, also a teen now, remembers his books positively but has no idea or concern for where they are. He is quite open about his adoption with us and others and occasionally launches into a series of origin story questions for me. For him, his books seem to have served as a jumping off point for further detailed discussion as he grows older.

My youngest child was the biological child who pointed out to me that she wanted her own book with her origin story (like her brother and sister), but as a preteen today, she seems to have forgotten the book exists. However, she smiles and rereads it when I presented her with it again. It appears that, for her, the creation of her book may have been more about affirming her equal specialness with her siblings (who already had books) rather than a need to have the details of her story written down.

These three very different responses to origin stories in children's books suggest to me that a child's response will likely be as different as the children themselves. But I do note with some relief that all of my children received their books and view their books positively, and given the complexities of motherhood and the rarity of right answers, that is, in itself, a relief. For our family, the act of writing down, illustrating, and binding all of our children's stories seems to have given their origins their respectful and rightful place in the rich tapestry that is our shared family story.

Postlude

Kerri S. Kearney and B. Lee Murray

All secrets come out eventually, if not in the telling then in psychosomatic responses, emotional disruptions, or inappropriate behaviour and reactions. Clarissa Pinkola Estes explains what happens when a woman finds her secret leaking out:

> She runs after it with great expenditure of energy. She beats, bundles, and burrows it back down into the dead zone again and calls her homunculi—the inner guardians and ego defender—to build more doors, more walls. The woman leans against her latest psychic tomb, sweating blood and breathing like a locomotive. A woman who carries a secret is an exhausted woman. (378)

And we may be exhausted, but we learn from our experiences. The authors in this volume have told their stories and hard truths, and they have become fierce and less afraid. They have fallen down, been bruised and injured, but they have stood up again, come back and have brought something good with them. They have found meaningful ways to share origin stories with their children and they continue to "run with the wolves."

Here are additional suggested questions for reflection:

1. What secrets of mothering are you still holding because of the normative discourse of the good mother?
2. How can you craft your own stories, or share your hard truths, in ways that matter for you and others?

Work Cited

Pinkola Estés, Clarissa. *Women Who Run with the Wolves: Myths and Stories of the Wild Woman Archetype.* Random House, 1992.

Notes on the Contributors

Evonne Garnett is an English and Psychology teacher and has taught all grades from kindergarten to university. She has a Bachelor of Education specializing in middle years' education, a Post-Graduate Diploma in Exceptional Education specializing in giftedness and language-learning disabilities, and a Master of Arts in Integrated Studies focusing on the connections between narrative and wellness.

Kate Greenway, MEd, PhD, has published on adoption in *Ephemera Journal*, *Adoption Constellation,* and in several Demeter Press anthologies; she has also presented at many MIRCI, NeMLA, and ASAC conferences. She has exhibited her adoption-themed glass art at the American Adoption Congress juried group exhibition (San Francisco), and as solo shows at the Samuel J. Zacks Gallery (Toronto), Toronto Public Library, and the M.O.M. Art Annex (St. Petersburg). Her awards include York Graduate Development Fund for Research; the *Toronto Star*'s Teacher Honour Roll; the inaugural MIRCI Outstanding Graduate Student Conference Paper; and the York Alumni Excellence in Teaching award.

Michael (Mick) Howard, PhD, is an assistant professor and writing center director at Langston University, located just outside of Oklahoma City. He earned his PhD in English from Middle Tennessee State University; while pursuing his degree, he created and co-organized the international conference Catwoman to Katniss: Heroines and Villainesses in Science Fiction and Fantasy. As a result of the conference, he co-edited a volume of essays titled *The Woman Fantastic in Contemporary American Media Culture*. His current research includes explorations of cyborg theory and its relationship to semiotics, webcomics and their social influences, and writing centers' impact on campuses.

Kerri Kearney, MBA, EdD., is an associate professor of higher education and student affairs at Oklahoma State University. Her professional experience is in both education and organizational consulting. Her research focuses on foster alumni (former foster youth) college students and other hidden college student populations, organizational issues, the role of emotions in human transition, mothering, and arts-based methodologies in qualitative research. She is the founder of the R is for Thursday Network of Oklahoma (education.okstate.edu/risforthursday) and holds the Christine Cashel Professorship in higher education and student affairs.

Sarah Symonds LeBlanc, PhD, is an assistant professor of communication at Purdue University Fort Wayne (PFW) and specializes in family and health communication, in particular identity negotiation. Her research examines the media's portrayal of PTSD and postpartum depression, new moms' perceptions of stigma communication, and how new moms negotiate their identity.

Sagashus T. Levingston, PhD, focuses her research primarily on literature; however, it is informed by theory and criticism from rhetoric, motherhood studies, and Black feminism. Her coffee table book, *Infamous Mothers: Women Who've Gone through the Belly of Hell and Brought Something Good Back*, was inspired by her related dissertation research, and so was Infamous Mothers, LLC, a social enterprise, in which Sagashus offers personal and professional development training meant to empower women who mother from the margins of society. Sagashus was the opening speaker for Women's March Madison, delivered a TED talk, and has spoken at several universities, domestic abuse shelters, and women's conferences. Her book was adapted to a sold-out stage play. She is the proud mother of six children—three boys and three girls—and partner of Tosumba.

Penelope Mendonça BA (hons), MSc, PhD, is a pioneering graphic facilitator and cartoonist with twenty years of experience promoting human rights, asset-based thinking, and co-production through visual practice. With a background in social care and advocacy, she facilitates strategic planning, public engagement, person-centred approaches, and works on gender, age, race and disability related campaigns. She lectures at University of the Arts London, where her PhD work helped to develop values-based cartooning as a research method for accessing and representing diversity, (in)equality, and inclusion. She has published with *Studies in Comics and Women: A Cultural Review*, and Jessica Kingsley is publishing *Values-Based Cartooning*.

B. Lee Murray, RN, PhD, is an associate professor at the College of Nursing, University of Saskatchewan. She is also a clinical nurse specialist (CNS) in adolescent mental health. Dr. Murray's clinical practice, research, and teaching is in the area of sexual health education for adolescents with developmental disabilities, individual and group counselling, interprofessional practice and leadership, and school health in the context of the role of the mental health nurse in schools. She also has a great interest and curiosity regarding mothering. To satisfy this curiosity, she uses autoethnography as methodology to explore the normative discourse of mothering in the context of her own experiences as a mom.

Elizabeth Cralley Wetzler, PhD, is an assistant professor at the United States Military Academy in West Point, NY. She earned her PhD in experimental social psychology from Tulane University in New Orleans, LA. Her dissertation research focused on stereotyping and modern sexism. Her recent research focuses on media depictions of threat, including the threats of nuclear terrorism and of infectious diseases, such as Ebola. She is also interested in qualitative methods, specifically the use of autoethnography.

Deepest appreciation to
Demeter's monthly Donors

Daughters
Naomi McPherson
Linda Hunter
Muna Saleh
Summer Cunningham
Rebecca Bromwich
Tatjana Takseva
Kerri Kearney
Debbie Byrd
Laurie Kruk
Fionna Green
Tanya Cassidy
Vicki Noble
Bridget Boland

Sisters
Kirsten Goa
Amber Kinser
Nicole Willey
Regina Edwards